Advance Praise for *Breaking the Constraints to World-Class Performance*

Bill Dettmer has found a way to take the tools of the Thinking Process and present them in a way even I can understand. Like "Windows for Dummies" and "Juggling for Dummies" this book could be aptly named "Thinking Process for Dummies."
>   Ed Young, Director of Process Improvement
>   Aluminum Ladder Company

Bill Dettmer has done it again! Another excellent book about Dr. Eliyahu Goldratt's Theory of Constraints (TOC) approach to management. This book shows detailed examples of how TOC's principles and structured thinking processes are applied to real situations in industry and everyday life.
>   Thomas B. McMullen, Jr.
>   Founding Chairman, APICS Constraints Management SIG

Dettmer's book succeeds in fully delivering the powerful knowledge of controlling complex organizations by identifying and focusing on the key issues...it has the right amount of depth for practical people who are busy looking for solutions, striving for breakthroughs, and appreciate true common sense. The reader shall find it all in this mind opener book.
>   Eli Schragenheim
>   Former partner with the A. Y. Goldratt Institute
>   Joint Managing Director, MBE Simulations Ltd.

Essential reading for those interested in using TOC techniques to solve their problems. Bill communicates clearly the tools and underlying assumptions of TOC.
>   Bob Fox, President
>   The TOC Center

Dettmer is a master teacher...and Breaking the Constraints...is full of creative discovery!
>   James R. Holt, Ph.D., PE., Associate Professor
>   Jonah-Jonah
>   Washington State University-Vancouver
>   Engineering Management Program

Unequaled are the book's real-life practical examples where using the TOC Thinking Process could not only have excluded millions of dollars of unnecessary expenditures, but also would have saved human lives, as most dramatically illustrated by The Challenger Accident and The Anatomy of an Airplane Crash case studies.
>   Bruno Lewandowski, Editor & Publisher
>   World Aero-Engine Review

Once again Dettmer provides the business world with an important publication. This book goes a step beyond his first which explained the how-to. Here, Dettmer adds breadth and depth as he seeks to bring reader insight into using and interpreting the Thinking Process application of Goldratt's TOC. It's another winner.

David T. Novick, Ph.D.
Technical Advisor-Process Improvement
The Boeing Company
Electronic Systems & Missile Defense

This book integrates theory of constraints logic with an executive viewpoint that has never before been presented in any published work.

Melvin J. Anderson, Ph.D.
University of Colorado, Colorado Springs

Alex Rogo, the hero of Eliyahu Goldratt's novels...would have wanted this book. It is a well illustrated and easy to read guide to the TOC Thinking Process logical tools originally developed by Goldratt.

Jack Goodstein, Program Management Office
Fabrication Division
Boeing Commercial Airplane Group

Dettmer's new book fills a gap that had been left unfilled—that is a book for managers and executives who have read introductory books on TOC...and are interested in knowing more about it without spending weeks of time. This exciting discipline is on its way to becoming a major power tool in every manager's toolbox.

Kimio Inagaki
NEC America, Inc.

In practice, utilizing these techniques has created greater understanding of the cause-effect relationships of our processes. It has also allowed development of breakthrough solutions while warning us of potential negatives prior to implementing the change. This is turn allows us to be proactive by addressing and preventing the negatives associated with change before they happen.

Michael J. Seifert
Plant Manager, Denmark, SC
NIBCO, Inc.

Through his gift of writing, Mr. Dettmer leads the reader through an understanding of Dr. Goldratt's Theory of Constraints from theory to application. This book is a must have for anyone wanting to learn the application of tools which will allow monumental improvements.

Jack L. Middleton, Quality Engineer
Aluminator Wire Company

Bill's skill with the logical thinking processes is clearly evident in his writing and the interest he generates, quite naturally, motivates the reader to agree with him and want to continue reading.

Dr. J. Wayne Patterson
Clemson University

Breaking the Constraints
To World-Class
Performance

Also available from ASQ Quality Press

Goldratt's Theory of Constraints: A Systems Approach to Continuous Improvement
H. William Dettmer

Mapping Work Processes
Dianne Galloway

Quality Quotes
Hélio Gomes

Understanding and Applying Value-Added Assessments: Eliminating Business Process Waste
William E. Trischler

Value Leadership: Winning Competitive Advantage in the Information Age
Michael C. Harris

The Change Agents' Handbook: A Survival Guide for Quality Improvement Champions
David W. Hutton

Quality Problem Solving
Gerald F. Smith

Avoiding the Pitfalls of Total Quality
Charles C. Poirier and Steven J. Tokarz

To request a complimentary catalog of ASQ Quality Press publications, call 800-248-1946.

Breaking the Constraints To World-Class Performance

H. William Dettmer

ASQ Quality Press
Milwaukee, Wisconsin

Breaking the Constraints to World-Class Performance
H. William Dettmer

Library of Congress Cataloging-in-Publication Data
Dettmer, H. William.
    Breaking the constraints to world-class performance / H. William
Dettmer.
        p.   cm.
    Includes bibliographical references and index.
    ISBN 0-87389-437-5
    1. Theory of constraints (Management)   2. Organizational change.
    3. Success in business.   I. Title.
    HD69.T46D48   1998   98-7622
    658.5—dc21   CIP

10 9 8 7 6 5 4

ISBN 0-87389-437-5

Acquisitions Editor: Roger Holloway
Project Editor: Jeannie W. Bohn

ASQ Mission: The American Society for Quality advances individual and organizational performance excellence worldwide by providing opportunities for learning, quality improvement, and knowledge exchange.

Attention: Schools and Corporations
ASQ Quality Press books, audiotapes, videotapes, and software are available at quantity discounts with bulk purchases for business, educational, or instructional use. For information, please contact ASQ Quality Press at 800-248-1946, or write to ASQ Quality Press, P.O. Box 3005, Milwaukee, WI 53201-3005.

For a free copy of the ASQ Quality Press Publications Catalog, including ASQ membership information, call 800-248-1946.

Printed in the United States of America

 Printed on acid-free paper

American Society for Quality

Quality Press
611 East Wisconsin Avenue
Milwaukee, Wisconsin 53202

DEDICATION

To Diane Dettmer, whose 30 years of continuous support, patience, perseverance, and encouragement, and love have been an inseparable part of my life.

Love bears all things, believes all things, hopes all things, endures all things.
—*1 Corinthians 13:7*

CONTENTS

PROLOGUE

Competition is eternal.
There is no such thing as winning
There is no end to the game.
Even if you compete and win today,
you must compete and win tomorrow.
—Kuniuasu Sakai
Chairman, Taiyo Kogyo

What constitutes *world-class performance?* In athletics, this is an easy question to answer. A world-class athlete is one who ranks among the best in the world—one who can go head-to-head with the best competition anywhere on a regular basis, with a reasonable probability of winning each time. It doesn't necessarily mean that the athlete *will* win every time, just that he or she will be able to give a good account of him- or herself against others at the highest skill level.

In tennis, for instance, a "top 50" ranking or higher might be considered world-class, since a field of only 50 competitors from among 5 billion people would clearly be rarified company. Within that top 50, it's unlikely that number 50 would beat number one in most encounters. But the possibility remains that, under the right combination of circumstances, the 50th-ranked contender might pull off the upset on any given day. What's probably more significant is that at the world-class level of athletic competition, often it doesn't require much of an overall performance improvement for number 50 to move up to the top 10, where repeated matches against the number one ranked player might be in doubt every time.

Breaking the Constraints to World-Class Performance is about making your system join the ranks of the world's best in your chosen field. But in business, what *is* world-class performance? Here the sports analogy falls short. It doesn't necessarily mean big, though size can sometimes convey a certain standing in the world. The Soviet Union was certainly big physically, militarily, and in population, but as an economic player in the world arena, it was well behind most western industrialized nations.

Quality might be considered a key element in world-class performance, but quality of service or product alone isn't enough to make an organization world-class. There are many small companies that produce outstanding quality, but they aren't even a blip on the world's radar screen. Lack of quality, however, would certainly be enough to eliminate a system from contention, so quality would clearly be a necessary condition.

Market share would be a prime characteristic of world-class performance. That share need not be as commanding as Intel's or Microsoft's. In fact, a company might be considered world class with less than 1 percent of the world's market. There are companies well down in the Fortune 500, or even 1000, that could be considered world-class.

A prominent characteristic of world-class performers is their reputation or standing in the eyes of their competitors. In other words, does world-class competition pay attention to what they do? Another characteristic would be at what level they choose to compete. Is their arena local, or is the world their stage? In summary, what makes a company world-class is probably a combination of all of these factors in varying degrees, depending on the chosen field. If an organization can successfully compete with any other player in the world at whatever it does, it should qualify as world-class.

Is your organization world-class now? If not, do you know why? In most cases, it would probably be accurate to say that something is limiting its performance. In other words, your organization's performance is *constrained* in some way. Just as the narrowest part of an hourglass constrains how much sand can pass from the top to the bottom, so, too, does an organization's constraint dictate how well it can perform. Obviously, the road to world-class performance (for those who are not yet world-class) requires breaking the constraints that impede them. But once you're there, you can't stand still and expect to stay there. There's always some other wolf biding its time to challenge for the leadership of the pack. Gordon Forward, CEO of Chaparral Steel, observed that to stand still is to fall behind. There is no such thing as staying the same. You are either striving to make yourself better or allowing yourself to get worse. So if you're already world class, staying there requires the same thing as getting there in the first place: breaking the constraints that keep you from doing even better.

Do you know where your organization's constraint lies? Believe it or not, most people don't. But knowing where that constraint is constitutes the first step in breaking it. This book is all about learning to think in terms of system constraints—not to allow them to limit you, but to make you ever cognizant that we live with them, always. Consequently, though we might break our system's constraint today, something else will come forward to confine our performance—at a higher level, perhaps, but confine it nonetheless. The process of constraint breaking is an exercise in incremental improvement. Sometimes the increments are large; other times they're small. But the key to successful world-class performance today is knowing where your constraint is today and how to manage it. To know where the constraint will be tomorrow is to ensure continued successful performance in the future.

H. William Dettmer
Sequim, Washington   June 1, 1998
gsi@goalsys.com   www.goalsys.com

ACKNOWLEDGMENTS

I would be remiss if I failed to acknowledge the many people who have contributed to this book. An author always runs a risk of leaving some deserving person out of a recounting such as this. If I have done so here, the omission is unintentional.

Dr. Van Gray, Baylor University, and Mr. Eli Schragenheim, my friends and colleagues, have expanded and enriched my understanding of constraint theory and its application. Dr. Mel Anderson, University of Colorado-Colorado Springs, reviewed this work and suggested valuable improvements, as did Dr. James Holt, Washington State University-Vancouver, and Mr. Steve Holt, Boeing Commercial Airplane Group. I'm grateful to Dr. John Caspari, who provided advice and the basis of the logic trees incorporated in the "Vector One" case study (Appendix D).

Jim Robinson, formerly CEO of the Butler Manufacturing Group (Canada), was kind enough to let me use the future reality trees (chapter 7) that he created to resolve a major problem in his company. Carl Johnson, Vice-President for Operations at Bethlehem Steel, Sparrows Point, was kind enough to give me an extensive telephone interview about his experiences with Throughput-Based Manufacturing. Jack Middleton, a quality engineer for a wire manufacturer in Arkansas, provided the details of his successful use of the thinking process. Ray Rerick, Harris Semiconductor, provided details on Harris's application of constraint theory at its Mountaintop, Pennsylvania, operation.

I could not fail to acknowledge the superlative professionalism and support of Roger Holloway, Jeanne Bohn, Cathy Christine, and the rest of the staff at Quality Press. They make it easy to be an author. I must also recognize the superlative, professional work of the staff at Shepherd, Inc., who deserve the credit for the layout and production of this book. Copyeditor Jane DeShaw scrupulously cleaned up all of my typing and grammatical errors. Rod Wiese, art and design manager, produced the final outstanding illustrations that bring my words to life. And Cristin Day, project editor, snapped victory from the jaws of defeat when major problems were discovered with the graphics very late in the game. Thanks, Shepherd team, for duty above and beyond the call!

Last, but certainly not least, I must acknowledge the contributions of Dr. Eliyahu M. Goldratt, who created the Theory of Constraints and its logical thinking process. Without his foundational work, this book would not have been possible.

Chapter 1
SYSTEM OR PROCESS?

He who innovates will have for his enemies all those who are well off under the existing order of things, and only lukewarm supporters in those who might be better off under the new.
—Niccolò Machiavelli

BETHLEHEM STEEL

A traditional smokestack industry, once the envy of the world, America's steel industry has largely gone into the tank over the last 25 years, the victim of foreign competition. U.S. Steel and Bethlehem Steel, once the flagships of American heavy industry, today are shadows of their former selves. Blistering competition from lower-priced competitors in Japan and Korea exposed the weaknesses of American steel producers. But after years of down-sliding, a bright spot appeared in big American steel: Bethlehem's Sparrows Point Division.

Sparrows Point is an *integrated steel plant,* meaning it processes iron ore from scratch into finished steel. In 1993, Bethlehem decentralized, allowing Sparrows Point to both produce and market its own products. In July of that year, Sparrows Point was able to deliver no more than 60 to 75 percent of their shipments on time. Order-to-ship cycle times ran eight to twelve weeks. The high backlog of late orders led to massive expediting, at the expense of any hope of production stability. All of these problems seriously wounded Sparrows Point's return on net assets (RONA), which ranged from negative numbers at worst to low single digits at best.

By mid-1995, the picture at Sparrows Point had changed considerably. On-time steel shipments had improved to the mid 80% range with two major products in the mid 90s, levels unheard of in the steel industry, where late deliveries are often the rule rather than the exception. Order-to-ship cycles dropped to four to six weeks or less. Expediting became the exception rather than the rule. Production stabilized. Sparrows Point became so competitive that for the first time in recent memory, they actually exported 500 thousand tons of steel—fully one-sixth of their entire output—into an international market whose blistering price competition had virtually shut out American steelmakers. And most important of all, RONA jumped from break-even levels to consistently positive.

What made the difference? Between September and December 1993, the staff at Sparrows Point learned about the theory of constraints (TOC) and the successes two other companies achieved in applying it: Federal Mogul, a Detroit auto parts manufacturer, and Columbus Stainless Steel in South Africa. Over the next year, union and management at Sparrows Point collaborated in building and communicating a new approach to steel production they called *throughput-based manufacturing* (TBM).

The TBM approach caused Sparrows Point to redirect its emphasis from producing tonnage to bringing in sales dollars. By identifying and breaking the constraints—both physical and policy—to achieving higher sales revenues, Sparrows Point was able to optimize the performance of the entire division as a whole, rather than its individual components.

FORD ELECTRONICS

Ford Electronics Division's plant in Markham, Ontario (Canada), manufactures many of the sensor, information display, and security components Ford Motor Company builds into its automobiles and trucks. In 1989, the management and staff of the modern 289,000 square foot Markham plant recognized the importance of becoming more responsive to their customers' needs. For almost a decade, the Ford Motor Company had committed itself to a significant corporate-wide effort to compete with Japanese automakers on the basis of quality. Since the early 1980s, Ford's motto has been *Quality is Job One.*

A major factor in virtually all quality improvement strategies is an emphasis on satisfying customers. Ford Electronics Division's primary customers are internal: the production plants that build Ford cars and trucks. But in the quality improvement paradigm, internal customers are no less important than external ones. So the Markham staff began a concerted effort to satisfy their automotive division customers. One of the most important factors for the auto production plants was how fast Markham could respond to new orders for electronic components. In 1989, Markham needed 16 days from receipt of an order until it was manufactured and ready for shipping. Four days of that time were consumed by order processing and production scheduling. The other 12 days constituted the manufacturing cycle—the time between the release of raw materials and the readiness of the finished product for shipping.

The Markham staff set about reducing manufacturing cycle time. Their early efforts were devoted to adopting a Japanese-style just-in-time production approach with *kanban* inventory control. Within a year, these efforts helped Markham reduce its manufacturing cycle time over 40 percent, from 12 to less than 8 days. In most ordinary circumstances, this would be the end of the line. But for the Markham plant, it was only the beginning.

In 1990, the Markham staff learned about the theory of constraints (TOC). The creation of an Israeli physicist, Dr. Eliyahu M. Goldratt, TOC had enabled a number of manufacturing companies in other industries to realize dramatic improvements in customer responsiveness during the 1980s, and commensurate increases in profitability. Despite the fact that these other applications of TOC had been in unrelated businesses, the Markham staff recognized the transferability of TOC principles to their own operations. Their aggressive efforts to apply TOC paid off handsomely.

By 1991, manufacturing cycle time had been reduced another *90 percent.* The fabrication of finished parts from raw materials now averaged only 0.88 day—*less than two shifts.* Material handling decreased by 50 percent. As a consequence of the reduction in manufacturing cycle time, the Markham staff also found they needed 25 percent less equipment to do the same volume of work and 50 percent less floor space, both of which could be diverted to other productive activities.

A SYSTEMS APPROACH

The successes of Ford Electronics' Markham plant and Bethlehem's Sparrows Point Division are dramatic, to say the least. Shorter cycle times make for agile businesses, which can be more responsive to the changing demands of customers, and better customer satisfaction can translate into competitive advantage. But how does the concept of constraints fit into the equation? Let's start with the basics.

Bethlehem Steel and Ford Electronics are both examples of complex systems, but what is a *system?* Since the concept of system underlies everything that follows, we'd better start by defining the term.

An unabridged dictionary would give nearly a dozen different definitions. For our purposes, however, we'll consider a system to be a number of connected or interrelated elements that could be seen as working together for the overall objective of the whole.[1] A system has a boundary that nominally encloses its components and separates them from the environment in which the system exists. A system takes inputs of some kind, acts on them in some way, and produces outputs. These outputs are supposed to have greater value than the sum of the inputs, so the system might be said to *add value* to the inputs as it turns them into outputs. Many systems also have feedback loops that allow the outputs to be evaluated for deviations from some desired standard. If deviations are found, the feedback loop provides adjustments of some kind, either to the inputs or to the system's components, until the outputs conform to the desired standards. Figure 1.1 illustrates a system similar to the one just described.

Notice that this characterization of a system is deliberately broad. It's intended to encompass a wide variety of systems, from mechanical and biological to organizational. The heating or cooling of your house is controlled by a system—an electromechanical system. The human body functions as a biological system. Manufacturing or service companies, universities, or government agencies also behave as systems—organizational systems.

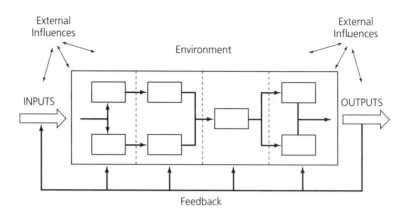

FIGURE 1.1 **Typical system.** From Dettmer, H. W., *Goldratt's Theory of Constraints: A Systems Approach to Continuous Improvement* (1996)

There are even combinations of types of systems. A manufacturing production line has electromechanical, biological, and organizational characteristics. Most of us operate in a variety of organizational systems. We may be part of a family, a civic group, or a church. We're often part of a department at work, as well as being an employee of the company in which that department resides.

This book is about the theory of constraints (TOC). TOC is a *system* philosophy. In these days of *process improvement,* TOC considers performance improvement from the system level, rather than the process level. Benjamin Franklin would probably have liked the systems approach. During the American Revolution, it was Franklin who advised his fellow patriots, "We must all hang together, or we shall surely hang separately." Sage advice about systems of any kind. Organizations also live or die as complete systems, not as individual components. An automobile, for example, functions as a complete system. It takes more than a well-tuned engine to ride safely, effectively, comfortably, and worry-free. The engine must work synchronously with the steering, suspension, wheels, brakes, electrical system, fuel system, even the climate-control system. You can maximize the performance of any one of these components without having any noticeable effect on the overall progress of the car toward its goal—a comfortable, worry-free ride.

WHAT IS THE SYSTEM'S GOAL?

Systems invariably exist for some purpose. Whether a system evolves naturally or is artificially created, it exists to fulfill some purpose. The heating or cooling system in your house has a well-defined purpose: to maintain your personal comfort while you're in the house. Organizational systems likewise serve some purpose. That purpose can be considered a *goal:* the objective or end toward which effort is directed.[2]

Determination or recognition of a system's goal is the first, most critical task of anyone who wants to improve a system. Why? Because improvement implies a change in the status quo. But changes can be either good or bad, so in order to know whether we're changing a system for better or for worse, we must know *relative to what?* Strange as it may seem, people tend to forget—or at least overlook—the system's goal when contemplating change. They are so tightly focused on components of the system that they fail to keep their eyes on the destination of the journey: the *goal.* Many organizations create trouble for themselves because of an inability to answer concisely and accurately the most important fundamental question: *what is the goal?* It's been said that it is more important to know where you are going than to get there quickly. In other words, don't mistake activity for achievement.

In any organization, there will be no shortage of ideas about what the goal is. Unfortunately, the problem is that many of these ideas won't coincide. So that people aren't working at cross-purposes, there has to be a single, undisputed goal that everyone can subscribe to. But who gets to set that goal? The members of the system? The system's leader? Or the system's customers? *The moral authority to set the system's goal resides with the system's owner.* If *you* owned a business, wouldn't you expect to have the right to decide what that business's goal should be? In a for-profit company, the system's owners are usually the stockholders, often represented by a board of directors. In a not-for-profit organization, it may be a little more difficult to decide who the owners are. A government agency usually exists to serve the public and could be considered to be owned by the taxpayers who foot the bill for its operation.

Whoever the system's owners are, and whatever goal they designate for the system, anyone bent on improving the system must know, first and foremost, what that goal is. *The first step is to define the goal.*

NECESSARY CONDITIONS AND CONSTRAINTS

No goal ever stands in isolation. Whatever the goal might be, there are always *necessary conditions* that must be satisfied in order to achieve it. These necessary conditions might be considered critical success factors. The common characteristic among such factors is *necessity*—the organization's goal can't be achieved if any one of them is absent. The number of necessary conditions will vary, depending on the nature of the goal. Some of these necessary conditions will be related to the goal-seeking activity itself. Others will be imposed by the environment in which the system operates. For example, the typical for-profit company's goal is usually profitability. For a company that sells a product or service, it makes sense that customer satisfaction is a necessary condition for selling the goods or services that produce profits. Since a well-qualified, motivated work force is usually necessary to produce high-quality goods or services that satisfy customers, this, too, might be a necessary condition. From the external environment come other necessary conditions in the form of government regulations: occupational safety and health, environmental protection, and so on. Satisfying necessary conditions, then, constitutes the foundation of achieving the goal (Figure 1.2).

Let's review what we've covered so far. A system converts inputs into outputs in some kind of environment. It does so to achieve some goal previously determined by the system's owners. Along the way to that goal, a set of definable necessary conditions must be satisfied. But if we're considering ways to improve the system's ability to achieve its goal (that is, to reach the goal more quickly or more decisively), we're implying that we're not there yet—that there's a difference between where we *are* and where we think we *should be*.

Assuming we know what the goal is, and assuming we can determine where we currently are in respect to it, the logical next question is, *What prevents us from achieving the goal?* There may be several specific answers to this question, but virtually all of them can be characterized by one term: *constraint*. A constraint is something that prevents us from satisfying a necessary condition or reaching our goal, or from reaching it more quickly or decisively. All systems—commercial corporations, not-for-profit or government agencies, even families—operate under constraints. The constraints in any system are the factors or elements that actually determine how much the system can accomplish.

SUBOPTIMIZATION

How does a system perspective relate to commercial business or a not-for-profit organization or government agency? Each of these is a system of some kind. Each has a goal, necessary conditions, and constraints. But many managers, while they might know what the system's goal is, tend to think in terms of organizational boundaries, or departments, rather than considering the system as a whole. So at the heart of the

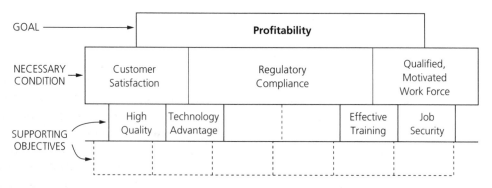

FIGURE 1.2   Goals and necessary conditions: A hierarchy.

problem of increasing system performance in any organization is the tendency toward *suboptimization:* the maximizing or fine-tuning of *a part* of the system, often to the detriment of the *entire* system.

Near the end of his life, W. Edwards Deming acknowledged the dangers of suboptimization. He observed the following:

> *Optimization is a process of orchestrating the efforts of all components toward achievement of the stated aim. Optimization is management's job. Everybody wins with optimization.*
>
> *Anything less than optimization of the whole system will bring eventual loss to every component in the system. Any group should have as its aim optimization of the larger system that the group operates in.*[3]
>
> *The obligation of any component is to contribute its best to the system, not to maximize its own production, profit, or sales, nor any other competitive measure. Some components may operate at a loss themselves in order to optimize the whole system, including the components that take a loss.*[4]

Examples of suboptimization abound. A sales department sets records for new orders while the company's profits improve only marginally, if at all. The star running-back on the pro football team amasses 1300 yards carrying the ball and earns a hefty contract boost the next year for his performance, but the team finishes the season with only five wins and eleven losses and doesn't make the playoffs. A company commits itself to a total quality management (TQM) philosophy, wins a prestigious award for quality, but subsequently files for bankruptcy. In every one of these examples, there are indications of suboptimization. And in each case, individual battles were won—perhaps with glory and honors for the foot soldiers—but the war was lost.

Sometimes suboptimization results from a lack of awareness. A system's managers might not realize how detrimental suboptimization can be. In other cases, management may deliberately pursue suboptimization, believing that it's the right thing to do. When this happens, it's usually because management operates on the assumption that maximizing the performance of each component part of the system will automatically maximize the performance of the system as a whole. As we'll see later, this isn't a valid assumption. If the assumptions aren't any good, the conclusions aren't likely to be any better.

ANALYTICAL THINKING

Suboptimization often results from what might be called *analytical thinking*. This kind of thinking carves complex problems into smaller, more manageable subproblems so that each can be worked on separately. After each subproblem is solved, often in isolation from the rest, the pieces are reassembled into a whole again. The underlying assumption upon which analytical thinking is based is the idea that if we make each of the parts of a system perform to its maximum capability, the system as a whole will benefit.

People often take for granted that partitioning complex issues and dealing with the parts in isolation is the best way to improve systems. In some cases, this approach might work. There's a certain appeal to the idea of disassembling something, spiffing up the parts, and gluing it all back together again. After all, isn't this what your repair shop does when it overhauls your car's engine?

But as systems become more complex, they quickly evolve beyond the purely mechanical, incorporating both human and organizational characteristics. At this point, the effectiveness of analytical thinking begins to break down. Two characteristics of systems conspire to compromise the effectiveness of analytical thinking: *variation* and *dependence.*

VARIATION AND DEPENDENCE

Variation basically means *inconsistency.* No part of a system will perform in exactly the same way every time. Instead, individual iterations will cluster around some desired value, much as the bullet holes in a target do (Figure 1.3).

Some individual performances will be very close to the desired value. Others might be somewhat farther away. Variation comes from two sources: common causes and special causes. We're normally more aware of special causes. These are assignable and occur for a specific reason. Operator fatigue, computer failure induced by weather, or inadequate training are all examples of special causes of variation. They may be unpredictable. Murphy's law (Whatever *can* go wrong, *will* go wrong) describes special cause.

Common cause variation results from the nature, or accuracy limitations, of the system's components. Common causes aren't assignable; they reside within the system's components and affect performance on every iteration. Both kinds of variation cause a system's performance to be other than expected.[5]

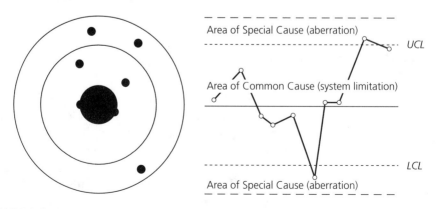

FIGURE 1.3 Variation.

When each component depends on one or more other components for the quality, accuracy, or efficiency of its own performance, they are considered dependent. Dependence is inherent in any system. Sometimes the dependent relationships are sequential, so that one part is affected by only a single predecessor and might itself affect only one other. In many situations, though, the systemic relationships can be quite complex, with one part affecting many others, or being affected by many others.

In Figure 1.4, the output of event *B* can be either 3 or 5, if it is considered exclusively on its own. Another way to express this might be that the mean of the possible outcomes of event *B* alone is 4. Notice that the same is true of event *A*. But if the output of event *B* is *dependent* on the output of event *A*, the performance of *B* can only deteriorate with respect to *A*. Thus, the mean of the two dependent events isn't 4; it's 3.5.

In complex systems, variation combines with dependence to turn analytical thinking into a nightmare. Because different components of a system naturally have differing capacities to begin with, an analytical approach can suboptimize every part. But because many parts are dependent, optimizing one part might be detrimental to its dependent part, even when both are operating perfectly. When we factor in the effects of variation in each component, the turbulence in system performance can become even more pronounced and unpredictable.

Complex systems become suboptimized through analytical thinking, especially when that thinking falls victim to interdependence and variation. However, analytical thinking isn't the only cause of suboptimization in a system.

HUMAN SUBOPTIMIZATION

Another often overlooked factor contributing to suboptimization is human behavior, particularly organizational behavior. No matter what goals or objectives an organization might set for itself, people always bring personal needs, objectives, and agendas to any situation.

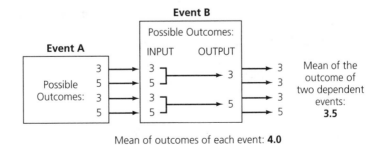

FIGURE 1.4 **Dependence.** This example provided by Dr. Van D. Gray. Used with permission

How many of us have witnessed a department head who is more concerned with how well his or her own department does than with the success or failure of the company? A typical attitude is, "Well, certainly the company didn't do very well this year, but *my* department had nothing to do with that. We pulled more than our share of the load. We swam while everybody else sank." A fairly reliable indication of suboptimization is bonuses awarded to key managers or executives even when the company as a whole doesn't do very well. Such a situation indicates the presence of a compensation policy that rewards or reinforces suboptimization, often at the expense of global system performance.

Since systems thinking is preferable and suboptimizing isn't, how can management avoid the suboptimization trap? How can executives ensure that the focus of everyone's efforts remains on system success? An answer to this question that has been used with great success by organizations such as Bethlehem Steel and Ford Electronics is *constraint management*.

> *All autonomous agencies and authorities, sooner or later, turn into self-perpetuating strongholds of conventional thought and practice.*
>
> —*Ada Louise Huxtable*

NOTES

1. Thomas H. Athey, *The Systematic Systems Approach* (Englewood Cliffs, N.J.: Prentice Hall, 1982), 12.
2. *Webster's New Universal Unabridged Dictionary,* 1989.
3. W. Edwards Deming, *The New Economics for Industry, Government, and Education* (Cambridge, Mass. Massachusetts Institute of Technology, Center for Advanced Engineering Study, 1993), 53.
4. Ibid., 99–100.
5. There's much more to variation than is offered here. For a more detailed discussion of variation try one or more of the following sources:
   W. Edwards Deming, *Out of the Crisis* (Cambridge, Mass.: Massachusetts Institute of Technology, Center for Advanced Engineering Study, 1986).
   Douglas C. Montgomery, *Introduction to Statistical Quality Control,* 3d ed. (New York, NY: John Wiley and Sons, Inc.,1996).
   Walter A. Shewhart, *Economic Control of Quality of Manufactured Product* (Milwaukee, Wis.: ASQ Quality Press, 1980). (Commemorative edition of original 1931 book.)
   Western Electric Company, *Statistical Quality Control Handbook,* 1956.

Chapter 2
THE THEORY
OF CONSTRAINTS

Courage is the power to let go of the familiar.

—Unknown

WHAT IS THE THEORY OF CONSTRAINTS?

One means of keeping everyone's eye on the ball is the theory of constraints (TOC), a system-level management philosophy developed by Dr. Eliyahu M. Goldratt. TOC might be described as the application of the scientific method to the challenges of managing complex organizations.

The theory of constraints did not spring fully formed from Dr. Goldratt's head. In much the same way that Deming's fourteen points coalesced over a lifetime of his experience in improving quality, TOC also evolved over a period of time. In a succession of situations over the past 20 years, Goldratt recognized some common characteristics and principles affecting the operation of systems. The collection and integration of these observations, coupled with some unique creative thinking on Goldratt's part, led to the gradual maturation of a body of knowledge Goldratt named *theory of constraints.*

TOC suggests that all systems are similar to chains—or to networks of chains. Each chain is composed of a variety of links differing primarily in their strength, or capability (Figure 2.1). In any independent chain,

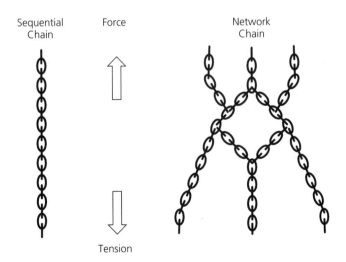

FIGURE 2.1   Systems as chains: One weakest link in each independent chain.

there is one link—and only one—that is weaker than all the rest: the *weakest link*. This weakest link limits (defines) the maximum performance of the existing chain. In other words, the weakest link is the *constraint* to system performance. If steps are taken to strengthen the weakest link (that is, to break the constraint), making it no longer the weakest link, then some other link will become the weakest link.

It's important to note that a weakest link can be defined only as such by considering the demand placed upon the entire chain. If we call upon a 12-ton rated chain to pull somewhat more than 12 tons, then a weakest link definitely can be identified: it's the point at which the chain will break. But if the chain is never used to pull more than 12 tons, then for all practical purposes, this weakest link is *not* a system constraint because it will always be stronger than the demand we might place on it. Therefore, the external demand imposed upon the system plays a key part in determining where a constraint might lie.

THE CHAIN ANALOGY: AN EXAMPLE

Let's see how this chain analogy applies to an organization. For simplicity's sake, we'll examine a manufacturing example, although TOC can apply equally well to a service organization. Our manufacturing company is very simple. It's a dental laboratory with a sequential process (Figure 2.2). It accepts orders for bridgework from dental practices, takes raw materials, and, using sophisticated equipment and the skill of its employees, produces artificial teeth to replace natural teeth.

There are seven steps, or processes, in this single, sequential system. The first step is the receipt and logging of the order. The next five steps constitute the manufacturing line, and the last step is packing and shipping.

The manufacturing process itself is made up of five sequential process steps: *opaque, plaster, wax-and-metal, polishing* and *porcelain*. These

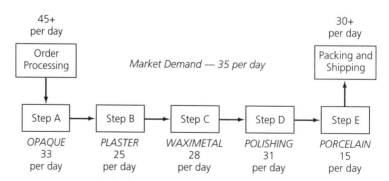

FIGURE 2.2   The dental laboratory: A simple chain. This example provided by Mr. Bryan Bloom. Used with permission

steps are capable of producing 33, 25, 28, 31, and 15 units per day, respectively. Based on what you can see in Figure 2.2, what is the overall daily capacity of the laboratory to produce bridgework? Where is the constraint—the link in the chain that limits the whole system's output? If you answered *15* and *process step E,* respectively, you're right. No matter how many units of work any of the other steps are capable of processing each day, the entire system can produce only 15 finished units per day, because that's all step *E* can produce at its best rate.

What will happen if the steps *ahead* of *E* produce more than 15 units? Say 25, for example. From Figure 2.2, it's clear that the others can all produce at least 25. The market demand is so high (35) that the lab owner has to turn away business. So for now, let's say that the boss has set 25 bridgework orders as the target. Since process step *E* can do only 15, the rest of the 25 units (10 to be exact) produced by the earlier steps will accumulate as partially finished work—completely unusable from the customer's standpoint—waiting for process step *E* to finish the job.

Suppose this work is done on Monday. On Tuesday, step *E* begins working on these leftovers from Monday. What are steps *A* through *D* doing in the meantime? They're *suboptimizing,* of course! They can't have the boss catch them doing nothing for two-thirds of the day while step *E* catches up on Monday's leftovers. So they begin work on 25 *more* new units. But by the end of the day, step E has only completed *five* of Tuesday's orders, because the first two-thirds of the day were needed to finish the Monday leftovers. Now instead of having 10 partially finished units left over from Tuesday, step *E's* operator finds *20 units* waiting on Wednesday, 30 units on Thursday, and . . . well, you get the idea. By the end of the week, the dental laboratory has a pretty hefty backlog of orders waiting to be done.

Of course, the boss would never think of turning away new orders, so the backlog mounts. But bridgework is a unique product. The customers (the dental practices) demand on-time delivery because the dentists have patients coming in at a prescheduled time for fittings. In other words, the *original equipment manufacturers* are depending on the supplier's dependability to maintain their own production schedule. (Is this beginning to sound familiar?) If a dental laboratory can't deliver its product on time to a dentist, both the dentist and the patient are inconvenienced. If this happens more than once, the laboratory can kiss the jilted dentist's business goodbye.

So what can the boss do to overcome this backlog? The knee-jerk reaction is *expedite*—try to have the employees work faster, or perhaps rearrange the production schedule to accommodate a particularly important customer. "Drop *that* for now! Work on *this* instead, and get back to *that* when you can!" However, a strange thing happens when an organization starts expediting. After some period of expediting, the worker never seems to get back to work on *that,* because some other order invariably needs priority. The result is that expediting becomes a way of life—the norm, rather than the exception.

It's like a juggler trying to keep an ever-increasing number of Indian clubs in the air. Eventually, one of them clunks the juggler on the head, and all the clubs fall to the ground. In other words, expediting can become an out-of-control infection. Pretty soon *everything* is expedited, and *nothing* is produced on a normal schedule. The stress within the system builds until a breaking point is reached.

There must be another way. Obviously, the desirable strategy would be to maximize the acceptance of new orders *without* getting into a backlog situation. But how can that be done?

THE THEORY OF CONSTRAINTS SOLUTION

Recall the TOC concept of a system: a chain with one *weakest* link. In our dental lab example, where's the weakest link? Obviously, it's step *E*. So if we could strengthen that weakest link, the capacity of the entire chain (laboratory process) to withstand a greater load would be improved. But what happens if we improve *E* so that it's not the weakest link anymore? Let's say we double its capacity to 30 per day and we accept an equal number of orders to match *E*'s new capacity. Usually, some other step in the process becomes the weakest link. Although its weakness occurs at a higher level of *system* performance, if the demand on the system exceeds the capacity of a link in the chain, the system *still* will be internally constrained. Can you tell by looking at Figure 2.2 where the *next* constraint in the system will be? Of course, it's step *B*, because its capacity is 25 units per day and our new production target is 30.

Now let's say that you improve step *B*'s capacity to produce. It's not the constraint anymore, either. What's more, you identify and break the next constraint, and the next, and you sequentially eliminate each one until you're able to handle more orders than you're receiving, say 39 for example. Now where's the constraint? In fact, it's not within your system anymore. As you increased capacity, you were able to take on more of that demand you were turning away, until demand petered out. The *market demand* (35 units per day) has become your constraint, because you have excess capacity for which there isn't a demand. That constraint can be broken, too, but it will require a different set of skills than those used to break the internal constraints. Let's talk about how we'd go about finding and breaking all these constraints.

THE FIVE FOCUSING STEPS

Goldratt has developed a five-step method for constraint breaking:[1]

1. Identify the constraint
2. Decide how to exploit the constraint

3. Subordinate everything else to the decision in step 2
4. Elevate the constraint
5. Go Back To Step 1, but avoid inertia

1. *Identify the Constraint.* The first step is to determine exactly what part of the system constitutes the weakest link. *What* needs changing? The constraint might be physical, as was step *E* in the dental lab example. It might even be an organizational policy.

2. *Decide How to Exploit the Constraint.* The key word is exploit. In this context, it doesn't have the negative connotation that it might have in a political or sociological context. Here, *exploit* means to wring maximum efficiency from the constraint in its existing configuration. Exploiting a piece of equipment usually involves eliminating all idle time on that machine. Don't shut it down during lunch hours. Do preventive maintenance on it at night so it doesn't break down during the workday. Quality-control the materials being fed to this machine, so that no constraint time is wasted on work that must be done over again or scrapped. In other words, make every minute the constraint is in operation count for the most—make it as efficient as possible *without* additional capital investment.

3. *Subordinate Everything Else.* Let the constraint set the pace. Once the constraint has been identified and you've figured out how to get the most out of it, synchronize all the other system components with the constraint. In almost all situations, this will require de-tuning parts of the system: accepting idle time as a way of life in some areas. This is a very difficult idea for most managers to accept, especially those accustomed to—and perhaps rewarded for—individual process efficiencies (that is, suboptimization).

4. *Elevate the Constraint.* At this point you have a decision to make. Did the first three steps break the constraint (that is, the originally identified constraint no longer limits the system's performance)? Often the exploitation and subordination steps are enough. If so, go on to step 5. If not, your next step must be to *elevate* the constraint. Since the original constraint is still limiting system performance despite your best efforts to make it as efficient as possible, the only remaining course of action is to *increase the capacity* of the constrained part of the process, and to continue to do so until the constraint is really broken. *Elevating* may mean buying another piece of equipment (a capital investment) or contracting out part of the constraint's load. Or it might be as simple as instituting limited overtime or adding a second shift.

The distinction between exploiting and elevating is simply this: *exploiting* means we change how we *use* the constrained resource without spending more money. *Elevating* means that we invest more money to increase the constrained resource's capacity. So if our idea involves *spending* more money than we're spending now to *make* money, we're elevating, not exploiting. But why spend money if we don't have to?

Clearly, it doesn't make much sense to elevate until we're sure we've exploited the constraint as best we can.

5. *Go Back to Step 1, but Avoid Inertia.* When the constraint is broken (in either step 3 or 4), return to the first step and begin the process again. Find the next constraint restricting the system's performance, and break it, too. The caution about avoiding inertia advises us to remember that the cycle never stops: there's always another constraint waiting behind the one we're working on now. Also, in successive cycles of the five focusing steps, we might have to revisit a constraint we thought we'd previously broken.

The five focusing steps enable a system's manager to remain focused on what's really important in the organization: the *system's* constraint. Why is the constraint the most important target? Obviously, it's the pacesetter for the entire system. No matter how fast the other components can do their job, the system can't produce at a rate faster than its slowest component. The chain is no stronger than its weakest link. But it goes well beyond this concept and into practice.

TOTAL QUALITY MANAGEMENT AND THE THEORY OF CONSTRAINTS

Many organizations today have adopted some kind of quality philosophy. *Total Quality Management* (TQM) and *Continuous Process Improvement* (CPI) are labels for a not very well standardized paradigm of prescriptions for quality improvement. The details of individual quality improvement efforts might vary from one organization to another, but there are some characteristics of TQM/CPI that remain more or less the same across company lines. One of these is an emphasis on process improvement. Another is bringing everyone in the organization into the fold or committing to improving a number of areas at once, maybe in some cases, everything at once. W. Edwards Deming himself emphasized the need to distribute efforts throughout the organization in his fourteenth point: Put everybody to work on the transformation. The transformation is everybody's job.[2]

Recall the chain analogy for a moment. We know that strengthening the weakest link produces an immediate improvement in system performance. But what measurable effect can we have on the entire system if we strengthen any links *other than* the weakest link? The entire chain is not any stronger, because the weakest link still constrains the system. By trying to improve all aspects of the system at the same time, we do two things, neither of which are very desirable.

First, we spread out our resources across the entire system, when only one part of it—the constraint—is capable of delivering immediate, measurable improvement. Second, by working on everything at once, tracing overall system improvement to a particular action becomes an almost impossible task.

Let's consider each of these outcomes in more detail. Who among us functions in an organization with unlimited resources to apply toward improvement activities? Answer: nobody. So in the first outcome, we may starve the constraint of resources vital to its improvement in the interest of getting the whole organization involved. If you don't have enough resources to do a job, either the job doesn't get done or it takes much longer to finish it. In the second outcome, because we're unable to trace the system improvement to a particular action or decision, we can never know for sure what we did that caused the improvement. And when it becomes necessary to refine system performance again in the future, we won't know which part of the system offers the most potential for improvement with the least commitment of resources. Remember the chain analogy: strengthening all the chain's links might make it heavier than it needs to be—and more costly!

Since TQM/CPI tends to spread resources across an organization in the interest of involving everybody, is it any wonder that real, measurable improvement seems to come so slowly? Even the most ardent adherents of TQM/CPI agree that it requires a long-term investment of time and effort and that it won't produce lasting results in the short term.

What about tracing an improvement back to the action that caused it? Why is it so important to make this connection? Deming observed that the transformation to an improved system is the product of *profound knowledge* about that system.[3] Two elements of Deming's profound knowledge taxonomy are *appreciation for a system* and an *understanding of the theory of knowledge.*

To appreciate a system, we have to recognize how the different components interact with one another to make the whole greater than the sum of its parts. Understanding the theory of knowledge addresses the questions of *how* we know *what* we know about our system, and how changes in one variable affect the performance of the whole system. If we can't isolate the effects of our actions on the system, how are we to differentiate between the important few and the trivial many? And if we try to improve everything at once, as most practitioners of TQM do, how can we ever know for sure what actions contributed most to the system's improvement?

Does it have to be this way? Is improving everything at once, and taking years to do it, the only way to realize the promise of TQM? Not necessarily. It's probably true that sooner or later every component of a system will need improving. The real question is, What's the difference between a parallel, or simultaneous, improvement strategy and a constraint-based approach? At the end of one complete improvement cycle, the same system elements are improved with either approach. But with a constraint-based approach, improvements come more quickly, they're incremental, and the increments are attributable to specific projects or activities. Figure 2.3 shows two different improvement curves. The upper one is a typical example of how improvement efforts produce progressively diminishing returns for the entire system.

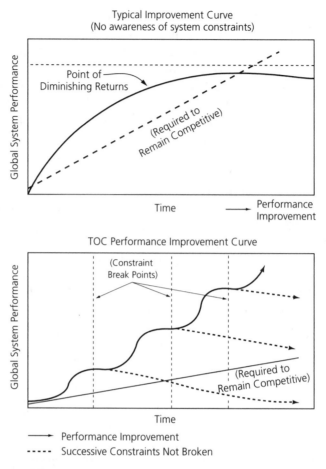

FIGURE 2.3 Two different curves.

When emphasis on improvement stops, the curve flattens out and even deteriorates as earlier solutions obsolesce.

The second curve is a typical constraint-based improvement curve, based on the five focusing steps. Note that as each constraint is broken, a surge in system performance occurs. But like the traditional curve, it begins to level off if the five steps are not repeated. Similarly, over time, the solution begins to obsolesce as the environment evolves, and performance begins to deteriorate. However, these diminishing returns can be avoided by starting the next iteration of the five focusing steps as the *rate* of improvement begins to level off.

TQM's shortcomings have been observed by a number of business and management authorities.[4] Terrence R. Ozan, a partner with Ernst and Young, said, "A lot of companies read lots of books, did lots of training, formed teams and tried to implement 9000 new practices simultaneously, but you don't get results that way. It's just too much." Many TQM believers discovered that although it works well in tweaking manufacturing processes to greater efficiency (suboptimization?), TQM is relatively difficult to apply to more complex, less structured functions. Moreover, many employees, weary of being "made over," have often seen TQM as just another ploy by underperforming CEOs desperate to report good news to shareholders—an impression that doesn't inspire willing cooperation.

INTRINSIC MOTIVATION

Besides the benefits of quicker, measurable improvement and knowing how to attribute results, there's an ancillary benefit to a constraint-based approach. Nothing motivates like success. The successes people achieve often inspire and encourage them to do more. What could be more intrinsically motivating to people in an organization than for them to see significant, tangible progress that they can *relate directly* to their own efforts? "The company is *X* percent ahead of where it was at this time a year ago, and our constraint-breaking efforts are a big part of the reason why!"

The lesson to be learned here is this: TOC is *not* a replacement for TQM. It's not an either-or situation. TOC provides the means to turbocharge TQM, to focus its efforts and realize its benefits without having to wait years for results. TOC doesn't compel you to build teams or empower people. It doesn't demand statistical process control. It doesn't require concurrent engineering or failure mode effects analysis. It has no dependency relationship with any of the traditional or new tools of the quality movement. Rather, it's intended to aim TQM efforts toward the part of a system that can potentially provide the most benefit for the least effort.

TOC can be much like an automatic radar tracking system. By the nature of its capability to zero in on the system's constraint—the critical one, as opposed to the trivial many—TOC helps decide what to work on first, which might suggest which of the host of TQM tools is appropriate for the situation. And management can be reasonably well assured of realizing the most bang for its improvement buck in the process.

POLICY CONSTRAINTS VERSUS PHYSICAL CONSTRAINTS

Thus far, we've established that most organizations function as systems, rather than as processes. We've seen that determining the goal of a system is the first critical step in improving it, and that necessary conditions must be satisfied in order to realize the goal. We've discussed the concept of systems as chains, with the constraint being the weakest link, and the advantages of breaking constraints sequentially using the five focusing steps.

But so far, all the constraints we've used as examples have appeared to be physical restrictions. It's relatively easy to locate physical constraints. They can often be found where backlogs of work-in-progress are high. Or they can be calculated based on the capacity or rate of each step in the process. In most cases, however, the real constraint to improved system performance is not physical, it's *policy.* A policy constraint is often the cause of a physical constraint.

What is a policy constraint? Anything that isn't tangible (physical), but restricts system performance, is probably a policy constraint. Most often, they're the rules, plans, procedures, measurements, or other guidance—usually written, but frequently oral—that prescribe "how things are done around here." Policy constraints can manifest themselves in training (or lack thereof). They can also be the benchmarks and measurements we use to assess our success—or failure. Let's consider some examples of policy constraints.

At one time or another, everybody has experienced, and probably complained about, the condition of America's highways. This highway system, once a model for the world to emulate, has fallen into such disrepair in the last 20 years that it will be difficult, if not impossible, to completely restore the entire system. The backlog of bad roads is so large that repair or replacement is deferred much longer than it should be. Repaired roads deteriorate again before the highway departments can get around to them.[5]

What's limiting our ability to maintain our nation's highways in good condition? It's a policy constraint. Federal funds support a large share of road maintenance in the United States. Federal funds are also attached by very powerful purse strings to federal law, and federal laws (many state laws, too) mandate that highway construction contracts go to the lowest bidder. Competition among contractors is keen, and each one cuts costs at every turn to remain competitive. While longer lasting, more durable road materials exist in the world today, highway contractors don't use them, because they invariably cost more, even though they may deliver far more than their cost in service life extension. The constraint is a policy that says, in essence, "We don't care how long our highway will last; we just care about how little we'll have to pay you up front."

Could we have better, longer lasting highways for less cost and aggravation to drivers and maintainers alike? Of course! The only thing we'd have to do is *change the policy* that says contracts must be awarded based on the lowest initial construction cost. Instead, the policy should specify the *lowest life-cycle cost.* They do this in Europe, and their highways last 40 years or more without needing major repairs or rebuilding.

Here's another example. A well-known high-tech company maintains a research facility in northern California.[6] Some of the best and brightest engineers and scientists in the world work there. They're given research opportunities that would turn most of their contemporaries elsewhere green with envy. And they've produced incredible results. The company, however, never developed or exploited many of the technology breakthroughs their researchers invented. Somewhere a policy (in this case, perhaps, a mind-set) said, "This is nice, but it doesn't really fit into our core competency. So just put it over there on the shelf for now."

Many of these breakthroughs were eventually licensed to other companies, some of which were turbocharged silicon valley start-ups. Others were noticed by sharks who swim in that high-tech environment and were subsequently reverse-engineered because they were never patented. In any event, the company never capitalized on any of these ideas—ideas their own people invented! And look what this company gave away because of a policy constraint: the original personal computer, the graphical user interface (which became the Macintosh "look," and Microsoft Windows™), the mouse, Ethernet, and the laser printer. As you can see, policy constraints can result in opportunity costs as well as real dollar costs.

One phenomenon Goldratt has observed over the 20 years he's been developing and applying the theory of constraints is that policy constraints are usually much more devastating than physical constraints. He's also noted that nearly every physical constraint results from some policy constraint. Here's one such example.

A manufacturing company in a very competitive industry accepts and evaluates proposals from within for developmental projects. A bright production engineer, fresh from a professional symposium where he saw a leading edge manufacturing process displayed, sends a proposal up-channel to senior management. The proposal suggests developing some proprietary equipment based on the new technology. The potential for decreasing manufacturing cycle time and increasing product quality is significant—an order-of-magnitude improvement. What a competitive advantage this application of new technology could provide! However, the engineer's proposal is rejected by senior management. It would take too long to pay off. The board of directors of this particular company reserved for itself approval authority on development projects. The board had established an internal rate of return of 20 percent in two years for all new development projects (policy constraint). Unfortunately, the proposal forecast a return of only 18 percent, and then only after three years, not two. So the company did not develop the new production technology. Three years later, in a desperate attempt to remain competitive, the company embarked on a crash project to do the same thing, costing significantly more than it would have originally. But it was too late. Competitive advantage had already been lost, and the company eventually filed for bankruptcy. The core problem behind their failure was an artificial measure of merit—a policy—that considered only short-term financial return but never took into account the consequences of failing to maintain technological competitiveness.

WHY POLICY CONSTRAINTS ARE THE TOUGHER CHALLENGES

From the standpoint of purely physical effort, policies are probably easier to change because, theoretically, they only require rewriting rather than the purchase of a new piece of equipment. But if your core problem—the entire system's constraint—is a policy, two things conspire against breaking it.

First, most people have difficulty identifying exactly *what* policy is causing the resultant effects in the first place. It's very difficult for most people to trace a complex chain of cause and effect back to a root cause, so unrecognized problems usually go unsolved. Sometimes efforts are focused exclusively on the obvious indicators, or undesirable effects, instead of their causes.

Second, it's not enough to accurately identify a policy as the constraint. The responsibility for it often lies in somebody else's domain—somebody whose willing cooperation is needed to change it. This is fairly common in organizations large enough to have several departments. Responsibility may even reside with the boss of the entire system. Persuading such people to act on a constraining policy they might be responsible for is not easy. It often requires policymakers to accept responsibility for poor organizational performance. Very few people are secure enough in their own positions and self-worth to be able to admit that they own a problem that's hurting the entire organization.

So you're likely to see two reactions from people when you show them the policy constraint. One is denial: "It's not really a problem—it's your imagination." The other is justification of the need for the policy constraint: "Well, maybe you're right . . . but we *need* to have this policy *because* . . ." (fill in the reason). Either way, people are likely to resist accepting responsibility or doing something about it.

If it truly is a system constraint, the inherent system interdependencies will inevitably cause the policy to affect other departments as well. Also, if the whole organization isn't optimized toward the entire system (which most aren't), chances are that it's suboptimized toward individual departments. For some departments, the policy may be very good or favorable. Those departments will argue against changing the policy constraint, and they'll probably make very persuasive arguments, certainly emotional ones if not logical ones. This is the human resistance barrier that total quality management and just about every other management innovation has come up against. It's also why some potentially very effective management innovations become no more than fads—here today, gone tomorrow. They can't beat resistance to changing the status quo.

This is one reason why Goldratt contends that policy constraints are significantly more difficult to identify and break. The highway construction case described previously is a typical example. The lowest bidder nearly always wins the contract, so contractors are eager to cut costs as much as possible to be competitive. They buy cheap materials to keep costs low, so these materials don't last. But the policy constraint is a federal law that requires the contract to be awarded to the lowest bidder. And the definition, by law, of *lowest bid* is lowest *initial acquisition cost.* Consequently, no effort goes into increasing quality. There's no benefit to the contractors in building higher-quality roads, and the law actually rewards those who don't. Could this policy constraint be broken by formally redefining the term *lowest bid* to mean *least life-cycle cost,* defining a life cycle as 40 years or so, and making contractors warrant their work? Current law doesn't allow warranties, either.

We know what the policy constraint is—it's a bad law. But have you ever tried to get a law changed? Not only do you have to persuade a majority of the U.S. Congress, you also have to overcome the resistance of special interests who have figured out how to make the current flawed highway acquisition system work to their advantage. They'll be not only in denial; they'll resist the change outright to preserve a system suboptimized in their favor.[‡7] So how do you overcome resistance to changing a root cause that is really a policy? The theory of constraints provides one very effective way to do it.

THEORY OF CONSTRAINTS AND WORLD-CLASS PERFORMANCE

So you want to be world-class? You want to compete with the best, and maybe win regularly? If you do, then you'd better know where your organization's constraint is *today* and where it will be *tomorrow*. You'd better be able to figure out *how* to break your constraints, both today's and tomorrow's. Once you have a good idea how to do that, you need to be able to execute it. And in executing it, you have to be prepared to swim against the tide of human resistance, sometimes the most formidable obstacle of all to real system improvement. But if you really want to be world-class—or *stay* world-class—the blueprint is in the chapters that follow, including the key to the shackles of human resistance.

> *Learning usually passes through three stages. In the beginning, you learn the right answers. In the second stage, you learn the right questions. In the third and final stage, you learn which questions are worth asking.*
>
> *—Unknown*

NOTES

1. Eliyahu M. Goldratt, *The Goal,* 2d ed. (Great Barrington, Mass.: North River Press, 1992), 307.
2. W. Edwards Deming, *Out of the Crisis* (Cambridge, Mass.: Massachusetts Institute of Technology, Center for Advanced Engineering Study, 1986), 24, 86–92.
3. W. Edwards Deming, *The New Economics for Industry, Government, and Education* Cambridge, Mass.: Massachusetts Institute of Technology, Center for Advanced Engineering Study, 1993), 94, 104–110.
4. Dan Vukelich, "The era of total quality management may be over," *The Press-Enterprise* (Riverside, Calif.: Scripps-McClatchy Western Service, January 4, 1996), D-3.
5. Betsy Dance, "Why Our Nation's Highways Go to Pot," *The Washington Monthly* (November 1991), reprinted in *Readers Digest* (May 1992), 121.
6. Robert X. Cringely, *Accidental Empires* (New York: Harper Collins, 1996), 82–92.
7. Betsy Dance, "Why Our Nation's Highways Go To Pot," *The Washington Monthly* (November 1991), reprinted in *Readers Digest* (May 1992), 124.

---

‡In 1991, the President and CEO of the American Road and Transportation Builders Association said, "I'm not sure it would be worth the effort. The current procurement system, as far as we know, indicates that there are no problems."

Chapter 3
THE TOOLS

Give me a lever long enough and a place to stand, and I will move the world.

—Archimedes

MANAGING CHANGE WITH TOC

The cases cited in the previous chapter show how damaging a policy constraint can be. Earlier we saw that physical constraints are fairly easy to identify and break using the five focusing steps. There's no shortage of literature on how to manage physical constraints.[1] But how can we identify an insidious *policy* that might be hurting us? The first of the five focusing steps is identify the constraint. When the constraint is a policy, or when we can't easily compare capacity to demand, how do we go about finding and breaking the constraint?

The same five focusing steps can be applied in breaking any constraint. But when the constraint is a policy, the first four steps are consolidated into three. We must determine

- *What* to change.
- What to change *to*.
- *How to cause* the change.

1. *What to change?* The answer to this question, obviously, is the constraint. Knowing what to change requires us to identify that constraint, which is the first of the five focusing steps.

2. *What to change to?* Answering this question is an exercise in creation and validation. Since we're working at the system level, with a system constraint, any change we might make is bound to have far-reaching effects on the components (and people) within the system. This will probably require more than just an incremental improvement. It's more likely to demand breakthrough thinking, which is a creative process. Since the configuration of the system might have to change, perhaps dramatically, the first part of determining what to change to involves creating this new system configuration.

However, any change carries with it some degree of risk. The bigger the change, the bigger the risk. More than one bright idea has been shot down by what might be charitably called the ready-fire-aim syndrome. Senior managers are often too quick to embrace a proposed change without first asking two questions: (1) Will this change really deliver the results we want, and (2) What adverse side effects can we expect? The answers to these questions provide *validation* that the proposed creative change is the right one. This step is a consolidation of steps 2 and 4 of the five focusing steps (*exploit* and *elevate*).

3. *How to cause the change?* Once you've validated the bright idea, you're faced with the most daunting part of constraint breaking: how to turn the idea into reality. The implementation stage is where almost every great idea is stillborn. Ideas are not solutions. They have to be converted into effective action. This demands that we answer three more questions:

1. What obstacles stand in the way of our implementing this bright idea?
2. How do we overcome these obstacles?
3. What must we do—and in what sequence—to turn our ideas into reality?

This step is a consolidation of steps 3 and 4 of the five focusing steps.

Answering these three questions—*what* to change, what to change *to,* and *how* to cause the change—is elemental to change of any kind. They can be considered the strategic navigation questions for the entire system. Their answers constitute the information a captain needs to know to steer a ship—or executives need to know to steer their organizations through an uncertain future.

When things aren't going as expected, when a system isn't performing as it should, there are four possible levels of response. The first is to do nothing, hoping that the problem will resolve itself and things will improve on their own. The second is to make minor changes in the system, or fine adjustments. Continuous process improvement is typical of this approach, which can be very effective if it's begun in time, if management is persistent, and if the problems aren't life threatening to the system.

The third level is to make major changes. When a heart bypass is necessary, incremental changes in life-style won't be sufficient. Such major changes have been the objective of *re-engineering.* The fourth, and most drastic, response is to throw out the existing system completely and begin all over with a new design. Understandably—thankfully?—this doesn't happen very often, because it's costly, and its effects on the people in the system are often devastating.

Our choices in responding to a system problem are to do nothing, make small changes, make large changes, or start over from scratch. Most executives and senior managers aren't willing to do nothing; after all, it's their job to improve things. But they usually avoid starting over from scratch, and for good reason: it's expensive, and the outcomes are usually uncertain. This leaves two choices for the majority of change decision: small changes or large ones.

Total quality management (TQM) generally focuses on the incremental smaller changes. Business process re-engineering has been used to address the larger ones. Neither approach has lived up to its advance billing. Earlier we saw one reason why so many organizations struggle with TQM—failure to work primarily on the system constraint. Re-engineering has fallen short of expectations, too, and because it deals with broader, more traumatic changes, its failures, and their related effects, are much more dramatic. Embarking on major changes without considering the related human toll can wound people's loyalty, motivation, and sense of security beyond repair.

As with TQM, the success of re-engineering lies in its execution. If TQM's odds of success can be improved by taking a constraint-oriented approach, could the same be true for re-engineering? Can the theory of constraints, and its tools, provide management the capability to effect major change in the system while mitigating or eliminating the adverse effects of that change? Experience suggests that it can. Change is never painless, but a judicious application of the TOC tools can dramatically smooth the transition and reduce discomfort.

THE THEORY OF CONSTRAINTS THINKING PROCESS

As he encountered more and more policy constraints in organizations, Goldratt realized that the five focusing steps alone weren't adequate to deal with the questions of *what* to change, what to change *to,* and *how* to cause the change. Over a seven-year-period beginning in 1985, Goldratt created and refined a logical thinking process to deal with the qualitative problems presented by policy constraints. Because the thinking process is logic based, it isn't confined to physical constraints, manufacturing systems, or for-profit organizations. The thinking process is applicable to *any* system, as long as you can define the goal of the system.

There are four criteria that must be satisfied in order to successfully apply this thinking process. First, you must have the motivation—a burning desire is preferred—to improve the system. Second, you must have a thorough knowledge of the subject—the system you want to improve. Third, you must have some degree of authority, or at least influence, to initiate change. Finally, you must understand the theory of constraints and the thinking process methodology and be self-sufficient in them. The first three are your responsibility to provide. The remainder of this book will start you on the road to the last.

The theory of constraints thinking process is composed of five basic logical tools, one subtool, and some logic rules. The five tools are the

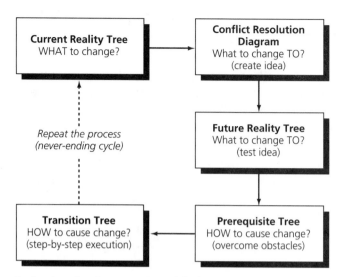

FIGURE 3.1 The five logical tools as an integrated thinking process.

current reality tree, the conflict resolution diagram, the future reality tree, the prerequisite tree, and the transition tree (Figure 3.1). The subtool, the negative branch, is an adjunct to the future reality tree. The logic rules, called the categories of legitimate reservation, guide the construction of our trees and ensure they are logically sound.

It's important to note that while Goldratt originally conceived of using these five logic trees as an integrated set, they are also well suited to use as individual tools. You can use an entire box of tools to build a house. Or, if all you need to do is to hang a picture on the wall, you can use just the hammer. Succeeding chapters will demonstrate how to use the five tools either as individuals or as an integrated set.

Current Reality Tree

It's been said that a well-defined problem is already half-solved. The current reality tree (CRT) is a problem identification tool. It helps us examine the cause-and-effect logic behind our current situation. The CRT begins with the undesirable effects we see around us, which tell us that we have a problem. It helps us work back to identify a few root causes, or a single core problem, which generate all the undesirable effects we're experiencing. The core problem is usually the constraint we're trying to identify in the five focusing steps. The CRT tells us *what to change*—the one simplest change to make that will have the greatest positive effect on our system. Chapter 5 describes the current reality tree in detail, gives relevant examples, and provides instructions on how to construct one.[2]

Conflict Resolution Diagram

Goldratt designed the conflict resolution diagram (CRD), which he refers to as an "evaporating cloud," to resolve the hidden conflicts that usually perpetuate chronic problems. The CRD is predicated on the idea that most core problems exist because some underlying tug-of-war, or conflict, prevents straightforward solution of the problem—otherwise, the problem would have been solved long before. The CRD also can be a *creative engine,* an idea generator that allows us to invent new, breakthrough solutions to such nagging problems. Consequently, the CRD provides the first part of the answer in determining *what to change to.*

Chapter 6 describes the conflict resolution diagram in detail, gives several pertinent examples from both personal and business situations, and provides guidance for using one to resolve conflict.[3]

Future Reality Tree

The future reality tree (FRT) serves two purposes. First, it allows us to verify that the action we'd like to take to resolve the core problem will, in fact, produce the ultimate results we desire. Second, through the negative branch (NB), it enables us to identify any adverse new consequences our contemplated action might have and nip them in the bud. These functions provide two important benefits. We can logically test the effectiveness of our proposed course of action before investing much time, energy, or resources in it, and we can avoid making the situation worse than when we started. This tool answers the second part of the question *what to change to* by validating our new system configuration. Used in this way, the FRT can also be an invaluable strategic planning tool. Chapter 7 describes the future reality tree in detail, providing examples and instructions on how to create one.[4]

Prerequisite Tree

Once we've decided on a course of action and verified that it will resolve the core problem without adverse consequences, the prerequisite tree (PRT) helps us execute that decision. It identifies the obstacles that might keep us from doing what we want to do and helps determine the best ways to overcome those obstacles. It also tells us in what sequence we need to complete the major milestones in implementing our decision. The PRT provides the first half of the answer to the last question *how to change.* Chapter 9 describes the prerequisite tree in detail and provides examples and procedures for constructing one.[5]

Transition Tree

The last of the five basic logical tools is the transition tree (TT). It helps develop the detailed step-by-step instructions for implementing our chosen course of action. Besides providing the steps to take (in sequence), it also displays the rationale for each step, which is often a critical factor in persuading people to help implement the change. The TT is essentially the detailed road map to our objective, and it answers the second half of the question *how to change*. Chapter 10 describes the transition tree, complete with relevant examples, and gives instructions on how to build one.[6]

Negative Branch

A subset of the future reality tree, the negative branch (NB) is designed specifically to keep us from jumping out of the frying pan and into the fire. While the FRT can tell us whether our idea for resolving the core problem will work, the NB tells us whether this idea will create new problems or worse problems than we already have. If the proposed idea really is a good one, the NB can tell us what we must do to keep the adverse consequences from developing in the first place. Chapter 8 describes the NB in detail as well, gives some interesting examples, and tells how to construct one quickly and effectively.[7]

Categories of Legitimate Reservation

Eight rules of logic govern the construction and validation of four of the five trees (CRT, FRT, PRT, and TT). A thorough understanding of the categories can also help us spot illogical assertions or statements of cause and effect in conversation, meetings, formal presentations, or written documents without even having to construct a tree. If you've ever been subjected to "smoke-and-mirrors", the categories of legitimate reservation (CLR) can help you see through the distractions.[8]

GLOBAL SYSTEM MEASURES

We've emphasized the value of a systems approach rather than analytical thinking. We've seen that the theory of constraints is, in fact, a systems approach, and we've examined the principles and tools that are part of the theory. But there's still a missing ingredient: *feedback*. In other words, How are we doing in our efforts to achieve our goal? Most systems have ways to feed back answers to that question. Figure 1.1 showed a feedback loop in its depiction of a system.

Feedback implies some kind of measurement against some predetermined standard. It's essential if we're to be able to control and correct a system in any significant way—otherwise, we'd just be shooting in the dark. If we're going to subordinate process efficiencies in favor of over-all system performance, we're faced with a problem: how do we relate the daily decisions we make at the operational level to real performance improvement at the system level? In other words, how can we be sure we don't expend nonproductive effort on a nonconstraint, or create unnecessary turbulence within the system? Conversely, how will we know when our improvements to the constraint are actually working?

To satisfy this need, Goldratt conceived three nontraditional system-level measures to aid in evaluating local daily decisions for their contribution to achieving the system's goal. Combined with a disciplined commitment to identify and concentrate on the system constraint, these measures can provide instant feedback on whether a given decision will actually benefit the overall system. These measures are throughput, inventory (sometimes referred to as investment), and operating expense.[9] The definitions of these terms warrant some attention because they aren't necessarily what they seem on the surface, nor are they used in traditional ways.

THROUGHPUT (T), INVENTORY (I), AND OPERATING EXPENSE (OE)

Goldratt defines *throughput* as the rate at which the system generates money through sales.[10] Another way of saying this might be all the money coming into a system from the outside. This definition excludes internal transfer pricing. If it hasn't been sold to somebody outside the company, it doesn't count as throughput. Most of this is the revenue the system generates through sales of its product or service, less the truly variable cost of generating the sale. Another way of saying this is total sales revenue minus variable cost.

$$T = SR - VC$$

For many organizations, the only real variable costs are the materials used to make the product or deliver the service. However, where other truly variable costs (for example, sales commissions, consumable supplies, and so on) can be identified, these should be subtracted as well. Rule of thumb: if it's an expense that is incurred as a direct result of producing a unit of the product or service, one that wouldn't be incurred if we didn't produce the product or service today, it should be included as a variable cost.

Goldratt defines *inventory* as all the money a system invests in things it intends to sell. The lion's share of this investment for a manufacturing operation is raw materials or purchased parts. However, Goldratt's definition of inventory excludes the added value of labor and overhead.[11] In a manufacturing system, inventory comes in three basic flavors: raw materials, finished products as yet undelivered, and things that are somewhere in between (work-in-process). Products built to stock (that is, no firm existing order against the finished item) might be considered *output,* but they are not throughput. As such, they must be treated as inventory until actually sold, at which time they can be part of the throughput calculation.

Inventory in a service organization may be quite different, but fixed assets and real property are still physical inventory, or as many organizations prefer, *Investment.* Even outdated equipment will eventually be sold when replaced by new, even if only at scrap value. When sold, the obsolete equipment actually contributes to throughput because the proceeds constitute money, however minimal, coming into the company.

The third measurement is *operating expense.* Goldratt considers this to be all the money the system spends turning inventory into throughput.[12] Essentially, this means all fixed expenses, including direct labor and overhead—those expenses the system would incur even if it never produced a single product or unit of service. The CEO's company car fits into this category, as do all the consumable office supplies and salaries, depreciation, interest, basic utilities, and telephone service. These *fixed* expenses may have accrued during some past accounting period, when the product was actually made. Keeping them under operating expense allows them to be charged to that previous period's operations and not lumped into unit costs and inventories that are sold later, or not at all. Allocating fixed expenses to production units sends an insidious, erroneous message to the plant: The more we make, the less each one costs, even if we don't sell them.

One operating expense worthy of special note is labor. In the past, it has been common practice to assign labor costs as variable product costs (for example, labor hour per unit produced). In the early twentieth century, before the advent of labor unions and hourly pay for employees, this undoubtedly made sense. Labor was clearly a variable cost of production when people were paid by the piece for their work. However, now that labor is paid by the punch of a clock or by salary regardless of the units of product or service produced, it makes much more sense to consider it a periodic fixed cost.

T, I, OE, AND TRADITIONAL FINANCIAL MEASURES

These measures may seem a little strange, but they *do* relate directly to the traditional measures of net profit (NP), return on investment (ROI), and cash flow (CF). Net profit is essentially throughput minus operating expense for a given period.

$$NP = T - OE$$

Return on Investment is net profit divided by inventory (or investment).

$$ROI = \frac{T - OE}{I}$$

Cash flow is net profit (throughput minus operating expense) plus or minus the change in inventory for the same period.

$$CF = T - OE \pm \Delta I$$

One might reasonably ask, Why bother with throughput, inventory, and operating expense? The traditional financial measures—net profit, ROI, and cash flow—tell us all we need to know. From a financial reporting standpoint, this is probably true. But daily operating decisions are made at the operational level, not usually in the finance office. It's not easy for line supervisors or middle managers to decide how their actions might affect net profit, ROI, or cash flow. However, throughput, inventory, and operating expense are more easily understood in relation to operational decisions. For example,

- Will the decision result in a better use of the worst-constrained resource?
- Will it make full use of the worst-constrained resource?
- Will it increase total sales?
- Will it speed up delivery to customers?
- Will it provide a characteristic of product or service that our competitors don't have?
- Will it win repeat business for us?
- Will it reduce scrap or rework?
- Will it reduce warranty or replacement costs?

If the answers to these questions are yes, the decision will improve throughput.

- Will we need less raw material or purchased parts?
- Will we be able to keep less material on hand?
- Will it reduce work-in-process?
- Will we need less capital facilities or equipment to do the same work?

If the answer is yes, the decision will decrease inventory (or investment).

- Will overhead go down?
- Will payments to vendors decrease?
- Will we be able to divert some people to do other throughput-generating work?

If the answer is yes, the decision will decrease operating expense. These are all decisions that middle management and line supervisors can make, assuring a favorable effect on net profit, ROI, and cash flow without even understanding those financial terms.

How T, I, and OE are used in operational decisions is as important as their definitions. Simple algebra tells us that net profit increases when T goes up or OE goes down. Furthermore, T can go up by increasing sales revenue or by reducing variable cost of production. Anything done to increase net profit also improves ROI, as long as I remains the same. If I can be decreased, ROI goes up even without an increase in net profit. In fact, the adoption of just-in-time/*kanban* systems is intended to do exactly that. Also, cash flow increases when either T goes up or the time to generate that T is reduced. The assumption here, of course, is that the time saved is productively applied toward generating more T.

MANAGEMENT PRIORITIES

Reducing OE and I are good things to do. Increasing T is, too. But in what order of priority? Common business practice is to focus on reducing costs as a way to make money and be competitive. This would tend to pull us toward OE as the overriding consideration. Since the mid-1980s, thanks to the Japanese, mainstream business has begun to recognize the significance of the tremendous investment in variable inventory and fixed assets, so there's also a strong pull toward reducing I, too. But there are some logical reasons why the traditional emphasis on cost reduction is misplaced.

The cost reduction emphasis is all around us. Downsizing and layoffs are probably the most visible indications. Some management philosophies emphasize hardware cost reduction as well, under the assumption that if costs are minimized, profitability from product or service will take care of itself. There are, however, some very good reasons why a cost reduction emphasis can be not only nonproductive, but harmful as well. Take a look at Figure 3.2.

The theory of constraints suggests all the money involved with a particular for-profit organization be assigned to one of three categories: T, I, or OE. We know that increasing T and reducing I and OE are desirable. But

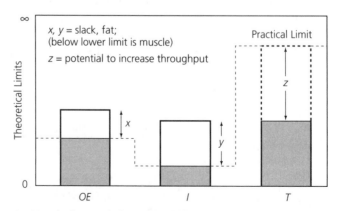

As *OE* and *I* decrease below practical limit, increasing trend of *T* is reversed

FIGURE 3.2 Limits to *T, I,* and *OE.* From Dettmer, H. W., *Goldratt's Theory of Constraints* (1996)

take a close look at the picture. Theoretically, OE and I could be reduced to zero, but from a practical standpoint, before we reach zero, we pass a point where reducing I and OE any further damages our ability to generate T. Remember the definitions? OE is spent to turn I into T. If we arbitrarily reduce OE, we may not be able to turn enough I into T to remain profitable. For example, most businesses would consider a 15 percent reduction in OE a dramatic cost saving. Any more than that is usually achieved only through severe slashes in the work force, division shutdowns, and major reorganization, all of which have direct impact on revenues and T.

So right from the beginning, we're faced with a fairly narrow range in which we can affect I and OE without degrading T. The first OE reduction may be significant in actual dollars, but with each cycle of I and OE reduction, we realize less and less benefit to the bottom line.

Inventory, or investment, also has a practical lower limit for most businesses. Although many firms have learned how to cut unnecessary material inventories in their factories and warehouses, daily fluctuations in demand still require safety stocks.

Now look at the part of Figure 3.2 representing T. The theoretical limit for increases in T is virtually infinite. Obviously, the practical limit is much lower than that, but it's still very high.

Consider a consumer appliance business, for example. It may be producing 60,000 toasters a year, but there are five billion people on the face of the earth. Even if only one out of ten could buy a toaster, that would still mean 500,000,000 potential customers. Certainly not infinite, but to the company producing 60,000 a year, it might as well be.

The point is that even though the possibilities for increasing T aren't infinite, they offer considerably more potential for improving net profit, return on investment, and cash flow than reducing I and OE. Besides, in reducing I and OE, we quickly reach a point of diminishing returns, which is not so when we increase T. So it makes sense that increasing T ought to be our first priority.

What should the second priority be? Historically, in the United States, reducing OE has always had a very high priority—the highest of the three, actually. So one might think that reducing OE would be the next most important thing to do. But in reality, there is probably more latitude, at least initially, for reducing I than OE in most organizations. Moreover, reductions in inventory show up *immediately* in the financials because inventory is directly translatable to dollars. For many companies, the investment in inventory is huge. The Japanese were quick to realize that money and space unnecessarily tied up in I weren't doing them any good, so they invented the just-in-time/*kanban* system to solve that problem. Doing so made their companies leaner and meaner very quickly.

It should be obvious by now that under a theory of constraints philosophy, reducing OE occupies third place on the priority list. This is not to imply that big savings aren't available in operating expenses. In fact, there's a seductive tendency to want to reduce OE first because its impact on financial condition is even more immediate than that of inventory reductions.

Traditional	Japanese	TOC
1. Decrease *OE*	1. Decrease *I*	1. Increase *T*
2. Increase *T*	2. Increase *T*	2. Decrease *I*
3. Decrease *I*	3. Decrease *OE*	3. Decrease *OE*

FIGURE 3.3 **Management priorities.** From Dettmer, H.W., *Goldratt's Theory of Constraints* (1996)

OE reductions are a one-for-one saving. Every dollar of OE saved goes straight to the bottom line. However, they won't produce the big gains in profitability that increases in T will. Moreover, the diminishing return phenomenon is even more pronounced in this area than in reductions in I. After all, in the competitive global economy we face in the 1990s and beyond, most organizations have already cut just about all the fat there is out of their systems. Any further reductions are likely to do nothing but cut muscle—the capability to produce more T. Therefore, after the first comprehensive pass at reducing OE, an organization's efforts are far more productive when directed primarily toward increasing T. Figure 3.3 compares traditional, Japanese, and TOC priorities.

If we increase T, reduce I, and reduce OE in that order, then net profit, return on investment, and cash flow will all improve at a faster rate. However, it's not very practical, or dignified, for senior management to run out onto the production floor yelling, Increase T first! Then reduce I and OE! To the supervisor at the operating level, these are still fairly abstract concepts. How will the people out where the "rubber meets the road" know whether the decisions they make on a daily basis are help-ing, hurting, or totally ineffectual? They need more relevant guidance. Figure 3.4 shows how traditional global measures of success can be con-verted, in stages, into criteria the working level can use to guide their local decisions.

As you can see, the matrix starts on the left with the traditional corporate-level measures of net profit, return on investment, and cash flow. In the second column, these are converted into their TOC equiva-lents, which are further reduced to individual factors that are usually assessable at the local level. The local measures are converted in the fifth column to yes-or-no criteria questions that can be used to evaluate local decisions. The arrows indicate the desirable direction in which the decision should drive the factor.

T, I, AND OE IN NOT-FOR-PROFIT SYSTEMS

Right now some of you might thinking, "But I'm not in a for-profit busi-ness. How does the concept of T, I, and OE apply to me?" This is a valid question. Goldratt conceived of these measures specifically to satisfy the needs of for-profit companies. They are easily applied to profit-oriented

Traditional global measure . . .	expressed in TOC terms . . .	and further reduced to . . .	produces the local measure . . .		which is expressed as a question about the decision being considered . . .		leading to the decision.
Net Profit	Throughput minus operating expense NP = T – OE	Throughput equals total sales revenue minus total variable cost of sales T = ΣSR – ΣVC NP = (ΣSR – ΣVC) – OE	Sales revenue Variable cost of sales Fixed costs	(SR) (VC) (OE)	Will it increase sales?	(ΣSR↑)	If yes, DO it.
					Will it speed up deliveries to clients?	(t↓)	
					Will it reduce backlogs?	(t↓)	
					Will it reduce our need for production materials?	(ΣVC↓)	
					Will it shorten production time?	(t↓)	If no, DON'T do it
					Will it reduce fixed expenses?	(OE↓)	
Return on investment	Net profit divided by inventory ROI = $\frac{NP}{I}$ or ROI = $\frac{T - OE}{I}$	Total sales revenues minus total variable cost of sales minus operating expense divided by inventory ROI = $\frac{(ΣSR - ΣVC) - OE}{I}$	Sales revenue Variable cost of sales Fixed costs Cost of product/ service-related consumable materials	(SR) (VC) (OE) (I)	Will it shorten the time between product/service delivery and time of payment?	(t↓)	
					Will it increase the volume of revenues received in the same time period?	(ΣSR↑)	
					Will it shorten the time between receipt of order and delivery to customer?	(t↓)	
Cash flow	Net profit (Throughput minus operating expense plus or minus the change in inventory) CF = T – OE ± ΔI	Total revenue from all products/ services actually delivered minus the total truly variable cost of products/service actually delivered +/– the change in inventory CF = ΣSR – ΣVC – OE ± ΔI	Sales revenue Variable cost of sales Fixed costs Cost of product/ service-related consumable materials	(SR) (VC) (OE) (I)	Will it free excess capacity?	(ΣSR↑)(I↓)	
					Will it make better use of the constraint?	(ΣSR↑)	
					Will we need fewer materials on hand?	(I↓)	
					Will we need less equipment?	(I↓)	
					t = time		

FIGURE 3.4 TOC decision matrix.

systems because the goal of such organizations is expressible in units of money. Consequently, metrics that can all be expressed in monetary terms are convenient and useful. But it doesn't make sense to try to jam not-for-profit organizations directly and completely into an evaluation concept that was specifically designed for profit-making enterprises.

Not-for-profit organizations, such as charities, foundations, and universities, don't have goals that can be expressed in financial terms. Neither do government agencies, such as public schools, the Department of Defense, social welfare agencies, or prisons. They may have elements of inventory and operating expense that can be quantified in dollars, but their throughput clearly can't because their goals can't. Nor are sales their source of money. In most cases, their operating budgets are allocated to them in some way by an outside source (Figure 3.5). Since throughput is the key indicator of progress toward the system's goal, what can such systems do to evaluate their progress toward their goals?

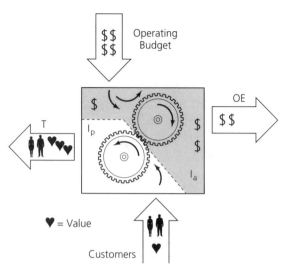

FIGURE 3.5 *T, I,* and *OE* in a not-for-profit. From Dettmer, H. W., *Goldratt's Theory of Constraints* (1996)

Goldratt has suggested one way that not-for-profit organizations or government agencies might still be able to use T, I, and OE productively, though not in the same way that for-profit businesses do.[13] Even not-for-profit organizations and government agencies have operating expenses that can be expressed in dollars, so OE can be handled the same way in both not-for-profit and profit-making businesses: reduce it where possible, but as a third priority.

Goldratt suggests not-for-profit organizations have two kinds of inventory: *active* and *passive*. Active inventory *acts* on something. This would be what we referred to earlier as the investment inventory—the fixed facilities and equipment the system uses in its operations. Active inventory can be quantified in financial terms and can be handled the same way as in a for-profit business: minimize it safely, but as a second priority.

Passive inventory is *acted upon* by the active inventory. This is the part of inventory that is turned into throughput, and is probably not expressible in monetary terms. Moreover, in a not-for-profit organization, it may not be productive to reduce it, unless the goal of the organization is to work itself out of a job.

Consider a hospital, for example. Its active inventory is the building, physical plant, furnishings, medical equipment, and stocked consumable supplies (which become a variable throughput cost once they're used). The costs involved in this part of inventory are relatively easy to quantify and manage in dollars. A hospital's passive inventory is sick patients. They're the raw material that the hospital turns into throughput—well patients—as it pursues its goal of a healthier society. This kind of inventory can't be valued in dollars.

Neither can the hospital's throughput. Well patients (that is, cured) aren't necessarily the only measure of throughput. As medical costs increase and health maintenance organizations abound, prevention efforts become more and more important. How does a hospital measure how many people *didn't* get sick today because of its preventive health care efforts? Such people clearly can't be discounted as throughput, because they definitely contribute to the hospital's goal of a healthier society.

How can we assess our success in managing passive inventory and throughput in this case? Until somebody invents a different surrogate for value as universally accepted as money, Goldratt suggests that the best we are able to do is manage by exception. System constraints are the root causes behind a system's failure to realize its goal. As we'll see later in chapter 5, such root causes aren't usually visible. They manifest themselves in *undesirable effects*. Undesirable effects are outcomes we don't want to occur; they indicate that the system isn't making maximum progress toward achieving its goal.

If breaking a constraint eliminates the root cause of these undesirable effects, then the effects themselves (visible indicators of lack of progress toward the goal) will go away. If we eliminate the visible undesirable effects with constraint-breaking efforts, then increased throughput—progress toward the goal—can be *assumed*. This may be somewhat indirect, but it's probably as good as we're likely to get.

In not-for-profit organizations and government agencies, the primary focus should be on breaking the constraints that cause the undesirable effects first, then managing facilities and equipment as efficiently as possible second, followed by carefully controlling operating expenses, but in doing so, not compromising the capability to produce throughput.

WHEN IS THE CONSTRAINT FINALLY BROKEN?

How do we know when we've broken a constraint? No matter what kind of system we're considering—for-profit business, not-for-profit organization, or government agency—there are some common tactical navigation markers that tell us how much progress we've made.

Constraints are a function of two variables: *capacity* and *demand*. A comparison of the two *at the system level* provides a reliable indicator of progress toward the goal. The following are some questions, the answers to which can tell us how far we've come and what to do next.

1. *Is the constraint internal or external?* Which is larger, demand or capacity? Is the system capable of fully and immediately satisfying the demand placed on it? The answers to these questions tell us whether the current constraint is inside or outside the system. If the system can't keep up with the demand, the constraint is internal—it resides within the system. If the system has slack capacity—the complete system, not just a few components—the constraint is external.

Note that there always will be a constraint, either internal or external, to improved system performance. Internal constraints are usually more under our control, while external constraints may be less so. As internal constraints are progressively broken, a point is eventually reached where nothing *internal to the system* limits system performance anymore. At this point, we can usually observe that capacity exceeds demand. However, the constraint is not gone; it's just moved outside the system, to the marketplace in the case of a commercial business.

So constraints are never really permanently broken. They merely migrate from one place to another. The physical resource that used to be the constraint still remains; it's just no longer the system constraint anymore. Once we've solved all of our capacity problems, demand becomes the constraint. To achieve even more system progress toward the goal, we have to break the demand constraint, which will inevitably return the constraint back *into* the system. Continued progress toward the goal then becomes a repeating cycle of breaking the internal constraint, which pushes the constraint out into the demand area (marketplace), then breaking the demand constraint, which pulls it back into the system again. The maximum rate of progress toward the system's goal is achieved when this out-then-in constraint migration oscillates in a very narrow band around the system's boundary, never getting too deeply embedded within the system or out in the demand environment.

2. Is the constraint physical or policy? Knowing whether our constraint is internal or external tells us where to focus our efforts and suggests what to do. If the constraint is external, it's almost certainly a policy. If it's internal, it could be either physical or policy. If it's a physical constraint, a policy might be the root cause behind it.

A current reality tree can tell us fairly quickly whether we're faced with a physical or a policy constraint. If the constraint is exclusively physical, we can follow the five focusing steps. If the constraint is a policy, the thinking process tools can help us reconfigure existing reality.

3. Has the constraint moved recently? A noticeable, sometimes abrupt, positive jump in system performance is a good indication that a constraint has been exploited or broken—if we've been bending efforts toward breaking the constraint. Traditional management measures and data collection can often pinpoint exactly when this happens, but a TOC measure—throughput—is probably a more reliable indicator that a constraint has been broken. Remember: constraints don't disappear; they only move somewhere else. So the jump in system performance should be regarded as nothing more than a cue to start the first step over again: identify where the system's constraint is now.

GENERAL MOTORS

General Motors competes with Ford, Chrysler, and the Japanese for a share of the U.S. market in automobile sales. Like other industries in highly competitive markets, the auto industry finds itself less able than ever before to compete on the basis of price alone. In the 1980s, the

Japanese drove Detroit to rethink its business philosophy. By delivering higher quality cars at lower prices than American automakers could, the Japanese forced American manufacturers to face seriously the issues of quality and customer satisfaction for the first time.

After billions of dollars of investment in quality improvements, the fortunes of the big three U.S. automakers began to turn. The competitive advantages of the Japanese—quality and price—had not been seriously threatened in the late 1980s, but by the early 1990s, the playing field had begun to level out. The differences in quality between American and Japanese cars became less pronounced, and, owing to a favorable dollar-yen exchange rate, American auto manufacturers enjoyed a slight price advantage.

With the various players at relatively equivalent competitive strength, General Motors (GM) began to search for a decisive advantage over the rest of the field. Using the theory of constraints, GM identified a way to provide a quantum increase in customer satisfaction and service while actually reducing the cost of providing cars to the buying public.[14]

Almost all automobile dealers in the United States make most of their money selling cars directly off their lots from on-hand stocks, which they buy from the manufacturers in a limited assortment of styles, colors, and optional equipment, but not all possible combinations. As a result, the odds are fairly high that most customers won't get exactly what they want in a car. They may get their preferred style and color, but not some desired optional equipment. Or, more likely, they may end up with equipment they don't really want. All automobile dealers face this problem, including those selling Japanese cars.

The American manufacturers accept custom orders from dealers, but most are incapable of delivering these made-to-order cars back to the dealers in less than 60 to 85 days. Most customers aren't willing to wait that long for a new car, so they often settle for something other than what they actually want. Dealers, too, prefer to sell off the lot, because they already have money tied up in the on-site inventory—money they need to recover quickly—and a custom order doesn't help them do that. Special orders aren't even an option with Japanese cars, which are usually offered in a few standard packages. The odds of a customer getting, and paying for, unwanted options are even higher than for American cars.

By building current reality trees to define the cause-effect relationship in the existing situation, senior GM executives were able to identify several root causes constraining their ability to deliver custom orders quickly. Using future reality trees, they developed and verified several creative solutions. They identified and trimmed negative branches and constructed prerequisite trees and transition trees to implement the solution.

GM found they could eliminate weeks of unnecessary delay in delivering a custom order. Theoretically, they thought, delivery time for about 15 percent of custom-ordered cars could be reduced to a maximum of 19 days.[15] By establishing regional distribution centers, they could deliver the remaining 85 percent in about *two days!* They set about testing the new process with Cadillac in the state of Florida. After an initial test period of several months, GM found that all but a very few vehicles had been delivered within the expected time, and those few were each only a day late. GM subsequently expanded the test to all Cadillac dealerships in the southwestern United States, with similar results.

By 1999, GM expects to roll out this concept to its other divisions as well.[16] The expectation is that most, if not all, cars eventually will be built to order, rather than to a sales forecast. In other words, big year-end unsold inventories would become a thing of the past, and dealers wouldn't have to maintain large on-site inventories. The final result could be a complete conversion of automobile production from a push to a pull system, which could yield savings of up to 20 percent in the cost of providing GM cars to the market.[17] Therefore, a concerted effort to improve customer satisfaction might actually provide a larger competitive pricing margin as well.

Whether GM ultimately succeeds in realizing this competitive advantage depends on three requirements, two of which they had already satisfied by 1995 through their use of the TOC thinking process. First, they were able to identify the constraints limiting dramatic improvements in customer satisfaction: in other words, *what* to change. Second, they were able to construct, verify, and "bulletproof" a workable solution *before* any money was invested in it: what to change *to*. Finally, they were able to plan implementation in detail, identifying and overcoming obstacles along the way: how to *cause* the change. GM's solution is there, and it's workable. Making the change happen now depends on their discipline and commitment.

SUMMARY

Let's review what we've covered so far.

- In chapter 1, we saw that organizations live or die as whole systems, and that systems are composed of interdependent parts.

- We also saw that understanding the system's goal is critical to the system's success and that setting of the goal is the sole purview of the owners of the system.

- We addressed the issue of necessary conditions for achieving the goal and the idea that constraints naturally restrict a system's capability to realize its goal.

- We saw that systems are often susceptible to suboptimization—the maximization of one component to the detriment of the entire system—and that human suboptimization is often the most problematic of all.

- We also discussed how analytical thinking carves up complex systems into manageable bites for problem analysis and improvement, and we saw how dependence and variation often conspire to make analytical thinking a disaster for goal achievement.

- In chapter 2 we learned that the theory of constraints is a *systems approach,* and that a system can be likened to a chain with a single weakest link.

- We also learned that the theory of constraints prescribes five focusing steps to keep our efforts always directed toward strengthening the weakest link in the system (the improvement that will deliver the most bang for a buck).

- We learned that a theory of constraints approach has the potential to make total quality management considerably more effective, with a commensurate effect on the intrinsic motivation of people within the system.

- We also discussed the fact that *policy* constraints are more insidious and usually more damaging to the system than physical constraints, and we saw why policy constraints are more difficult to break.

- In chapter 3, we learned about the theory of constraints tools and how they are applied in breaking constraints. We learned about the importance of knowing *what* to change, what to change *to,* and how to *cause* the change to happen.

- We were introduced to the current reality tree, the conflict resolution diagram, the future reality tree, the prerequisite tree, the transition tree, and the categories of legitimate reservation.

- We learned about the concepts and operational measurements of throughput, inventory, and operating expense and their crucial role in helping determine how well the system is progressing toward its goal. We also saw that these measures can be useful in solving the difficult problem of relating local decisions to overall system improvement. And we saw that T, I, and OE can be useful to not-for-profit organizations and government agencies as well, though they aren't as readily transferrable.

- Finally, we learned that constraints never really go away. As we break one, another emerges. Eventually, the system constraint moves from inside the system to outside and back again.

The balance of this book will be devoted to giving the reader a thorough understanding of the theory of constraints logical thinking process, which has proven so useful to so many organizations in breaking the policy constraints that inhibit the major improvements in system performance required to achieve world-class status.

> *Excessive dependency on past policies, however successful, is dangerous in time of rapid change.*
> —*Michael J. Kami*

NOTES

1. The following is a partial list of books concerned with managing physical constraints:

   Eliyahu M. Goldratt, *The Goal,* 2d rev. ed. (Croton-on-Hudson, N.Y.: North River Press, 1992).

   Eliyahu M. Goldratt, *The Haystack Syndrome: Sifting Information Out of the Data Ocean* (Croton-on-Hudson, N.Y.: North River Press, 1990).

   Eliyahu M. Goldratt and Robert E. Fox, *The Race* (Croton-on-Hudson, N.Y.: North River Press, 1986).

   M. L. Srikanth and Scott A. Robertson, *Measurements for Effective Decision-Making* (Conn.: Spectrum Publishing, 1995).

   M. L. Srikanth, *Regaining Competitiveness: Putting the Goal to Work* (Conn.: Spectrum Publishing, 1993).

   Robert E. Stein, *The Next Phase of Total Quality Management: TOM II and the Focus on Profitability* (New York: Marcel-Dekker, 1994).

   Robert E. Stein, *Re-engineering the Manufacturing System: Applying the Theory of Constraints* (New York: Marcel-Dekker, 1996).

   Michael L. Umble and M. L. Srikanth *Synchronous Manufacturing: Principles for World Class Excellence* Conn.: Spectrum Publishing, 1995).
2. H. William Dettmer, *Goldratt's Theory of Constraints: A Systems Approach to Continuous Improvement* (Milwaukee, Wis.: The Quality Press, 1996), ch. 3.
3. Ibid., ch. 4.
4. Ibid., ch. 5.
5. Ibid., ch. 6.
6. Ibid., ch. 7.
7. Ibid., ch. 5.
8. Ibid., ch. 2.
9. Eliyahu M. Goldratt, *The Goal,* 2d ed. (Great Barrington, Mass.: North River Press, 1992), 60–61.
10. Eliyahu M. Goldratt and Robert E. Fox, *The Race* (Great Barrington, Mass.: North River Press, 1986), 28.
11. Ibid., 28.
12. Ibid., 28.
13. Conversation between Eliyahu M. Goldratt and the author on July 16, 1995.
14. Duncan Maxwell Anderson, "Thinking Revolutionary," *SUCCESS* Magazine, (Jan/Feb 1995), 40.
15. Gabriella Stern and Rebecca Blumenstein, "GM Expands Plan to Speed Cars to Buyers," *The Wall Street Journal* (October 21, 1996), A3.
16. Ibid., A3.
17. Gabriella Stern, "GM Expands Its Experiment to Improve Cadillac's Distribution, Cut Inefficiency," *The Wall Street Journal* (Wednesday, February 8, 1995).

Chapter 4
A LOGICAL FOUNDATION:
The Categories of Legitimate Reservation

Enthusiasm without knowledge is like running in the dark. You might get there, but you might also get killed.

—*Unknown*

W. Edwards Deming observed that effective transformation of a system isn't possible without *profound knowledge* of that system.[1] In order to have such profound knowledge, he said, we must be well versed in its four components: appreciation for a system; knowledge about variation; theory of knowledge; and psychology of individuals, society, and change. Moreover, he asserted, these four elements are inseparable. While it wasn't conceived with Deming's profound knowledge in mind, the theory of constraints does fit that paradigm remarkably well.

In chapters 1 through 3, we discussed appreciation for a system in some detail and saw how the theory of constraints can be used to appreciate a system's complexities. We also briefly visited the topics of variation and dependence. As we begin to dig more deeply into the TOC logical thinking process, we can't help but consider its relationship to what Deming called the *theory of knowledge.*

What did he mean by that? In essence, understanding the theory of knowledge means answering the question, How do we know *what* we know about our system? Did we just guess? Did we observe? Did we generalize our observations into a hypothesis? Can we say for sure that one thing causes—or doesn't cause—another to happen? How good is our data? Do we understand the distinction between data, information, and knowledge? Simply put, our confidence in our knowledge about our systems springs directly from the source, structure, and reliability of that knowledge. There are many different facets of the theory of knowledge, but one of the most important is cause and effect.

CAUSE AND EFFECT

One of the basic rules of a method of dealing with teenagers called STEP (Systematic Training for Effective Parenting) is the lesson of natural and logical consequences.[2] As parents practice this rule, children learn the natural consequences that will inevitably result from their actions. Desirable behavior is reinforced with pleasant consequences. Undesirable behavior is discouraged by applying unpleasant ones. Eventually (faster for some, slower for others) children internalize a basic lesson in cause and effect: *If* I don't do what I'm supposed to do, *then* I won't like what happens to me. But even with prior verbal warnings by parents, it's usually a lesson fully learned only by trial-and-error testing.

Unfortunately, responsible adults don't have the luxury of learning about cause and effect by time-consuming trial and error. Irresponsible adults, on the other hand, are often *forced* to make the time, whether they think they have it or not. It's been said that good judgment comes from experience, and experience comes from bad judgment. This is really an indirect way of saying, Pay attention to cause and effect. We make mistakes in the first place because we have an incomplete understanding of cause and effect. If we're reasonably intelligent, we learn from those mistakes, and that's often referred to as learning at the school of hard knocks. If we make an active effort to learn from the mistakes of others, we can often avoid the school of hard knocks altogether. Any understanding of cause and effect we can absorb from the wisdom or experiences of ourselves or others (not always pleasant experiences, either) is that much less we'll have to learn the hard way.

Our education system doesn't formally teach cause and effect. That's unfortunate. Many lives could be saved and untold suffering eliminated if it were. Our entire existence in reality, from birth to death, is an exercise in cause and effect, sometimes simple, other times complex. We're fish in a lake of cause and effect. Just as fish are oblivious to the water around them, for the most part people aren't conscious of the cause and effect at work around them either, except in the most superficial way.

Some people, though, are very much aware of cause and effect on a daily basis and how complex it can be. Doctors, for example, employ cause and effect in diagnosing and treating illness. And safety investigators use cause and effect to figure out why accidents happen. The following account describes an aircraft accident. The accompanying logic tree (Figure 4.1) shows how complex cause and effect can be. Although some of the contributing causes were present before the plane attempted to take off, nearly all of the 22 levels of cause and effect shown in the logic tree dropped like falling dominoes within a space of less than 30 seconds.

THE ANATOMY OF AN AIRPLANE CRASH

The military airplane had been flying for more than seven hours. Its mission was nearly completed. All that remained was for the crew to land briefly at its home base and, without even shutting down its engines, pick up a pilot evaluator to finish an annual proficiency check, then take off again for one nonprecision instrument approach and a final landing.

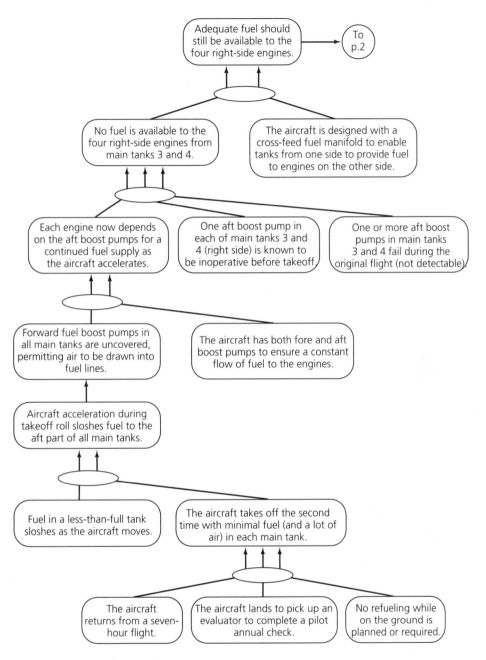

FIGURE 4.1.1 Airplane crash.

The landing to pick up the evaluator was uneventful. After seven hours of flight, the aircraft was light and responsive. The evaluator was waiting near the takeoff end of the runway as the plane taxied back from the landing. The evaluator boarded, and the hatch was closed.

The plane's four rectangular main fuel tanks (Figure 4.1.4), full at the time of the original takeoff, had about 10,000 pounds of fuel remaining in each one—more than enough to complete a lightweight takeoff, an instrument approach, and a final landing. But even at 10,000 pounds, the tanks were considerably less than half full. Located in the wings (two on each

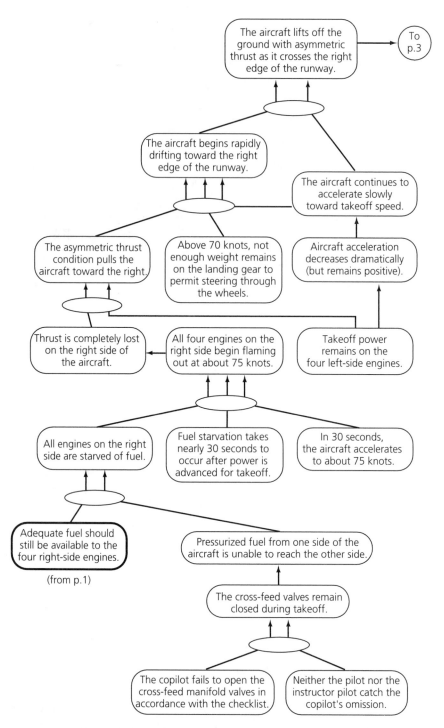

FIGURE 4.1.2 Airplane crash.

side), the main tanks had fuel boost pumps in each corner of the rectangle to provide fuel under pressure to the main pumps of the engines. The strategic location of these boost pumps ensured that even when fuel shifted in partially empty tanks, much as water shifts when a person tries to walk while carrying a pan, one or more of the boost pumps would

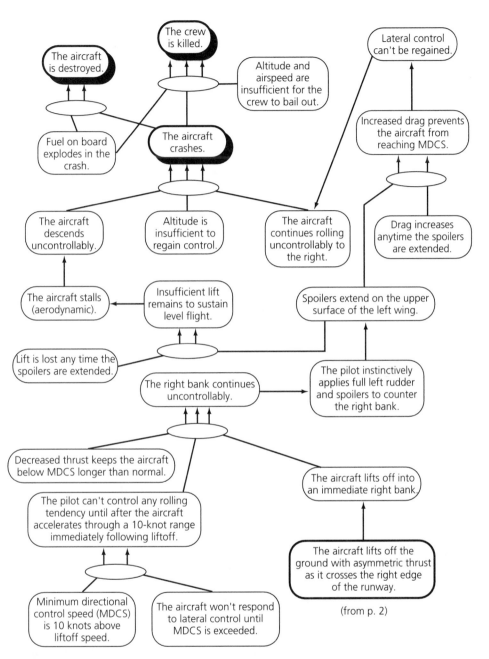

FIGURE 4.1.3 Airplane crash.

remain covered with fuel. Air might be drawn into uncovered boost pumps, but as long as at least one boost pump remained covered with fuel, an uninterrupted supply of fuel to the engines was guaranteed.

However, even if no fuel should be available from a particular main tank, the continued operation of the engines was ensured by a design feature called a cross-feed manifold. This was nothing more than a 4-inch pipe running in the leading edge of the wing and connecting all four main tanks on both sides of the aircraft. If one tank happened to run dry, fuel from another tank could feed the engines usually served by the dry tank,

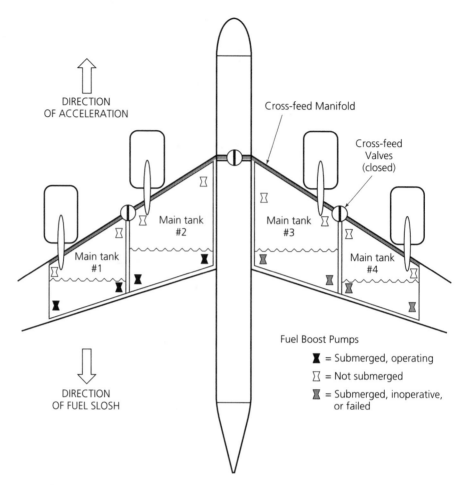

FIGURE 4.1.4 Aircraft fuel tank diagram.

as long as the isolating cross-feed valves located in the pipe between each tank were open. It was the normal operating procedure to open those valves whenever the total weight of the aircraft decreased below a certain level. This level had not been reached when the plane landed to pick up the evaluator pilot.

As the plane prepared to take off the second time, the copilot completed the taxi-back checklist. One of the steps called for the cross-feed valves to be opened. But for some reason, the copilot didn't complete this step. Neither the pilot nor the evaluator caught the omission. Normally, this would not have posed a problem, but one of the two boost pumps in the back (aft) of each main tank in the right wing had been written up in the maintenance records as being inoperative prior to the original takeoff. Because of system redundancy and the cross-feed procedure, this deficiency was not considered serious enough to cancel the original flight. Also, during the first seven hours of that day's flight, one or more of the other two aft boost pumps apparently failed, leaving none—or at most, one—of the boost pumps at the back of the tank operating.

The pilot advanced the throttles for takeoff. The copilot confirmed eight good engines operating, and the airplane, at its light weight, accelerated rapidly down the runway. With the acceleration, all the fuel shifted to the back of the main tanks. The front boost pumps in the main tanks were uncovered by the shift. The aft boost pumps in the left wing functioned normally. The aft pumps in the right wing were inoperative. And because the cross-feed valves were closed, no emergency source of fuel was available to the engines on the right side of the plane. It took about 30 seconds for the right-side engines, at full power, to suck all the fuel from the lines between the tanks and the main pumps. The crew, however, was unaware that all this was happening.

At about 75 knots, things started to go horribly wrong. The four engines on the right wing began flaming out in rapid sequence. Because of the noise level of the remaining engines, the only indication of the engine failure was the rapid unwinding of the tachometers for those engines. But that wasn't immediately noticed by the crew. What the pilot did notice was that the plane started veering toward the side of the runway, a consequence of the lack of thrust on the right side, coupled with the full thrust on the left.

The pilot immediately applied left rudder, which, on the ground, also steered the nose landing gear. But at that light weight, above 70 knots the wings had enough lift to take most of the plane's weight off the wheels, so the wheels turned but with no effect on the plane's direction. It kept drifting toward the right side of the runway—and accelerating. Even with the loss of four engines, at that light weight the plane continued to gain speed, but at a much slower rate. Since the airplane was already at nearly 100 knots and drifting rapidly to the right, it became obvious that it would not stay on the paved surface if the pilot tried to abort—a certain disaster. But the plane was only about 10 knots from liftoff and still accelerating, albeit slowly. The pilot instantly elected to try to get airborne.

The plane lifted off about the time the main landing gear touched the dirt on the right side of the runway, and as it slowly rose into the air, the right wing dipped dangerously because of the asymmetric power condition (no thrust from the right side, full thrust from the left). The pilot instinctively applied full controls to the left in an attempt to level the wings. But the plane's turning motion was governed by spoilers, designed to induce the airplane to roll one way or the other by disturbing the aerodynamic lift on a particular wing. Spoilers are like hydraulically operated "barn doors." When they're extended, they create much air resistance. As the spoilers on the left wing extended fully, two things happened. First, the aerodynamic drag increased to such a degree that the plane stopped accelerating and actually started losing speed, just above the point of aerodynamic stall.

Second, though the plane was going fast enough to fly (minimally), it wasn't going fast enough for the lateral controls to be effective in leveling the wings. That required another 10 knots of airspeed, which the airplane would never achieve because of the tremendous loss of thrust in the dead engines and the increase in drag from the spoilers.

The plane continued to roll uncontrollably to the right, at an altitude of about 30 feet. The right wing tip dragged the ground, and the plane cartwheeled. The physical stress broke the airframe and fractured the main fuel tanks, explosively igniting nearly 40,000 pounds of jet fuel. The aircraft was destroyed, and all seven crew members were killed.

INSTRUCTIONS FOR READING A LOGIC TREE

Cause-and-effect trees are easy to read. Every statement at the tail of an arrow is read with the word *If* . . . preceding it. Every statement at the head of an arrow is preceded with the word . . . *then* . . . . When two or more arrows pass through an ellipse between the cause and the effect, the multiple causes are read, If . . . and . . . then . . . . The first effect then becomes the cause for the next higher effect. Appendix A offers a simple humorous example on which to practice.

Causality as complex as the aircraft accident is virtually impossible to fully comprehend as it is happening. Yet many of the most important situations in our lives—business, family, personal, professional, or safety—unfold with equivalent speed. Understanding how cause and effect works can be critical to our success, perhaps even to our survival.

Even professionals who use cause and effect daily usually do it intuitively. They don't normally employ a formal, rigorous logical taxonomy to guide them. This makes it much more difficult even for professionals skilled in cause-and-effect analysis to transfer this knowledge of the workings of cause and effect to others. Doesn't it make sense that if a straightforward set of logical rules were available, more people, such as homemakers, students, teachers, businesspeople, and elected representatives and government bureaucrats, might benefit from a better understanding of cause and effect?

The theory of constraints thinking process has such a logical foundation, called the *categories of legitimate reservation.* Understanding and being able to apply these categories are crucial to our success in using the powerful theory of constraints logic trees. Those trees provide answers to the questions what to change, what to change to, and how to cause the change. The categories of legitimate reservation are deeply rooted in classical, or traditional, logic.

THE LOGIC OF ARISTOTLE

Logic isn't new. It's been around for thousands of years. It comes in many varieties, some of which pertain more to its application than to any real difference in its form. Logic can be practical, epistemic, deontic, temporal (of which two component parts are megaric and stoic), deductive, and inductive. These can be categorized as either pure logic or applied logic. Perhaps the most renowned practitioner of logic was Aristotle, who lived in ancient Greece during the fourth century B.C. Aristotle conceived of the kind of logic with which most of us are familiar, the kind that many popular logic puzzle books employ: syllogistic logic.[3]

Most people have seen the syllogism at one time or another. It starts with at least two related premises, p_1 and p_2, and from these proposes a conclusion, C. Here's a typical example:

p_1: *All male Hare Krishnas have bald heads.*
p_2: *John is a male Hare Krishna.*
C: *John has a bald head.*

It works fine going in this direction but not the other way around:

p_1: *All male Hare Krishnas have bald heads.*
p_2: *John has a bald head.*
C: *John is a male Hare Krishna.*

Clearly, John could be congenitally bald but not be a Hare Krishna. Or he could be a skinhead, which would explain his baldness but not in any way make him a Hare Krishna. Aristotle recognized the differences in these conditions, and he created the sophistical refutations (seven material fallacies, five verbal fallacies, and two formal fallacies) as a kind of logical benchmark with which to verify the validity of the conclusion that issues from two related premises.

Syllogistic logic has a major drawback, which might explain why more people don't use it on a regular basis. It has no widely accepted graphical means of presentation. The example above is expressed in text form. While that might be sufficient for a single simple relationship, or even two, it becomes impractical to express a cause-and-effect relationship as complex as the airplane crash example in a syllogistic form. We simply can't hold it all in our heads.

The logic employed in the theory of constraints thinking process is based on cause-and-effect relationships, rather than the conditions of inclusion or exclusion inherent in Aristotle's approach. The thinking process logic has some elements in common with Aristotle's syllogistic, but there are enough differences that a direct transference is difficult, if not impossible. So if you're confident that you're already knowledgeable in Aristotle's version of logic, you're in for something a little different. You'll see some similarities, but much of it will be new to you as well. Even if you don't know logic from lima beans, don't worry. Cause-and-effect logic is easier to understand than syllogistic logic anyway. Also, as we'll see later, the cause-and-effect logic of the theory of constraints can be represented graphically in a way that makes it much easier to visualize than the syllogism.

CAUSE AND EFFECT: INTUITION VERSUS SUBJECT MATTER KNOWLEDGE

We've seen, in the airplane crash example, how complex cause and effect can be, and why it's important for us to understand its nature. It's absolutely critical in making good decisions. Cause and effect is inherent in the appreciation for a system that Deming considered so important to his concept of profound knowledge. However, if we're to understand cause and effect in our systems, we have to have some understanding about how those systems work to begin with, some knowledge of the subject. For example, to some degree you know how the organization you work for operates, at least your part of it. Everybody else who works there has some knowledge of it, too, though theirs may be different from yours.

Let's say something has gone wrong in your organization, something that affects you. When you try to figure out what happened, or predict what might happen in the future, you naturally draw on your knowledge—the experiences and perhaps your understanding of some theory that pertain to the situation. The more *subject matter knowledge* you bring to the analysis, the more confident you are likely to be of accurately identifying cause and effect. The more accurate your knowledge, the higher your probability of making a firm prediction about the future success of a decision.

In some situations, however, we have only limited experiences or knowledge to draw upon, or maybe none at all. In such circumstances, the best we may be able to come up with is a gut feeling, or a wild guess. Obviously, in such situations, the accuracy of our analysis and prediction about the future is suspect. There's a wide range of possible levels of knowledge that we might bring to any situation. Figure 4.2 shows how this range might affect our decisions about changing a system.

We could consider the possible range of our knowledge to lie on a line of indefinite length—a knowledge continuum. The line extends to the right toward increasing uncertainty, which results from little or no knowledge about a topic. As we move to the left, we approach certainty, which is the result of absolutely perfect knowledge. Somewhere in between, we pass through a domain of risk, in which we have imperfect knowledge—some, but not all, of what we need to know. When we try to answer the question *why* about something, our position on the continuum is established.

The closer we are to complete uncertainty, the more we rely on our intuition. As Figure 4.2 indicates, intuition can be as vague as a pure gut feeling, as solid as an educated guess based on experience and some understanding of theory, or somewhere in between. As our knowledge and experience improve in reliability, we move farther to the left on the continuum. Somewhere along the way, we shift from the high end of intuition to the low end of subject matter knowledge. The more concrete our knowledge becomes, the farther to the left we move along the knowledge continuum, in the direction of certainty.

What helps us to continue that progress? Each step builds upon the one before it. Observations of reality take us from pure gut feeling to perhaps a wild guess. Experience moves us from a wild guess to a somewhat educated guess. A more educated guess results from experience backed by theory. And when we overlay empirical evidence and logic on our experience and theory, we begin to approach a firm prediction in which we have high confidence. Understanding the logic of cause and effect goes a long way toward helping us make that last jump to high

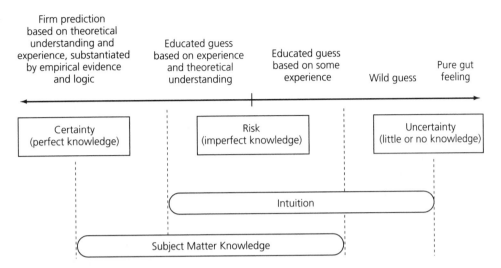

FIGURE 4.2 Knowledge continuum.

confidence in our predictions of future outcomes—the objective of Deming's theory of knowledge.[4]

CORRELATION VERSUS CAUSE AND EFFECT

Sometimes people confuse cause and effect with *correlation*. They're not the same, but people often fail to differentiate between the two. Cause and effect is a verifiable one-way relationship in which one element, condition, or action makes another exist when it would not have done so on its own. Correlation is the observation that something changes when another does, but a verifiable causal connection between the two hasn't been established. What initially seems to be just a correlation might eventually turn out to be a cause-effect relationship, but more rigorous testing is required before that can be confirmed. W. Edwards Deming provided the following fable to illustrate the difference between correlation and cause and effect:

> *The barnyard rooster Chanticleer had a theory. He crowed every morning, putting forth all his energy, flapped his wings. The sun came up. The connection was clear: His crowing caused the sun to come up. There was no question about his importance.*
>
> *There came a snag. He forgot one morning to crow. The sun came up anyhow. Crestfallen, he saw his theory in need of revision.[5]*

TWO EXAMPLES OF CORRELATION MISTAKEN FOR CAUSE AND EFFECT

The following are a couple of examples of correlations that seem like cause-effect relationships but really are not. In the 1980s, many investors (not a few of them bankers) observed that people who had bought junk bonds made a great deal of money. That was a correlation: as junk bonds are bought, money is made. But many of those who got on the junk bond bandwagon were rudely introduced to the difference between correlation and cause and effect. A time came when buying junk bonds turned into a sure way to *lose* money. Because the investors never firmly established a valid cause-effect relationship (they mistook correlation for cause and effect) many of them lost their money, some much more than they could afford to lose. (There's that school of hard knocks again!)

Here's another example. Some years ago, a man bought a Pontiac from a local dealer.[6] Before it was two weeks old, he had problems starting it. Several visits to the dealership turned up no apparent problem, so he wrote directly to the Pontiac Division of General Motors. He said, "I bought one of your cars, only to discover that it's allergic to vanilla ice cream. What are you going to do about it?" Naturally, the carmaker did what any sane person would do upon receiving a letter like that: they trashed it. But after the customer's third inquiry, the engineering department sent a representative to see the man.

The customer described how his family would jointly decide what kind of ice cream to have for dessert after dinner each evening, and he'd drive to the local ice-cream parlor to get it in the new car. Every time he tried to come home with vanilla ice cream, the car would refuse to start. Every time he brought chocolate, strawberry, or some other flavor out of the store, the car started up just fine. So, he concluded, the car must be allergic to vanilla ice cream.

The engineer accompanied the man to the ice-cream parlor on two consecutive days. Sure enough, the day the man bought chocolate ice cream, the car started normally. But on the day he ordered vanilla, it didn't. However, the engineer took notice of several other factors besides the ice-cream flavor. He noticed that the most popular flavor sold in the store was vanilla, and the proprietor had set up a separate counter near the door to serve only those customers ordering vanilla. All the other flavors were served from a larger counter near the back of the store. Also, because he was shorthanded, the customers wanting other flavors than vanilla waited considerably longer to be served. Those buying vanilla were in and out in just a minute or two. That, combined with the ambient warm temperatures and humidity, induced a vapor lock in the new car's carburetor when the engine was turned off. The vapor lock had plenty of time to dissipate if the man ordered any flavor but vanilla. But when he ordered vanilla, he was in and out of the store so fast that the vapor lock hadn't had time to clear, and the car wouldn't start. There was no cause and effect between the vanilla ice cream and the car not starting, but there was a correlation.

The most serious pitfall in not accurately distinguishing between correlation and cause and effect is the wrong decisions that can result. In some cases, the impact might be no more than trying to treat a car's allergy with Benadryl™. But in other cases, it could result in the loss of life savings.

Correlation is an improvement over nothing at all. On the knowledge continuum in Figure 4.2, it lies somewhere in the domain of risk. In other words, it's probably better to establish a correlation than it is to operate on a gut feeling alone. But it's not as good as being able to verify a cause-and-effect relationship. Deming considered a thorough understanding of cause and effect to contribute significantly to profound knowledge of a system. Correlation resides firmly in the part of the knowledge continuum dominated by *intuition.* Understanding cause and effect can translate our position substantially to the left, into the realm of *subject matter knowledge,* where predictions based on experience and theory have a higher probability of validity than they do farther to the right on the continuum. Decisions based on theoretical understanding and experience can be pushed significantly toward the certainty end of the continuum by supporting them with empirical evidence and logic.

It's clear that cause and effect is more useful than correlation. But why did the man with the flavor-conscious Pontiac have trouble distinguishing between correlation and cause and effect? One major reason is that he had no simple rules to guide his reasoning. Without fixed rules as a benchmark, evaluating each new situation becomes an adventure in uncertainty.

THE CATEGORIES OF LEGITIMATE RESERVATION

The theory of constraints thinking process is based on the concept of cause and effect, not on correlation. Cause and effect is built on a foundation of constancy provided by certain rules. In Aristotle's syllogistic logic, these rules are called *fallacies.* In our use of cause and effect, the rules are called the *categories of legitimate reservation* (CLR).[7] The CLR serve two purposes. They help us to construct our own logical relationships, and they enable us to evaluate the logic of others. Additionally, the CLR can help us communicate any disagreement we might have to others in a way they'll easily understand without antagonizing them.

Categories of legitimate reservation is certainly a mouthful. What the term is trying to imply is that there is a limited number of types of logical errors a person can make in formulating cause and effect. This is the *categories* part of the term. *Reservation* means *doubt, hesitancy, qualm,* or *uncertainty.* If somebody has a reservation about something, it means they're not convinced about it. *Legitimate* basically means *allowed.* So the categories of legitimate reservation are really a limited number of types of logical flaw that we're allowed to express our doubts about. Another way of saying it is that all possible logical errors fall into a limited number of general types. In the theory of constraints thinking process, this number is eight, of which we'll see only seven in graphical logic trees. The eighth, however, is quite real, but it's exclusive to spoken conversation. We'll look at each of these categories in detail.

Aristotelian logic has three categories of fallacy: material, verbal, and formal. This means that logical errors were related either to the subject

Aristotle's Logical Fallacies	Goldratt's Categories of Legitimate Reservation
Material Fallacies (sophistical refutations)	
Improper application of the general rule (inclusion)	(no corresponding category)
Improper application of a special rule (extension)	(no corresponding category)
Irrelevant conclusion (six subordinate cases)	Causality existence, cause-effect reversal, tautology
Circular argument	Tautology
False cause	Causality existence, additional cause, predicted effect
Many questions	Additional cause
Non sequitur	Causality existence
Verbal Fallacies	
Equivocation	Clarity
Amphiboly	Clarity
Accent	Clarity
Composition	Entity existence
Division	Entity existence
Formal Fallacies	
Denial of the antecedent	(no corresponding category)
Affirmation of the consequent	(no corresponding category)

FIGURE 4.3   Aristotelean and cause-effect logic: A comparison.

matter of the statement, the way the statement was communicated, or the structural form of the relationship between premises and conclusions. There are some similarities between the CLR and the classical fallacies. One of the eight CLR is *clarity,* which is another way of describing the communication, or verbal, quality of a statement. Another is *entity existence,* which bears a more than passing resemblance to Aristotle's material grouping. The remaining six CLR address different aspects of *causality,* which correspond loosely to Aristotle's formal fallacies. (See Figure 4.3 for a direct comparison of the categories of legitimate reservation and the classical logical fallacies.)

Clarity

In traditional communication theory, there's a sender, a message, and a receiver. The sender *encodes* a message, using some form of symbol, and transmits it through some kind of medium to the receiver, who *decodes* the message and interprets its meaning. *Clarity* is the first of the eight CLR, and its preeminence reflects the importance of accurate communication in presenting logic. Many questions people might have about our logic will actually stem from a failure on our part to communicate effectively.

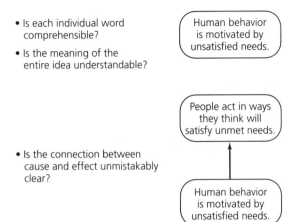

- Is each individual word comprehensible?
- Is the meaning of the entire idea understandable?

Human behavior is motivated by unsatisfied needs.

People act in ways they think will satisfy unmet needs.

- Is the connection between cause and effect unmistakably clear?

Human behavior is motivated by unsatisfied needs.

FIGURE 4.4   **CLR 1: Clarity.**

Just as the sender of a message has a responsibility to the receiver to encode it in a way that gets the meaning across—that is, it doesn't confuse—so the logical communicator, or tree builder, bears the responsibility of ensuring that the logic is understood. This means that someone stating a cause-effect relationship must take care to ensure that others will (a) understand the individual words used, (b) comprehend the meaning of the entire idea, and (c) see a clear connection between the cause and the effect (Figure 4.4). So, if we're building a cause-and-effect tree similar to the one concerning the aircraft accident earlier in this chapter, we have to be sure that our audience (the readers of our tree) will understand the words we've used, comprehend the idea we're trying to convey, and recognize the connection between the cause and the effect. The latter means that we don't jump over, or ignore, intervening effects just to get more quickly to the one we really want.

If we do this job well and avoid the logical problems inherent in the remaining reservations, a reader should be able to pick up our tree, read it all the way through to conclusion, understand what we're trying to convey, and accept our reasoning, all without any verbal explanation from us. This is a real challenge, but it's doable.

Entity Existence

Entity—an unusual word. In the context of the TOC thinking process, it requires definition because it doesn't mean what most people might think it means. In common usage, it means something having "a real existence . . . distinct, independent, or self-contained."[8] That's true for the TOC usage as well, but it doesn't tell the whole story. The thinking process logic trees are composed of text enclosed in some kind of geometric shape, with the shapes connected by cause-and-effect arrows. Every one of these shapes filled with text is considered an entity, but each entity must meet three criteria to be considered legitimate (Figure 4.5).

1. The text must be a complete, grammatical sentence. A complete sentence contains an independent idea or thought. At a minimum, this means it must have a subject and a verb. It may also have an object and modifiers, too.

2. The sentence must not be a compound or complex sentence. In other words, only one idea per entity is allowed, and the more simply expressed, the better. For example, "John goes to the store, and Jean goes to the tennis court" wouldn't qualify as a single entity, because it's really two different ones: "John goes to the store" and "Jean goes to the tennis court."

Complex sentences are also excluded because they tend to have if . . . then statements embedded within them. For example: In order to keep my car clean, I park it in the garage. This looks like one statement, but it's really two: *If* I park my car in the garage, *then* my car stays clean. Why is this distinction important? Because it makes it easier for us to consider other ways to keep the car clean besides parking in the garage. In other words, it opens new possibilities that we might have missed had the two entities remained locked in a single complex sentence.

3. The idea contained in the sentence must be valid. It must be true, or at least perceived as true by most people familiar with it. For example, most people would consider "Stop signs are red" to be a valid statement. But they probably would not say the same about "The moon is made of green cheese."

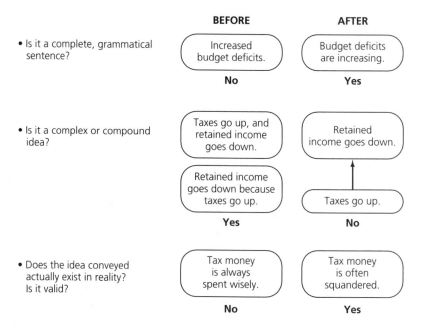

FIGURE 4.5 CLR 2: Entity existence.

If each of our statements in a cause-and-effect tree meets these three criteria (a complete sentence, no compound or complex sentences, and valid content), then they successfully meet the *entity existence* test.

Causality Existence

Causality existence is a test of the *connection* between two statements, rather than the statements themselves. A suggested cause-effect relationship must meet one very basic criterion: does the proposed cause really produce the observed effect? If it does, then the relationship is said to have causality existence. Cause-effect relationships must be *direct* and *unavoidable.* If an intermediate step (or effect) is overlooked, the observed effect is not the direct and unavoidable outcome of the proposed cause (Figure 4.6).

A good analogy would be the public interest some years ago in people who would set up thousands of dominoes just to see the chain reaction that resulted when they fell, which often took 15 minutes or more. These demonstrations succeeded only because the dominoes were so closely spaced that each successive domino's fall was the direct and unavoidable outcome of the preceding domino's fall.

Similarly, an effect must be in such close proximity to the cause that there is no doubt in anybody's mind that causality exists. For example, consider the following cause-effect statement: *If* I win the lottery, *then* my worries are over. It's quite possible that winning the lottery might eventually lead to your worries being over. Of course, there are those who might say they're just beginning, too! But in either case, there are some *direct and unavoidable* intermediate steps missing, such as collecting the money, using some of it, saving some of it, but keeping much of it. So the test of causality existence is: Does the cause lead directly and unavoidably to the effect? If so, causality is said to exist. If not, keep looking—you've missed something.

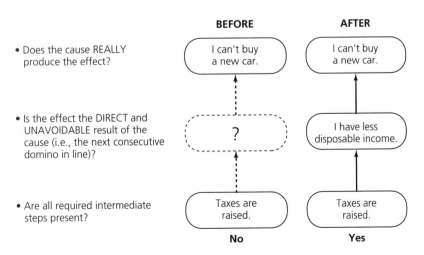

FIGURE 4.6   CLR 3: Causality existence.

Cause Insufficiency

The word alone says it all: *insufficiency*. It implies that there are several factors acting in concert to produce the effect. When you build a cause-and-effect tree, you must be sure you've identified and included all the major contributing causes. A contributing cause is like any single leg of a three-leg stool: if it isn't there, you don't have a stool. It takes all three to have the stool. The absence of any one renders the stool mere firewood. In the same way, a contributing cause is considered major if its removal would cause the effect to not exist anymore. In fact, this is the definitive test of cause insufficiency: If I take away each cause, one at a time, do I still have the effect?

For example, what does it take to produce a fire? Combustible fuel, oxygen, and a source of ignition. Take any one of those away, and you don't have a fire. No one of them, or even two, is sufficient. It takes all three. To be considered *contributing*, the causes must *depend* on one another (Figure 4.7).

The test for cause insufficiency is twofold:

1. Is my proposed cause enough by itself to deliver the effect, or does it need help from something else? An answer to this question ensures you haven't missed anything critical.

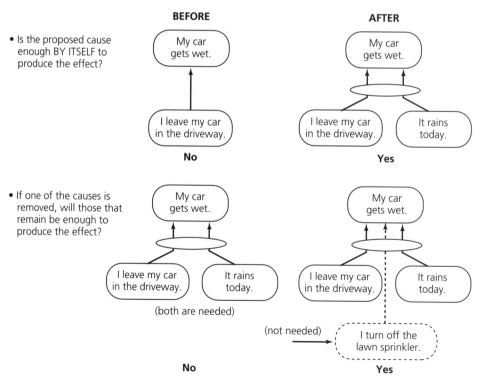

FIGURE 4.7   CLR 4: Cause insufficiency.

2. If I take away one of the proposed contributing causes, will I still have the effect? The answer to this question ensures you haven't included more than you need to get the effect.

In cause-and-effect trees, cause *sufficiency* (that is, the presence of two or more dependent contributing causes) is indicated by drawing the cause-effect arrows to pass through an ellipse. The presence of the ellipse is critical when it comes to problem solution: *it signifies that only one of the causes must be removed to eliminate the effect.* If the effect is undesirable, it makes the job of eliminating it that much easier!

Additional Cause

How many different ways can you skin a cat? This question implies the idea of *additional cause.* Every time you observe or hypothesize an effect, you're remiss if you don't consider all the possible *independent* causes of that effect. Every independent cause is an additional cause, and every additional cause must be capable *by itself* of producing the effect (Figure 4.8).

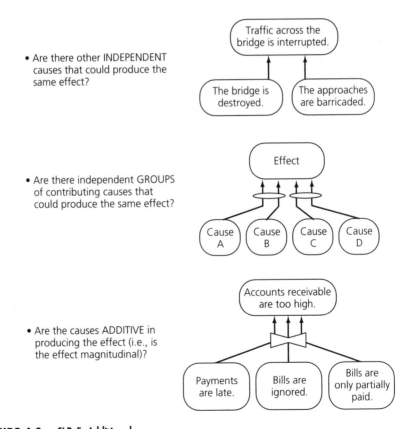

FIGURE 4.8   CLR 5: Additional cause.

For example, how many different ways can you think of to interrupt automobile traffic crossing a bridge? One, obviously, is to destroy the bridge, and there are many independent ways to do that alone. Another is to barricade the road on both sides of the bridge. A third might be to pay people to use an alternative route, or perhaps scare them into doing so. Any of these ways, independently, could produce the effect of stopping traffic from using the bridge. They're all potential additional causes.

There are two special situations that need emphasis at this point. First, an additional cause may, itself, be made of several contributing causes (cause sufficiency). If two such causes existed, there might be six different arrows leading to the effect, but only two additional causes. In other words, all the arrows enclosed by an ellipse, taken together, constitute an additional cause.

The second situation is considerably different. It's the idea of a *magnitudinal* increase to the effect produced by each independent cause. Consider the effect that accounts receivable are too high. There might be three causes of such an effect: (1) customers are late paying their bills, (2) customers ignore their bills, and (3) customers only partially pay their bills. Each of these should be treated independently, because the cures are likely to be different. Each alone could cause accounts receivable to be too high. But each one added to the others actually increases the magnitude of the effect. Accounts receivable that were too high with one of the three causes become much too high with the addition of the other two.

There's a subtle difference between the magnitudinal combination of causes and cause sufficiency. In sufficiency, the causes are all dependent of one another. Take just one away, and all the others are rendered inoperative as well. In a magnitudinal situation, the causes are independent but additive. If you take away one, you still have the others, as you do with straight additional causes, but since the magnitude of the effect decreases, at some point you may reach a threshold of acceptability. "No need to get rid of any more causes—we can live with this level of effect."

To distinguish between magnitudinal causes, cause sufficiency, and a pure additional cause, we'll use a bow tie symbol to indicate a magnitudinal relationship.

Cause-Effect Reversal

Have you ever seen a situation where an effect was mistaken for a cause, or vice versa? Here's an example:

> *If students' standardized test scores are low, then the qualifications of students are poor.*

At face value, this looks like a reasonable statement. But let's take a closer look. The *if* part of the statement is supposed to be the cause; the *then* part is the effect. Now ask yourself, Did the low test scores *cause* the poor qualifications, or were they the *result* of them? It should be pretty obvious that the cause and the effect have been reversed in this case. The test

FIGURE 4.9   CLR 6: Cause-effect reversal.

scores are the indication that student qualifications are poor. Something else is causing the poor qualifications. Here's another example:

If I have a pain in my side, an elevated white blood cell count, and a fever, then I have appendicitis.

Did the pain, the white blood cells, and the fever cause the appendicitis, or was it the other way around?

The easiest way to safeguard your logic trees from this deficiency is to ask yourself the question, Is the cause I'm proposing an *indication*, rather than a cause? Could it really be the reason I know that something else is actually the cause? This is the test for cause-effect reversal. (Figure 4.9).

Predicted Effect Existence

Causes rarely have just one effect. If we look closely enough, we can usually find others. Take an automobile accident, for example. As a cause, it can produce several effects: damage to the vehicles involved, injury to the drivers and passengers, disruption of traffic, damage to other property, and perhaps even psychological trauma—five effects from the same cause.

Each of these effects could be anticipated in an auto accident, so each could be considered a *predicted effect*. Let's say you didn't actually see the accident, but you saw two damaged cars close to one another, injured people lying beside the wreckage, a knocked-down fence under one of the cars, and traffic slowing down as it passes the scene. What would your conclusion be about the cause? Of course! A collision. You saw the wrecked cars and postulated that an accident had occurred. You looked for other confirming evidence that your postulate was correct, and you found it: injuries, property damage, and traffic slowing down. So you concluded, with a high degree of confidence, what the cause was without even having seen it.

Predicted effects are used specifically to verify the existence of an intangible cause (one that isn't directly observable or measurable). For example, astronomers use predicted effect to substantiate their hypotheses about invisible planets a long way from earth. If such a planet is really there, but they can't see it directly, they would look for other effects of

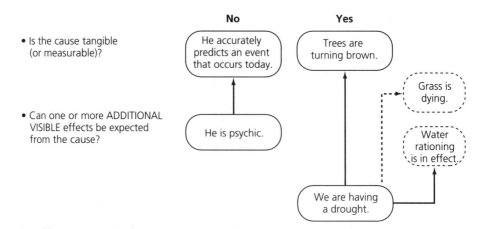

FIGURE 4.10 CLR 7: Predicted effect existence.

its presence, such as perturbation of the orbits of other planets. Th
how Uranus and Neptune were discovered in our own solar system.

The purpose of the predicted effect reservation is to help us estab
causality. In other words, is the observed effect really the result of
proposed cause (Figure 4.10)? This means that some causal relation
must be proposed first, before we can use this reservation to confir
refute it. There are four possible conditions for predicted effects:

1. The predicted effect *should* be there and *is* there. In this case,
   cause is confirmed.
2. The predicted effect *should* be there but *isn't* there. In this cas
   the cause is refuted.
3. The predicted effect *shouldn't* be there and *isn't* there. Again,
   cause is confirmed.
4. The predicted effect *shouldn't* be there but *is* there. And again
   the cause is refuted.

Tautology

Tautology is also known as *circular reasoning*. It's never seen in gra
cal representation of logic, such as cause-and-effect trees beca
there's no distinctive way to depict it. It's actually not likely to em
as circular reasoning until causality existence is challenged first, usu
when the follow-up question *why* is asked. Tautology is somewhat n
common in spoken conversation. In fact, that's where we're most li
to encounter it. What is circular logic? Basically, it's a situation in w
someone offers the effect as the rationale for the existence of the ca
Here's an example:

> *The fisherman brought home several large fish because the fishing was goo
> [How can you be sure the fishing was good?]
> Well, he brought home some big fish, didn't he?*

That's circular reasoning. The effect is taken as unquestioned proof alone that the cause exists (without ever considering possible alternatives, such as a stop at the fish market on the way home). You can watch for tautology in conversation with others, but when you're building cause-and-effect trees, the other cause-related reservations will be all you'll need.

SUMMARY

These are the eight categories of legitimate reservation: clarity, entity existence, causality existence, cause insufficiency, additional cause, cause-effect reversal, predicted effect existence, and tautology (Figure 4.11). They're the rules of engagement used in constructing logic trees. Every

1. Clarity
Are the
  • words
  • idea
  • causal connection
  clearly obvious?

2. Entity Existence
Is it
  • a complete sentence?
  • NOT a compound or complex idea?
  • valid, at face value?

3. Causality Existence

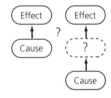

  • Is there REALLY a connection?
  • Are intervening steps missing?

4. Cause Insufficiency

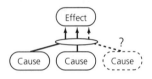

  • Are ALL contributors included?
  • Are TOO MANY included?

5. Additional Cause

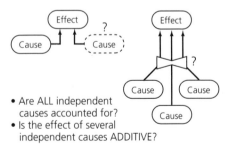

  • Are ALL independent causes accounted for?
  • Is the effect of several independent causes ADDITIVE?

6. Cause-Effect Reversal

  • Is the effect REALLY the cause?
  • Is the effect really HOW WE KNOW some other cause exists?

7. Predicted Effect Existence

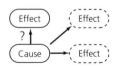

  • Are there other effects that could be expected from the same cause?

8. Tautology

  • Is the effect offered as the rationale for the existence of the cause?

FIGURE 4.11 The categories of legitimate reservation: A summary.

connection (arrow) we create between a cause and an effect is measured against the first seven of them. If the connection passes these tests, we can consider it valid. Try not to feel overwhelmed at the prospect of having to assess each connection seven times. In practicality it doesn't work that way. In some cases your connection will pass muster just by quick visual inspection. In others, you'll have to give special attention to perhaps three or four possible reservations. But all the categories of legitimate reservation give us the confidence to know that our cause-and-effect logic is sound.

Now it's time to start building trees.

The understanding of systems never lies in the system.

—*Russell Ackoff*

NOTES

1. W. Edwards Deming, *The New Economics for Industry Government and Education* (Cambridge, Mass.: MIT Center for Advanced Engineering Study, 1993), ch. 4.
2. Don Dinkmeyer and Gary D. McKay, *The Parent's Guide—STEP/Teen: Systematic Training for Effective Parenting of Teens* (Circle Pines, Minn.: American Guidance Service, 1983), 123.
3. *Encyclopedia Britannica,* 15th ed. (Chicago, 1979), Macropaedia Vol. 11, 28–77.
4. Deming, op. cit., *The New Economics,* 105.
5. Ibid., 105.
6. *Bits and Pieces* (Fairlawn, N.J.: The Economics Press).
7. H. William Dettmer, *Goldratt's Theory of Constraints: A Systems Approach to Continuous Improvement* (Milwaukee, Wis.: ASQC Quality Press, 1996), ch. 2.
8. *Webster's New Universal Unabridged Dictionary* (N.J.: Barnes and Noble, 1989), 476.

Chapter 5
IDENTIFYING THE SYSTEM CONSTRAINT:
The Current Reality Tree

Managers who attack results without analyzing causes usually make matters worse rather than better.

—Unknown

The title of this book is *Breaking the Constraints to World Class Performance*. A worthy objective, but before we can break a constraint, we have to know what our constraint is. Often that's not easy to determine. What's the constraint that limits the performance of *your* organization? Is it the market? Or your production capacity? How do you know? A gut feeling? An educated guess? Are you confident enough in your identification of the constraint that you're willing to commit valuable, maybe irreplaceable, resources to breaking it?

Remember in chapter 4 we considered the knowledge continuum, a scale that ran from *uncertainty* to *certainty* (Figure 4.2). Our gut feelings lie toward the uncertainty end, while educated guesses are closer to the center, in the region of risk. However, breaking constraints warrants considerably more than educated guesses. Why? Because breaking a constraint requires change. Sometimes that change can involve a significant financial investment. Even if it doesn't, breaking a constraint often represents such a significant change to the way business is done that it results in considerable organizational turbulence or confusion. Whether the effect is financial or functional, it makes no sense to commit to such change unless we're sure we're working on what's really constraining our system, because we know from chapter 1 that there's not much profit in working on nonconstraints.

For decisions of this import, we need more than educated guesses. We need the confidence that comes from theoretical understanding, experience, evidence, and cause-and-effect logic. Theoretical understanding comes from education. Experience is a function of how many times we've been around the block, and evidence comes from what we measure, both inside and outside our organizations. But where do we find cause-and-effect logic, and how does it relate to identifying constraints?

Anyone who has battled a dandelion or other weed problem in their front yard has had a first-hand exposure to cause and effect. Dandelions are the bane of many homeowners' existence, especially those who take pride in the appearance of their lawns. In fact, the dandelion is an excellent metaphor for cause and effect.

Like many effects, the dandelion's blossom is highly visible and bright, clearly showing above the surface. Like many causes, the roots are complex, hidden below the surface, and hard to eliminate. Many homeowners cut down the offending dandelions with a mower or weed trimmer. The effects (the yellow blossom and green leaves) are gone temporarily, but the cause (the root) remains alive and well, concealed beneath the surface. Because we haven't eliminated the cause, the effects will be back eventually. The homeowners who are really successful in clearing dandelions from their yards are the ones who figure out how to destroy the roots—the cause of the dandelions.

Obviously, not all effects are bad. Clearly, we don't want to get rid of the good ones. But life isn't usually as simple as a dandelion. This is especially true in complex organizations, or society as a whole. How do we eliminate what we don't like, while retaining what we do? Understanding cause and effect can help us separate the wheat from the chaff. It enables us to get to the hidden causes of the effects we don't like and differentiate them from the causes of those we do. If those effects are indications of less than maximum system performance, the hidden causes we find are likely to be system constraints. So a comprehensive cause-and-effect analysis can help us identify system constraints, particularly if those constraints are faulty policies.

In order for us to make change decisions with the highest possible degree of confidence that they'll break our constraints, we need the answers to three key questions:

- *What* should we change?
- What should we change it *to?*
- *How* should we make the change happen?

Our structured cause-and-effect analysis will provide the answers to these questions.

The theory of constraints thinking process is based on the idea that we can positively identify what we don't like about a situation and trace it back to some underlying cause. What we don't like is referred to as an undesirable effect (UDE). The underlying cause is a *root cause*. Sometimes a number of intermediate effects, which are themselves causes, can lie between a root cause and an undesirable effect (Figure 5.1). The impression is similar to a series of dominoes lined up in close sequence. The effect of knocking over the first domino is that it triggers the fall of the second, which knocks over the third, and so on, until the last domino falls.

Before we can effectively solve a complex system problem, we must thoroughly understand the cause and effect behind the reality of our cur-

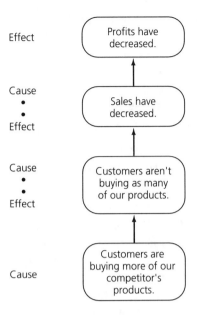

Effect → Profits have decreased.

Cause
•
•
Effect → Sales have decreased.

Cause
•
•
Effect → Customers aren't buying as many of our products.

Cause → Customers are buying more of our competitor's products.

FIGURE 5.1 Intermediate levels of cause and effect.

rent situation. The current reality tree gives us a way to expose that cause and effect. Before we jump into the current reality tree, let's consider how we'll define some key terms we'll be using: undesirable effects, root causes, complex causality, core problem, and causality arrow.

UNDESIRABLE EFFECTS

The easiest place to start is with what we can see each day: the undesirable effect. What's an undesirable effect? The meaning would seem obvious at face value, but it's not quite as simple as it seems.

Effects can be either desirable, neutral, or undesirable, but they can be categorized only by comparing them to some designated standard. Obviously, we must have already determined what that standard is before we can label an effect desirable, undesirable, or neutral. Since we're interested in optimizing a *system,* the benchmark must be related to system performance, whether that system is personal or organizational. In chapters 1 and 2, we said the system goal and the necessary conditions for achieving that goal would be the focus of our constraint-breaking efforts. It only makes sense that to begin our analysis of what to change in our systems we should start with these same factors. The standards against which we measure undesirability should be the system's goal, necessary conditions, and measures of merit for each of them.

If we're part of a for-profit system, either the goal or one of the necessary conditions is clearly to make money. Consequently, "profits increase" would be a desirable effect. "We lost money in the first quarter" is obviously negative in light of the same standard. Most people trying to build a current reality tree have the most difficulty with neutral effects. They may be exactly that—neutral—or they might seem to be somewhat positive or negative. Following are four examples of effects. Which are positive, negative, and neutral?

- The door is closed.
- People in the office are sweating from the heat.
- My in-basket is overflowing with paperwork.
- Everyone in the office enjoys the birthday party.

The first one seems reasonably neutral. The next two seem somewhat negative, and the last seems positive, *but in comparison to what standard?* If our goal is to make money, and the three necessary conditions are customer satisfaction, a high demand for our products, and regulatory compliance, then what bearing do the effects listed previously have on those benchmarks? By themselves, none! That makes them all neutral effects, even the ones that seem positive or negative.

On the other hand, if we define the system to be *ourselves,* we're dealing with an entirely different goal and different necessary conditions. Your personal goal might be happiness, however you choose to define it. One necessary condition might be personal comfort. Another might be avoidance of excessive stress, and a third might be rewarding personal interactions. In this case, the first effect, listed previously, is still neutral. The second is clearly undesirable, as is the third. The last one is definitely desirable.

The principle here is simple. Before a determination of undesirability can be made, we *must* know the system boundary, its goal, and the necessary conditions. These are the factors that determine whether the effects we observe in the situation we're analyzing are positive, neutral, or negative. This is the *most important step* in building a current reality tree, because if we fail to do this step well, we risk suboptimizing the system. If we build a cause-effect analysis around the wrong undesirable effects, we should be neither surprised nor disappointed when our corrective actions fail to improve the system! It's been said that a well-defined problem is more than half-solved. Defining that problem depends absolutely on starting from the right undesirable effects, and the only way to do that is to be certain that they are truly undesirable from the perspective of the system's goal and necessary conditions.

To summarize, here are two effective rules of thumb for differentiating undesirable effects (UDEs) from neutral effects:

- *What bearing does the effect have on the system's goal?* UDEs are negative in relation to the goal or necessary conditions of the system involved, or the key measurement of progress toward that goal. If the effect is truly undesirable, progress toward attainment of this goal is hindered or completely obstructed. In a profit-and-loss example, it can be assumed that the goal of the company is to make more money. That's the benchmark that enables us to say "We lost money in the first quarter" is an undesirable effect. It's also what enables us to say that "My department is not fully staffed" is neutral, and "Sales are up 25 percent" is positive.

• *Does the effect pass the* So what? *test?* UDEs are negative on their own merit. The simple statement of the effect alone is enough to convey negativity. No further explanation why is required. Any person reasonably familiar with the situation—and the system's goal and necessary conditions—would consider the effect negative at face value. "We lost money in the first quarter" would certainly be considered negative by almost anyone associated with a company.

ROOT CAUSES

As we discussed earlier, the true underlying cause may reside several layers of cause and effect beneath the undesirable effect. Remember the airplane crash example in chapter 4 (Figure 4.1)? The ultimate cause of the destruction of the aircraft and death of the crew—both definitely undesirable—lay 22 levels beneath these effects. Our challenge is to identify those causes—root causes—that produce our undesirable effects.

If we have so many layers of cause and effect, how do we know when we've reached a root cause? When do we stop? Theoretically, we could trace causality back to a quotation that reads, "In the beginning, God created the heaven and the earth. And the earth was dark and without form . . . ."[1] Likewise, we could consider the scriptural history of other religions and the scientific big bang theory to be a root cause of everything that transpires today. If we went back that far, then no problem would ever be solved. There has to be some intermediate point between the creation of the universe and the undesirable effects we see—terrorism, genocide in Bosnia, Chernobyl, and so on—where the chain of cause and effect can be effectively broken. That point is what we'll consider to be the root cause, and we'll indicate it in the current reality tree as a round-cornered box with an arrow coming *out* of it, but no arrow going *into* it.

Of course, since we'd like to be the prime movers in the breaking of an undesirable chain of cause and effect, it would be nice if the break point were at least under our influence, if not under our outright control. So for our purposes, we'll define the root cause as *the lowest cause in a chain of cause and effect at which we have some capability to cause the break*. Yes, there will undoubtedly be causes below this that someone else would consider the root cause, and from that person's standpoint, they could be considered root causes. But the same two characteristics still apply:

• It's the lowest point at which human intervention can change or break the cause.
• It's within our capability to unilaterally control, or to influence, changes to the cause.

For example, lightning striking an electrical transformer would clearly be the root cause of the transformer's destruction. The existence of a lightning stroke itself is well beyond our ability to change or influence. But the fact that it *strikes the transformer* isn't. So we can, to some degree, preclude the undesirable effect (the destruction of the transformer) by exercising our influence to ensure that the lightning strikes something harmless—a lightning rod, for example. *Redirecting* the lightning is the lowest point at which human intervention can break the chain of cause and effect.

COMPLEX CAUSALITY

From the examples you've seen so far, it's probably obvious that cause and effect isn't often as simple as a single chain of dominoes waiting to fall. There will always be many root causes in a current reality tree, because existing reality invariably has many underlying causes.

Some of these are independent; that is, they can make the cause-and-effect dominoes start falling all by themselves. In chapter 4, we saw that these independent causes are called *additional causes*. Their singular characteristic is, in fact, their independence, and they're identifiable in a current reality tree by a single arrow coming from the independent cause. The lightning strike is an independent additional cause, because it's enough by itself to cause the electric power transformer's destruction.

Most causes, however, contribute to the effect *in concert* with some other cause. These are *interdependent* causes, because each one needs the help of the other to produce the effect. With the loss of either one, the effect ceases to exist. We called that *cause sufficiency* in chapter 4, and we indicated it with an ellipse enclosing the arrows issuing from two or more causes. For example, putting a fishing line in the water isn't enough to catch a fish. There have to be fish present, and they have to be attracted to whatever you're using for bait. All three are required. Removing any one of them is enough to warrant changing the dinner menu to hamburgers.

We also saw in chapter 4 that in some cases, causes have characteristics of both contributing and independent causes. For example, your poor gasoline mileage could be the result of an improperly tuned engine, your lead foot on the accelerator, or the size of your engine's displacement. Any one of these could be enough to cause the undesirable effect (bad gasoline mileage). But in combination, they add to, or magnify the effect. By the same token, taking any one of them away won't get rid of the undesirable effect, as it would with the additional cause and cause sufficiency. It would reduce only the magnitude of the effect. However, sometimes in problem solving that's good enough. When independent causes combine to increase the magnitude of an effect, we indicate that relationship in the current reality tree by use of a bow-tie-shaped figure.

CORE PROBLEM

A core problem is a unique kind of root cause. It's one that can be clearly traced to an exceptionally large percentage of the undesirable effects we see in our system. How big a percentage? One rule of thumb is 70 percent. If you can find a root cause that produces 70 percent of your undesirable effects, you may have a core problem. But 70 percent is a somewhat arbitrary number. If it seems too much or too little, use a different threshold, as long as it's a majority.

One other weakness in using a purely quantitative criterion to determine a core problem is that undesirable effects are *not* all created equal. Some are much, much worse than others. Let's say that you've identified ten undesirable effects and found one root cause that accounts for seven of them. But one of the remaining three UDEs is a really critical one—a success-or-failure factor for the organization, and perhaps due to the circumstances, it doesn't result from the same root cause that produced the other seven undesirable effects. Should we be worrying about the 70 percent core problem, or might we be better off dealing first, or at least simultaneously, with the root cause that produces our game-breaker UDE? It's possible that leaning on the 70 percent crutch could lead us astray. However, if we've properly identified the *real* undesirable effects—the ones that are defined in terms of the system's goal—the core problem will, in all likelihood *be* the system's constraint, whether it accounts for the 70 percent or not.

In a situation like the one just described, you do not have a single core problem; you have *at least two* root causes you must deal with. Many people don't even bother identifying a single core problem at all. Instead, they evaluate the undesirable effects and select the minimum number of root causes they must address to get rid of them. The only real virtue in identifying a single core problem is what military strategists call *economy of force:* it delivers the maximum total benefit to your system for the minimum investment in resources—the most bang for your buck.

The moral of this story is this. By all means, look for a core problem among your root causes. In most cases, it's probably the system constraint. But don't get locked into the idea that a purely quantitative criterion determines what the core problem might be. Assess the gravity of the undesirable effects in each situation and make a subjective determination for yourself. If you have a root cause that accounts for a majority of your UDEs, and if your most burning UDE lies within that group, you'd be a fool to work on anything else first!

CAUSALITY ARROW

The arrows in a cause-and-effect tree seem so inconsequential. They're nothing but thin lines with barbs at one end. Our attention is inevitably drawn away from the arrows and toward the contents of the entity blocks, the words that give life to our reality, current or future. But there's a wealth of meaning embedded within each arrow. That meaning has two components, each of them alone as important as what's written in the boxes.

One component of the arrow is the categories of legitimate reservation, our acid test of validity for the proposed cause-effect relationship. Seven categories (all but clarity) are implicit in that arrow, because it's a valid arrow only if the proposed cause-effect relationship passes all seven tests of logic. Failure of just one of the tests breaks the relationship—in other words, it renders the arrow invalid. So every time you see an arrow, it should trigger your mind to remember to apply the tests of logic—the categories of legitimate reservation.

The second component of the arrow is the *implied assumptions* it represents. Even a cause-effect relationship that appears simple and straightforward has unstated, but implied, assumptions associated with the arrow. For example, consider the lightning strike situation again (Figure 5.2). It looks very simple:

If lightning strikes the transformer . . ." (cause)
↓
. . . then the transformer is destroyed. (effect)

However, think about the assumptions we've unconsciously made (about either the cause or the effect) in proposing this relationship. Here are a few:

- The weather is capable of generating lightning.
- The transformer is on top of a telephone pole (that is, exposed, above ground level).
- The electrical discharge is of sufficient power to destroy the transformer.
- No provisions are made in advance to shunt the charge away from the critical transformer parts.

Each of these assumptions affects either the cause or the effect, and each has one of three characteristics: (1) it's *valid,* (2) it's *invalid,* or (3) it's valid, but we can *make* it invalid. In cause-and-effect problem solving,

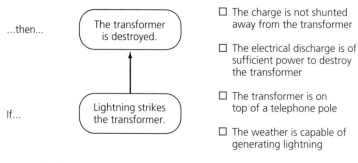

FIGURE 5.2 Implied assumptions.

when any assumption is either invalid or can be made invalid, the potential for breaking the cause-and-effect chain at that point rises dramatically. For example, among the assumptions mentioned previously, the first and third are likely to be valid. But the second and fourth, though perhaps valid now, could be made invalid by putting the transformer underground or by attaching a grounded lightning rod to the top of the pole. So besides considering the categories of legitimate reservation, when we see an arrow, we should be asking ourselves, What unstated assumptions are hidden there that we might use to break the chain at this point?

NEGATIVE REINFORCEMENT

At one time or another, most of us have encountered a situation where a negative effect of some cause, often several steps removed, has a reinforcing effect on the cause itself. For example, the negative effect of a large fire in a building might actually reinforce the behavior of the pyromaniac who set the fire, to cause more, and possibly worse, fires. While negative reinforcement isn't common, it can be found if we have the motivation to look for it. Figure 5.3 shows an example of a negative reinforcing loop as part of a logic tree. Really bad problems—negative effects that seem disproportionately magnified—are often good places to look for negative reinforcement. While negative reinforcing loops aren't likely to make a core problem or root cause any more difficult to solve, identifying them points out situations where much greater improvement might be possible when the problem is eventually solved.

AH-CHOO!: A PRACTICAL EXAMPLE‡

We've talked about undesirable effects, root causes, complex causality, core problems, causality arrows, and negative reinforcing loops. Let's see how they all come together in a typical current reality tree.

Who among us hasn't been afflicted with the common cold? The undesirable effects of a cold are obvious: uncontrollable coughing and sneezing, congested sinuses, a runny nose, and a general feeling of fatigue. If I saw you at your desk, suffering from these symptoms, and asked you what was wrong, you'd probably reply, "I've got a really bad cold." For you, the cold is the cause of your misery. But is the cause and effect really that simple?

Tim Sellan related his experience with some hard-working immigrants on a farm some years ago. In spite of the common nature of the cold, these hardy people reported never having had one! So although the cold

---

‡The author is indebted to Mr. Tim Sellan of Windsor, Ontario, Canada, for his creation of this example and his permission to use it here.

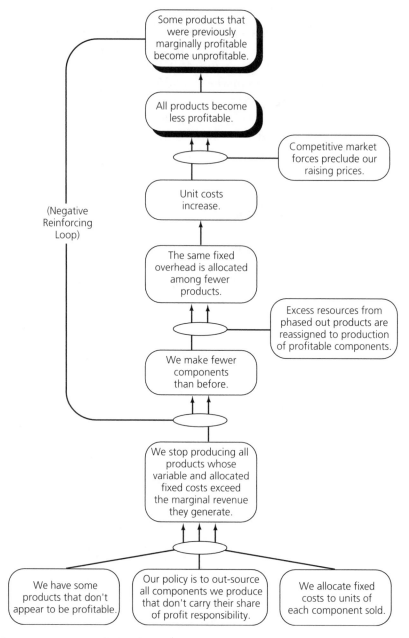

FIGURE 5.3 Negative reinforcing loop example.

virus is undoubtedly the cause of the undesirable effects, it's probably not an independent root cause. But if not, then what is?

Let's look at the current reality tree in Figure 5.4. We normally trace cause and effect back from the undesirable effects to the root causes. That's how this tree was built. However, when we read the completed tree, we normally read it from bottom to top. So we'll do that here, starting with the box numbered 100.

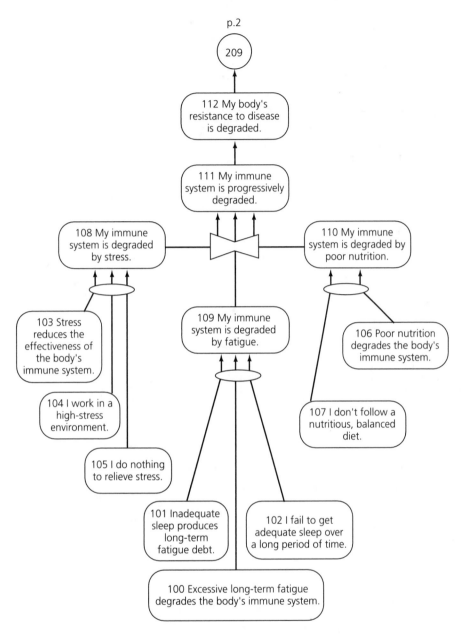

FIGURE 5.4.1 Ah-choo!: A current reality tree.

HOW TO READ A CURRENT REALITY TREE

Let's quickly review how to read a cause-effect tree. Start with a root cause (a box with an arrow coming out of it, but none going in). Read the statement in the box verbatim, preceded by the word *If* . . . . After that, read the statement in the box the arrow is pointing to, preceded by the word . . . *then* . . . . When two or more arrows are enclosed by an

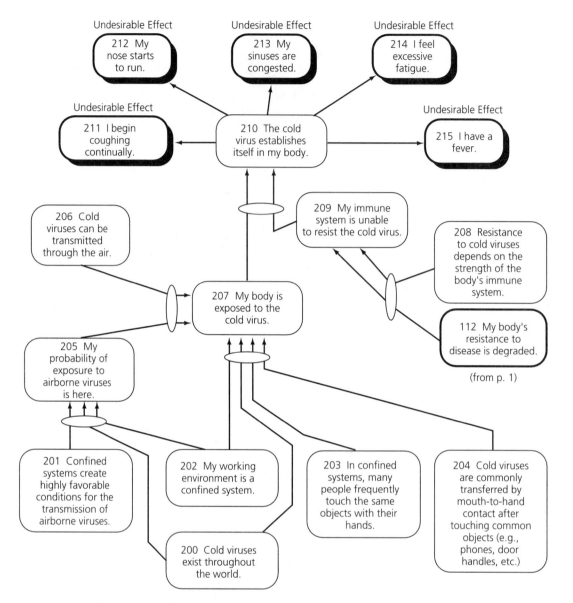

FIGURE 5.4.2 Ah-choo!: A current reality tree. The author is indebted to Mr. Tim Sellan, of Windsor, Ontario, for the use of this tree and his participation in preparing it

ellipse or a bow-tie shape, read all causes with If . . . before reading the effect with . . . then . . . . For example:

> *If (100) excessive long-term fatigue degrades the body's immune system,*
> *and*
> *(101) inadequate sleep produces long-term fatigue debt,*
> *and*
> *(102) I fail to get adequate sleep over a long period of time,*
> *then*
> *(109) my immune system is degraded by fatigue.*

Continue reading boxes 103, 104, and 105 the same way, and also 106 and 107. Keep reading the cause and effect in If . . . then . . . form until you reach the undesirable effects (indicated by the shadowed boxes). Each . . . then . . . becomes an If . . . for the succeeding level of cause and effect.

There are some noteworthy observations to be made about this tree. First, what we tended to cite as *the* cause (I have a really bad cold) is actually an intermediate cause (block 210). Since there's currently no cure for the common cold, if we don't take our cause-effect analysis any farther than that, we're faced with treating only the symptoms. In fact, that's what most of us usually do: we take decongestants, cough medicine, antihistamines, and maybe even chicken soup, and eventually the undesirable effects (blocks 211–214) go away— temporarily, until the next cold virus comes along! Since we've never even attempted to dig deeper into the causality of the situation, we haven't made any effort to break the chain of cause and effect at the lowest practical level over which we have control. So we can be relatively sure that we're going to go through this experience again, perhaps sooner than we'd like.

Second, if we look immediately below block 210 (The cold virus has established itself in the victim's body), we see that the tree diverges into two distinctly separate branches at that point. In reading the general tone of each branch, we can see that one branch relates to exposure, while the other relates to resistance. In other words, *exposure* to the cold virus is an important cause, but it's *not sufficient alone.* It must be combined with a failure of the body's immune system to resist the virus.

Third, there are a number of causes that look like they could be root causes (100 through 107, 200 through 204, 206, and 208). However, if we look carefully at 100, 101, 103, 104, 106, 200, 202, 203, 204, 206, and 208, we'll see that our ability to influence them is virtually nonexistent. We can't do anything about the fact that stress reduces the effectiveness of the body's immune system (103). We can't change the fact that poor nutrition does the same (106). Nor can we change the fact that confined systems promote the transmission of cold viruses (202). Our ability to change the high-stress nature of the work environment (104) or people's tendencies to touch their faces and then other commonly handled objects (203, 204) may be likewise limited. So to find the *real* root causes—the ones we have some hope of influencing—we have to search a little harder. There are several over which we might exercise some control, 102, 105, 107, and 201, for example. These are the real root causes, the ones we want to focus our energy on.

Fourth, notice that the causes of a degraded immune system (108) are *additive* in nature. With enough severity, each one alone can cause the degraded immune system. But together they produce a highly degraded immune system, which then increases the likelihood of infection from exposure.

Finally, notice that in this case there's no single core problem. We have to eliminate all the magnitudinal causes of the degraded immune system, which might not be possible to do completely. Or we have to eliminate the exposure problem, which could be even more difficult. One might say, "Well, the core problem is the cold virus itself; it's the one factor that affects both the exposure and the resistance branches." And that's true. Eliminate the cold virus and resisting it becomes moot. So does exposure to it. But for the foreseeable future, that's a cause somewhere closer to ". . . the earth was dark and without form . . . ." So why waste energy on that? We should focus our effort where it will do the most good quickly—let's move to Canada and live with the hardworking immigrants!

SPAN OF CONTROL AND SPHERE OF INFLUENCE

Our definition of a root cause included the condition that it be within our capability to control or influence changes in that cause. This definition implies the existence of some arbitrary boundaries, which we'll call our *span of control* and our *sphere of influence*. These two boundaries are like concentric amoebae (Figure 5.5). They're larger along some axes than others.

Our span of control is the region of our lives, our company, our society, or the world at large over which we have unilateral authority to change things. It would be really nice if all of the root causes we ever had

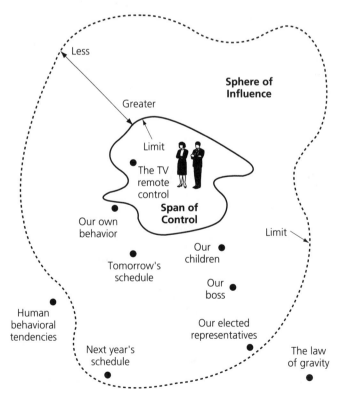

FIGURE 5.5 Span of control and sphere of influence.

to deal with lay within this variable radius. But in reality, most of us labor with a fairly limited span of control—even the chief executive of a company or a head of state. Given how high in the hierarchy they're supposed to be, it's often surprising to find out how little unilateral authority they have to change their domains. When a root cause falls within our span of control, it should be cause for celebration, because we have the power to solve that particular problem *right now.*

Unfortunately, more often than not, this is not the case. The root cause is more likely to lie within our sphere of influence. This means that we can bring pressure to bear to change the situation, but we can't completely control or effectively mandate it. The farther toward the boundary of our sphere of influence a root cause or core problem lies, the less influence we are likely to have over it. For example, a chief executive officer doesn't *control* the company's external suppliers, but he or she probably can exert a powerful influence over them. That same CEO might be able to influence a particular congressional representative to sponsor legislation favorable to his or her company, but influencing enough members of congress to pass the bill is probably much less certain. So the supplier lies just outside the CEO's span of control, in an area of great influence. Congress probably lies a little farther out, and the majority needed to pass a bill might lie right on the outer boundary of the sphere of influence—if not outside it altogether.

Success in business or any personal endeavor, then, becomes a continual game called "Let's see how far outward I can push my sphere of influence." The current reality tree is the first of five logical tools that will help us do that.

HOW TO BUILD A CURRENT REALITY TREE

We've defined the key elements of the current reality tree: undesirable effects, root causes, core problems, causality arrows, and assumptions. We've discussed how causes and effects relate through cause sufficiency (an ellipse), independent cause (a single arrow), and magnitudinal cause (a bow-tie). Now it's time to see how these all combine to produce a current reality tree.

What *is* a current reality tree? Consider it a snapshot of reality as it exists at a particular moment in time. As with a photograph, it's not reality itself, just a picture of reality, and, like a photo, it encloses only what we choose to aim at through the camera's viewfinder. Have you ever wondered why the pictures of the Grand Canyon you shot on your vacation, while beautiful, don't convey the breathtaking image your eyes beheld when you stood on the South Rim? You see much more when you look directly at reality than you do when you look at a picture of reality.

In the same way, the current reality tree is a picture of reality. By aiming our logical camera at the undesirable effects and their root causes, we're essentially cropping out all the details that don't relate to them. So the printed image, while detailed in what it does show, doesn't portray the richness of our firsthand view of reality. In other words, what's outside the viewfinder doesn't show up.

For our purposes, however, this is probably a good thing. One of the most valuable features of a current reality tree is that it gives us a detailed, *focused* look at the logic of *only* what involves our designated undesirable effects. Unrelated elements of reality are left out. This helps us avoid information overload, but it also demands that we be absolutely sure that we've correctly identified the undesirable effects to begin with, or we'll be tracing branches down to root causes that don't actually cause the system to hurt the most.

Let's see how the construction process works and look at some real-world examples. Each step in the building process will be explained, using an actual example as an illustration. That example is based in part on an article entitled "Why Our Roads Go To Pot."[2] The content of many of the entities in Figures 5.5 through 5.14 comes from facts reported in that article. The content of other entities was extrapolated from the author's own knowledge of the situation.

1. *Define the System Boundaries and Goal.* Our efforts to portray current reality in a tree begin with defining the goal and boundaries of our system. You'll recall from our earlier discussions of undesirable effects that we need a benchmark against which to assess the negativity of the effects we observe. This means that we have to know, first, what boundaries we'll use to define our system. Is our system a national, economic, or societal system, a discrete organization, a family, or an individual? For example, are we considering the economy of the United States or just the commercial corporation of which we're a part? If we are considering the latter, is this a corporate problem we're trying to solve, or is it just divisional? By establishing the boundaries, we're aiming the viewfinder of our camera.

When defining the system boundaries, two words of caution are in order: *avoid suboptimization!* Remember in chapter 1 we said that systems often fall victim to suboptimization—the idea that if we thoroughly polish every process to its highest shine, the entire system will perform at its maximum. That's the underlying assumption that total quality management is based on, and because of variation and dependence, it's an invalid assumption. Call it friction, tolerance backlash, unequal capacities, or whatever you choose, but where system performance is concerned, the whole isn't equal to the sum of the parts, or processes.

The trap here is that if you define your boundaries too low in the system (for example, around a process, such as production, marketing, or finance), you might be suboptimizing—improving that part of the system at the expense of another part, and doing so might not be what's best for the system as a whole. Never forget that the theory of constraints and the thinking process, as methods, are completely blind to the nature of the organization and its structure. They can't know

Boundary: U.S. national highway infrastructure

Goal: Safe, expeditious vehicle transportation (auto and truck) for economic, social, and political purposes

Necessary Conditions:
1. Maximum number of roads in good condition; minimum number of roads undergoing maintenance
2. Minimize direct and indirect cost to taxpayers

Measures:
1. Miles of roads needing repair
2. Miles of roads under repair
3. Drive-times between standard points
4. Average length of traffic delays
5. Total cost of traffic delays
6. Road repair backlogs

FIGURE 5.6   Step 1: Define the system's boundary, goal, necessary conditions, and measures of progress.

whether you're suboptimizing the system or not. Only you can know that. As a result, if you let it, the methodology can do an outstanding job of suboptimizing, to the detriment of the system as a whole. In other words, TOC and its tools can be abused as readily as they can be constructively used. It's all in the skill and intent of the user.

Once the system's boundaries have been explicitly defined, we must determine the benchmarks against which to measure the negativity of our proposed undesirable effects. From our discussion earlier, we know that these are the goal and its associated necessary conditions. Figure 5.6 provides examples of the boundary, goal, two possible necessary conditions, and some typical measures of progress for the highway infrastructure system.

2. *State the System Problem.* Once we've defined our system's boundaries, goals, and necessary conditions—the context of the problem—we're ready to tackle the problem statement. Since we haven't started our cause-and-effect analysis yet, it would be premature to presume that we really know anything beyond the visible indicators that something isn't quite right. To keep us focused on the cause and effect that will follow, we'll formulate our problem statement as a *why?* question. For example:

*   Why are we having trouble increasing sales?
*   Why are deliveries to customers taking so long?
*   Why are we getting so many customer complaints?

Whatever the big indicator is that you don't like about the system's performance, state it as a *why* question. Write it at the top of a piece of paper. Or, if you're working on the problem in a group, write it at the top of a whiteboard or flip-chart.

Why are America's highways failing society?

FIGURE 5.7 Step 2: State the system problem as a question.

After you've written your problem statement, review it carefully. Is it clearly related to your system goal, one of the necessary conditions for achieving that goal, or one of your key measurements—*throughput,* for example? If it is, you're ready to continue.

In the case of the highway example, Figure 5.7 indicates one possible statement of the problem.

3. *Start Three Columns: Causes, Negatives, and Why.* Below the problem statement, create three columns, from left to right, entitled *Causes, Negatives,* and *Why.*

4. *List Negatives, Why, and Causes.* Starting with the Negatives column (in the center) list all the things you *don't like* about the way the system is performing. Emphasize the visible indicators that tell you performance isn't up to snuff. Include in your list of negatives the things that make it more difficult for you to do your job. For example, you might know that production has a three-week backlog of orders. That would be a negative that relates very closely to throughput. Another might be, "One-third of our finished products fail final inspection," a second indication that throughput is being compromised. A CEO might come up with one that says, "Status reports all look good, but our major customers are calling me directly with complaints." A sales manager might suggest, "We can't get training for our inexperienced salespeople," which makes the sales manager's job tougher to accomplish. After you've completed a list of five to ten negatives, number them in sequence starting with number 1. Don't worry about prioritizing them. The numbers are arbitrary and temporary, to help you keep track of related causes and effects.

Go now to the *right* column, the one labeled *Why.* Reread your list of negatives, one at a time. As you read each one, ask yourself the question, "*Why* is this bad in relation to our goal, a necessary condition, or a key measurement such as throughput, inventory, or operating expense?"

You'll be inclined to respond, "Well, because Negative 1 limits our ability to sell more products, which in turn hurts throughput. And Negative 2 degrades our ability to make more money, which is our goal." Write each of these *becauses* down in the Why column. There might be more than one for each negative. Number them to correspond with the number you assigned to the negative, in the center column. If there are several whys for the same negative, add a letter to the number (for example, 1a, 1b, 1c, and so on).

After you've come up with reasons why each of the negatives are bad, move to the *left* column, labeled *Causes.* Starting at the top, with the first negative in the center column, ask yourself, "What's causing this negative? Why does it exist?" If a reason doesn't immediately spring to mind, you might need to research the negative, to find out more about it. In most cases, however, you'll find that it's fairly easy to identify reasons why the negative exists. Take the negative, "One-third of our finished products fail final inspection," for example. *Why* is that happening? If you don't know off the top of your head, chances are your quality control department can tell you what failure modes are most commonly found during inspection. There might be several. Each of them, stated separately, becomes a cause to be listed in the left column.

Let's say the two most common causes of failure in your final inspection are: circuit boards frequently fail to pass continuity tests and throttle linkages frequently jam during acceleration. Both of these cause the negative, final inspection failure. List them beside the negative they apply to, and number them to correspond with it, too. To distinguish *causes* from *whys*, you might reverse the labeling; for example, A1, B1, C1, and so on.

Once you've completed listing all the causes for each negative and all the reasons why that negative is bad for the system, you're ready to begin construction of the current reality tree itself. All the *causes, negatives,* and *whys* will be your initial building blocks.

Figure 5.8 shows the causes, negatives, and whys for the highway deterioration problem. Notice that in some cases there is more than one *cause* and *why*. These elements are labeled with upper- and lowercase letters as well as numbers.

Causes	Negatives	Why?
A1. Road repair budgets are limited.	1. More roads need repairs than can be funded.	1a. Road repairs and budgets become backlogged.
A2. Highway contractors use low-durability paving materials.	2. Paving materials used require more frequent repair.	2a. Highway repair costs exceed budgets.
A3. Backlogged repairs are delayed in their completion.	3. Roads are in worse condition when repairs start.	3a. Repair delays and excessive repair costs double the life-cycle cost of a road.
A4. Too many lanes are closed for repair on too many roads.	4. Congestion is aggravated by road maintenance.	4a. Traffic congestion costs the U.S. $30 billion annually in travel delays and fuel consumption.
B4. Main roads are busy.		4b. Risk of accidents increases.
A5. Paving material cracks easily.	5. Pavement is disintegrating.	5a. Heavily traveled roads have many potholes.
B5. Water infiltration causes disintegration.		5b. Cars and trucks are damaged when they hit potholes.

FIGURE 5.8   Step 4: List negatives, why?, and causes.

5. *Convert All Negatives, Whys, and Causes to CRT Entities.* From the examples you've seen of current reality trees, it's clear that they're combinations of words, geometric figures, and arrows. It's this graphical nature of current reality trees that makes complex cause and effect so easy to visualize. So our next task is to convert our list of causes, negatives, and whys into graphic blocks, or *entities.*

Throughout this book you'll see references to the word *entity.* Don't let it confuse you. An entity is no more than an idea stated in words and enclosed in some kind of geometric figure. It might be a cause, effect, undesirable effect, core problem, obstacle, objective, or action of some kind. All of these are entities, for the purpose of discussing logic trees, and they're usually identifiable by a number, a letter, or a combination of the two.

Perhaps the most tedious aspect of building current reality trees is managing the entities. Since we have to convert written causes, negatives, and whys into graphical entities, how do we manage all these blocks of information? There's a low-tech way and a high-tech way. Each offers its own advantages and disadvantages.

The low-tech method is to use stick-on paper, such as the Post-it™ notes manufactured by the 3M Corporation. If you elect to use Post-it™ notes, don't use anything larger than 1½ inches by 2 inches. The low-tech method gives you complete visibility on the entire tree as it develops. It also enables you to move entities around easily or reposition them as necessary. Because the notes come in a variety of colors, you can assign different colors to undesirable effects, the core problem, or other discrete kinds of entity. But the best advantage is that it's not expensive.

The biggest drawback to the low-tech approach is logistical. You need oversized paper (maybe the size of a sheet from a flip-chart) because even the small Post-it™ notes can consume a large amount of space in some trees. You have to handwrite the causes, negatives, and whys onto each sticky-note, and since you'll undoubtedly be polishing wording at some point, it means rewriting as well. Once your tree is under way, you're faced with a portability problem: how to carry a large sheet of paper around? Rolled up is usually the best way, but it can be inconvenient. And rolling the paper sometimes causes the little sticky-notes to fall off.

The high-tech way is to use a computer. Notebook computers can solve the portability problem, but the digital solution is obviously more expensive. Even if you already have the hardware, you'll need software that will give you the efficiency and flexibility to create free-form structures of entities. There are many software packages that will do a creditable job of creating theory of constraints logic trees. Flow charting programs are usually the best. Which one you choose is likely to be a matter of personal taste. Graphic programs offer some definite advantages. The output is cleaner and more readable than handwritten sticky-notes. This is particularly important when you want to present your trees in formal meetings. Software programs lend themselves to partitioning complex trees into manageable pages. Editing is easier, quicker, and cleaner, and

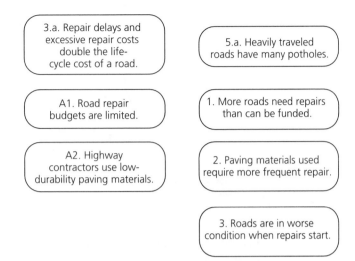

FIGURE 5.9 Step 5: Convert all negative, whys?, and causes to CRT entities.

software files can be carried on a diskette or transmitted by electronic mail. But it's not as easy to achieve the overall visibility, or big picture effect, that you have with the sticky-notes and flip-chart paper.

The primary disadvantages of building logic trees on computers are the risk of losing or corrupting a data file and the possible financial investment in the software. However, it's worth noting that excellent flow charting software packages for both PC and Macintosh are available for about $100 or less.

Whether you choose the low-tech or high-tech solution, your job at this point is to transfer all of those causes, negatives, and whys to a graphical form. When you do this, be sure to transfer your initial numbering scheme as well. Once this is done, you're ready for the next step.

Figure 5.9 shows how a few of the causes, negatives, and whys of the highway problem look when converted to graphical form (round-cornered blocks).

6. *Designate the Undesirable Effects.* Now it's time to determine which of the negatives and whys are undesirable effects. They need to be highlighted in some way. If you're using the low-tech method, you might put a red star on the entities that are clearly undesirable on their own merit, or you could use a different color Post-it™ note. If you're working on a computer, most graphic programs offer drop-shadow capability for geometric shapes. Either way, differentiate the undesirable effects from all the other entities in some fashion.

How do you decide which are really undesirable? If you did your homework in step 4, virtually all of the *whys* will be undesirable effects. Review them to make sure that some other person reasonably knowledgeable about the system would also consider the entity negative at face value and obviously detrimental to achievement of the system's goal. If so, mark it as a UDE. Set aside any *whys* you didn't mark as UDEs. They might

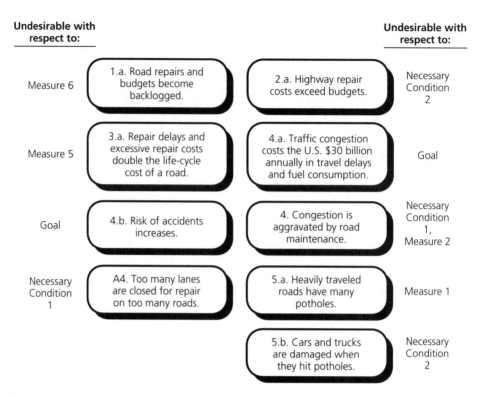

FIGURE 5.10 Step 6: Designate undesirable effects.

still be usable in your tree. Look, too, at the *negatives*. Some of them—probably a fewer number than the *whys*—might actually qualify as undesirable effects, too. If so, highlight these entities the same way.

The nine undesirable effects indicated by drop-shadows in Figure 5.10 were selected from among the 19 entities created from Figure 5.8. Notice that they are all clearly undesirable in relation to one or more of the goal, necessary conditions, or measures of progress toward the goal.

7. *Group Entities in Clusters.* From this point on, building the current reality tree is going to be very much like assembling a jigsaw puzzle. The entities are the pieces. Most of us learned to assemble jigsaw puzzles by color and cluster. That is, after laying all the pieces faceup on the table, we grouped the blue pieces near the top, because they were obviously part of the sky. Then we grouped the green pieces together, because they were clearly grass and trees. Then came the red pieces, which made up the old mill and waterwheel. Finally, at the bottom, we placed the pieces that were undoubtedly the reflection of everything in the picture off the surface of the water.

Once we grouped all the pieces into clusters by color, we began searching for pieces *within clusters* that obviously fit together. Little by little, we assembled each colored cluster into part of the overall picture. Finally—inevitably—we reached a point where the linkages between clusters were obvious, we made the connections, and the puzzle was complete!

We're going to use the same approach with the current reality tree. Our initial numbering scheme allows us to immediately group related entities into clusters. Practitioners of total quality management will recognize the similarity of this task to the building of an affinity diagram.[3] Once we've segregated all the entities into groups of the same basic number, we position the entities within each cluster. This is similar to grouping the white and the blue parts within the sky cluster in the jigsaw puzzle analogy. Align the undesirable effects horizontally at the top of each cluster, in no particular order. Then center each *negative* directly below the undesirable effects. Below the *negatives,* do the same with the *causes.* The clusters are now framed, much as a house is. They're ready for you to put on the walls and roof.

8. *Connect the Causes, Negatives, and Undesirable Effects.* Using a dotted line, connect the *negative* individually to each of the undesirable effects. Then connect the *causes* to the *negative.* Repeat this until all entities in each cluster are connected by dotted lines. Don't worry about trying to tighten your logic with the categories of legitimate reservation yet. For now, these simple temporary connections are good enough.

Figure 5.11 shows how the entities created from Figure 5.8, including the undesirable effects, are clustered and connected with dotted lines.

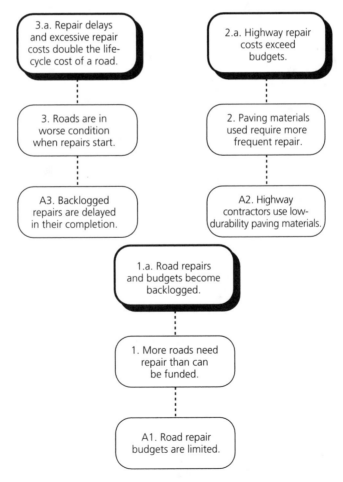

FIGURE 5.11   Step 7: Group entities in clusters by number. Step 8: Connect the causes to the UDEs.

9. *Group Related Clusters Together.* In our jigsaw puzzle, we knew that some of the pieces had both blue sky and red from the mill in them, or blue sky and part of a green tree. Knowing that the sky would be at the top of the final picture, we could then move the entire green cluster to be close to the part of the blue cluster that had some green on the pieces, and we could do the same for the red pieces. We're going to do the same thing with our current reality tree. At this point, we need to look for two clusters that seem to be related and relocate them so they're beside one another. For example, if we had a cluster on production backlogs and one on customer complaints, there's a good chance that the complaints would be related to late deliveries caused by the backlogs. So we should move those two clusters, as groups, to be right next to each other.

Once this is done, start looking for likely places to bridge the gap between clusters: places where a connection is very likely to develop. Again, use a dotted line to temporarily complete this connection without worrying yet about cause sufficiency, additional cause, or missing intermediate effects.

In Figure 5.12, we've moved three related clusters near one another and found possible connection points between them. Notice that these dotted line connections are not logically sound because we haven't

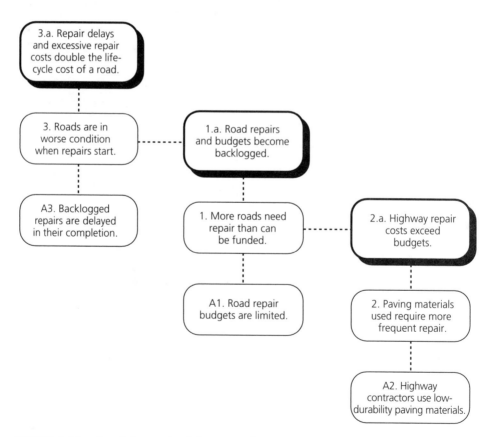

FIGURE 5.12   Step 9: Group related clusters together.

tested them using the categories of legitimate reservation. However, the dotted lines clearly show a general causal relationship between entities that will eventually be solidly connected.

10. *Scrutinize and Finalize Connections. Now* it's time to go back and solidify the logic of each causal connection, using the categories of legitimate reservation. Pick a cluster to start with and begin with the cause at the bottom. Look at the effect that the dotted line connects it to, and ask yourself:

- Is *this* cause enough, by itself, to create that effect, or does it need help from something else we haven't identified yet? If so, what is that contributing cause?
- Is there a step (entity) *missing* between this cause and that effect? If so, create a new entity, insert it between the cause and the effect, and recheck *both* connections for cause sufficiency (in other words, whether it needs help from another dependent cause).
- Is there another *independent* cause that could realistically produce the same effect, without help from this one? If so, create a new cause entity, place it below the effect, and connect it. Recheck the connection for causality existence (that is, it actually causes the effect) and cause sufficiency.

Add ellipses to show cause sufficiency or bow-ties to show magnitudinal effects where they're needed. When you're satisfied that a connection is logically sound enough to withstand criticism from someone else with knowledge about the system and the problem, change the dotted lines to solid lines and move on to the next connection.

The part of the current reality tree (for at this point it has become a tree, not just related clusters) in Figure 5.13 shows how the original entities, with numbers in the blocks, have been logically connected by adding contributing causes and their associated ellipses. Note that the newly added dependent causes don't have numbers assigned to them yet. Also note that one dotted-line connection has been rerouted to make for a better logical connection. The rerouting takes it through an intermediate cause (in this case, 2.a., an undesirable effect).

11. *Look For Additional Causes.* As you evaluate your cause-and-effect connections, be especially watchful for additional causes. You must determine whether there could be a different probable cause of the same effect. As you read each effect, ask yourself, "Besides the cause I already have here, what else could realistically produce the same effect?" If you find one, add it to the tree and solidify the logical connection immediately, using the categories of legitimate reservation.

Notice in Figure 5.14 that when we asked that question about entity A2, there were two completely independent causes that could produce A2. Both of these causes are the beginning of separate branches that continue downward along different paths.

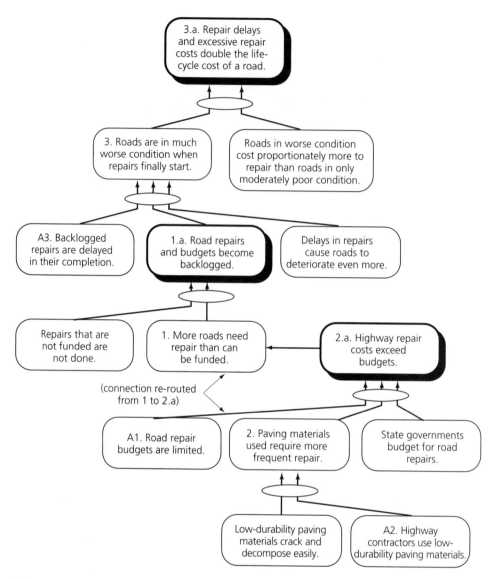

FIGURE 5.13   Step 10: Scrutinize and finalize connections.

12. *Continue Building Downward.* Repeat step 10 for all connections within each cluster. Then do the same for the temporary connections you made between clusters. If you haven't already been able to do so, try to find places where all clusters can be connected to one another to form a single tree. This might require you to build on several cause-and-effect layers below your original causes.

Keep building each cluster downward, one layer at a time in rotation. As you add a layer to each cluster, compare the new addition to every other cluster. You're looking for a new place where unconnected clusters might be linked to the main body of the tree with a lateral connection. If the clusters don't directly connect laterally, you'll have to continue building downward until you reach a V-shaped connection point. Stop when you have all clusters joined into a single tree. Scruti-

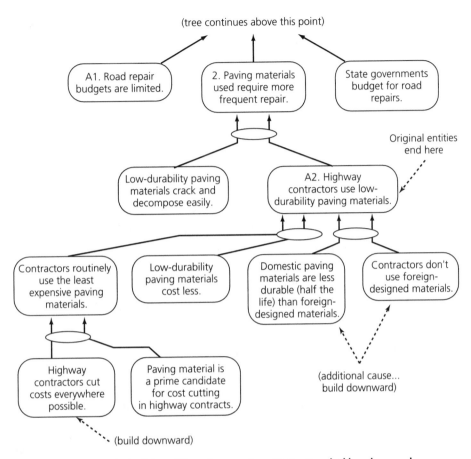

FIGURE 5.14 Step 11: Look for additional causes. Step 12: Continue building downward.

nize each new connection for logical soundness using the categories of legitimate reservation.

In Figure 5.14, we see that with the cause entity labeled A2, we've reached the end of the line for the entities we originally started with in Figure 5.8. But if you read the content of that entity, it fairly begs the question, "Well, *why* don't contractors use more durable materials?" Clearly, there's still more to this problem than meets the eye, and probably more that the states could have influence over. So we must dig deeper; we have to continue building downward. We're not at a root cause yet, much less a core problem.

13. *Redesignate Undesirable Effects.* By the time your clusters are all joined into a single tree, considerably more of the cause and effect of your current reality will be visible. In fact, enough of it might be visible that the character of your tree could have evolved to some extent. Also, some things you originally considered undesirable effects might no longer seem undesirable when considered in the context of the entire tree. Maybe they've reverted to just being negatives. Or, in adding entities to complete your connections or solidify your logic, there might be new undesirable effects in addition to those you originally identified.

So now is a good time to go back through the whole tree, from top to bottom, asking yourself the following questions:

- Are all my original undesirable effects bad enough to be still considered undesirable? If so, leave them alone. If not, remove their UDE designation.
- Are there any other effects in the tree, not previously identified as undesirable, that might now qualify as negative with respect to the goal on their own merit? If so, designate them as UDEs.

Once this is done, you're ready for the next step.

14. *Look for Negative Reinforcing Loops.* As we discussed earlier, a negative reinforcing loop can dramatically amplify the seriousness of undesirable effects. Though negative loops are not common, their presence would be grave enough to warrant an examination of the tree to see if one or more might be present. To find a negative reinforcing loop, look carefully at each undesirable effect and one or two layers of causes immediately below it. Based on what you know about the causes and effects farther down in the tree, ask yourself whether anything at this higher level might aggravate a cause-effect statement at a lower level. If so, draw in the loop to the appropriate place and verify the connection using the categories of legitimate reservation, as you would any other logical connection.

15. *Identify All Root Causes and a Core Problem.* Start looking at all the blocks in the tree that have arrows coming out of them, but none going into them. Decide which ones are facts of nature that you have little or no probability of changing, and which are within your sphere of influence. Highlight the latter in some way. When you examine the content of these entities, it may become apparent that you haven't yet built all the way down to the lowest level of cause over which you have substantial influence. If this is the case, keep extending the tree downward until you reach that point. This is the *real* root cause. Remember: where undesirable effects are concerned, we want to pull the tree out by the roots, and we want to get as much of the root as we can.

When you've reached the lowest level of cause within your sphere of influence, start tracing the cause-and-effect path back up the tree to the undesirable effects. Determine how many each root cause eventually produces. If you find one root cause that results in a majority of the undesirable effects, you *may* have a core problem *if* that majority includes the worst of the undesirable effects.

The completed current reality tree is provided in Figure 5.15. Note that all the entities have been renumbered in a similar sequence to make following the cause and effect easier. Two possible root causes appear on the first page, near the bottom: numbers 101 and 103. Why are there two possible root causes, in sequence? If you work at the state level and you think your chances of getting federal contracting law (101) changed are remote, you might want to work on the way your state awards contracts instead. But if you have significant influence in Washington, D.C., you might want to attempt changing federal law.

Notice, however, that in no case is entity 100 a root cause. By our definition, it probably doesn't meet the second requirement of a root cause: that it be within our sphere of influence to change.

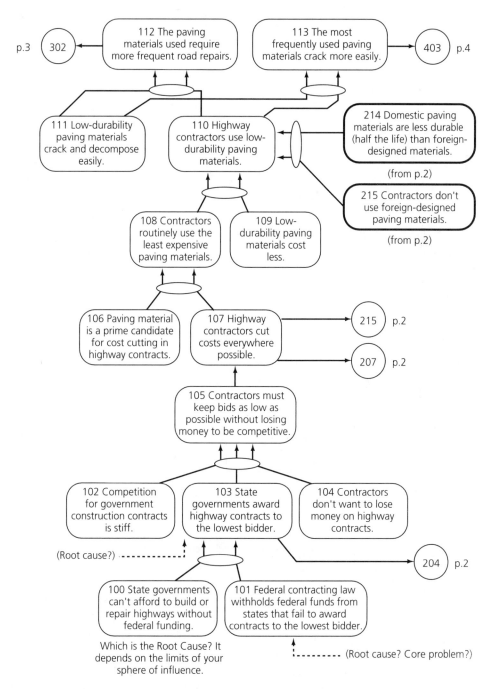

FIGURE 5.15.1 **Why our roads go to pot.**

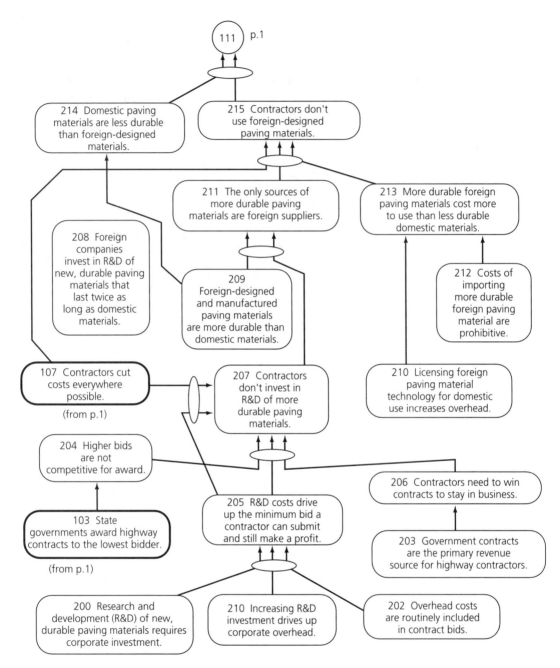

FIGURE 5.15.2 Why our roads go to pot.

16. *Trim Nonessential Entities.* When you redesignated the undesirable effects in step 13, you might have rendered some branches of your tree neutral, or not essential for connecting the remaining undesirable effects. If this happened, for housekeeping purposes, eliminate all such entities. You should be left with only those needed to link the undesirable effects to the root causes. This makes for a clean, logically tight tree— one that won't confuse people.

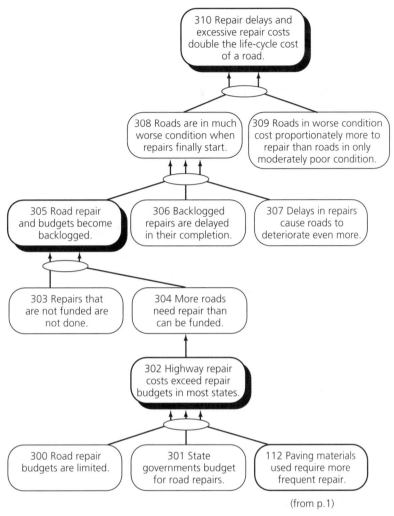

FIGURE 5.15.3 Why our roads go to pot.

17. *Choose the Root Cause(s) to Attack.* It's decision time now. You have a clear depiction of the cause-and-effect relationship inherent in your existing reality. You can see what problems are causing the indications you don't like in your system. One of those root causes—probably the core problem, if there is one—is the constraint in your system: the one factor that, by itself, is keeping you from making any better progress toward your goal.

The nature of the cause-and-effect logic is such that if you remove this root cause, the chain of cause and effect will be broken. In the same way that the dominoes fell from the root cause to produce the undesirable effects, eliminating the root cause now also eliminates all the intermediate effects that in turn produce the undesirable ones. Because of cause sufficiency (the ever-present ellipse), you don't even need to eliminate all the contributing causes to get rid of an effect. Eliminating any *one* of the arrows passing through an ellipse will be enough.

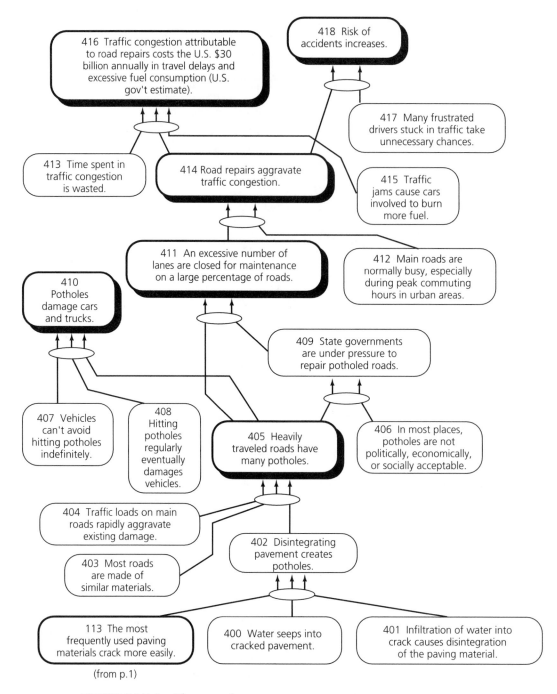

FIGURE 5.15.4 Why our roads go to pot.

Now it's time to select which root cause you're going to try to change. You might decide that you're better off dealing with them all, eventually. But one should stand out as so important, because of it's ultimate impact on the goal, that you'll want to take that one on first. Three rules of thumb for deciding which root cause to attack first include the following:

- The one with the highest probability of your being able to influence
- The one that accounts for the *most* undesirable effects
- The one that accounts for the *most critical* undesirable effect

Look at Figure 5.15 again. Since both entities 101 and 103 eventually lead to every undesirable effect in the tree, either one you choose to attack could be considered a core problem. Both of them meet the second and third criteria. So whether you choose 101 or 103 will depend on how far you think you can push the limits of your sphere of influence.

That's the current reality tree, in a nutshell. With it we can build, from a completely unstructured, *qualitative* situation, a rigorous network of cause and effect that clearly shows the real root cause of the problem indicators in our system—the system constraint that keeps us from moving on to world-class status. The current reality tree does this even when that constraint isn't something physical, such as a piece of machinery or a facility. *Identify the constraint* is the first of the five focusing steps of the theory of constraints. The current reality tree tells us *what to change* about our system.

Just as important as the analysis of the problem, the current reality tree provides a structured, easy-to-follow visual aid that we can use to communicate our understanding of the problem to others, perhaps influential others whose help we need to make the change.

USING THE CURRENT REALITY TREE

The current reality tree is a powerful way to display the details of complex cause-and-effect logic behind any situation. Current reality trees can be very flexible. They can be simple or detailed. They can be used as the first step in solving a problem, or they can enhance our understanding by explaining why reality is the way it is—or was. In the latter mode, they might be considered knowledge trees, piecing together the lessons of the past to make sure we don't have to repeat them in the future. As George Santayana once said, "Whomever cannot learn from the past is condemned to repeat it."

The current reality tree begins with a clear determination of our goal and the indications that we're not achieving it, or at least not making as much progress as we could. It then works backward from those indicators, or undesirable effects, through some intermediate effects, to the root causes that produce them. If we're extremely fortunate, we can find one root cause that accounts for the worst of the undesirable effects we see. That so-called heavy hitter becomes a core problem, most likely the system *constraint* and the one factor that we can change that will produce the maximum positive effect. Because we started with the *system's* goal rather than a departmental objective, the root causes or core problem are the system's constraint, and we avoid the pitfall of suboptimization. Suboptimized systems *never* make it to the world-class level. Because we have clearly identified the real causes behind our undesirable effects, we know we won't be wasting time, energy, and resources on a nonconstraint that won't produce any short-term visible improvement in the situation. Our efforts to change things, whether they're quality related or not, should produce immediate progress toward achieving the goal.

The current reality tree can be a powerful tool for system improvement when used properly. But let's not lose sight of the fact that the current reality tree, and all the other logic tools, can be abused as easily as they can be productively used.

Much like a computer, the trees can't tell you when your entering arguments are flawed. In the hands of someone who's determined to subvert the system for personal or departmental ends, the logical tools can do a superb job of suboptimization. Only two safeguards exist to preclude that from happening. Much as an informed electorate is the watchdog of democracy, so can (1) a clear understanding of the system's goal and (2) informed scrutiny of the logic trees prevent suboptimization.

Appendix B contains another current reality tree. This one is a detailed analysis of the Challenger space shuttle disaster, based on the Rogers Commission report. Appendix C is a knowledge tree, showing how ill-advised tax policy in ancient Rome contributed, in ways the Roman senate couldn't comprehend, to the downfall of the republic.

Appendix D is a case study that shows how one company used the entire thinking process to salvage a dying total quality management effort. The current reality tree was the first step in doing so. You might take time now to read about Vector One Corporation's current reality tree, then revisit the case study after learning about each of the five logic trees.

In chapter 6, we'll see what the conflict resolution diagram is and how it can be used not only to resolve conflict, but also to help figure out how to deal with the root causes and core problems identified in current reality trees.

> *We flatter ourselves by claiming to be rational and intellectual beings, but it would be a great mistake to suppose that people are always guided by reason. We are strange, inconsistent creatures, and act quite as often, perhaps oftener, from prejudice or passion.*
>
> —*John Lubbock*

NOTES

1. The Holy Bible (King James version), Genesis 1:1–2.
2. Betsy Dance, "Why Our Roads Go To Pot," *Readers Digest* (April 1992), 121–124, (condensed from *The Washington Monthly,* November 1991).
3. *The Memory Jogger Plus* (Methuen, Mass.: Goal/QPC, 1993).

Chapter 6
GENERATING
BREAKTHROUGH IDEAS:
The Conflict Resolution Diagram

Creative thinking may simply mean that there's no particular virtue in doing things the way they have always been done.
—Rudolph Flesch

Everybody knows what conflict is. We see it around us every day. It happens on highways, as one motorist signals displeasure with the driving of another by using universal sign language. It happens when we argue with others, or they with us. Sometimes we actually see people in physical conflict. More often, conflict is less overt, though it might still be confrontational. For example, in a meeting, one person might assert a position or opinion with which another takes issue. One department manager might try to thwart a course of action proposed by another because it causes problems for the first one.

There probably isn't one of us who hasn't been involved in a confrontation of some kind, certainly verbal if not physical. Though most people focus on the confrontation itself, it's the underlying conflict that really causes the problems we experience. What's the difference between confrontation and conflict? Confrontation is only the outward expression of conflict; the conflict itself might not be conspicuous. However, in the same way that working on undesirable effects doesn't do anything to address their root causes, focusing on the confrontation alone does nothing to resolve the underlying conflict.

THE NATURE OF CONFLICT

The outward indicators of conflict might include sharp words, maybe even shouting, anger, retaliation, hard feelings, or clearly opposing positions. A classic example of obvious conflict is rancorous labor negotiations leading to a strike. In cases like this, the conflict is so overt that special techniques, especially designed for the purpose, are trotted out to help resolve it: collective bargaining, negotiation, binding arbitration, and so on.

In most cases, however, conflict is even more often likely to be subtle, or unspoken, maybe even internal to oneself. It might be more like different opinions on the same subject, the difference between what you *want* to do and what you're *allowed* to do, or two different parties competing for exclusive use of the same resources (time, money, manpower, equipment, and so on). In situations like this, the conflict frequently goes unrecognized, so nobody is aware that an underlying conflict with a life of its own is even affecting the situation. As a result, the problem may be difficult or even impossible to effectively resolve.

TWO TYPES OF CONFLICT

Because *conflict* has such a pejorative connotation, most people tend to think only of the overt indications of conflict. But for identifying and solving hidden problems, it's sometimes better to think in terms of *competing forces*. These competing forces are usually of two types: *opposite conditions* and *different alternatives*.

Opposite Conditions

If the conflict is one of opposing conditions, one force pulls us to *do this*. The other force pushes us to *not do this* (or to do something which is the diametric opposite). An opposite condition conflict is *mutually exclusive:* the two sides can't exist in the same space at the same time. For example, on one hand we might be driven to save money, while compelling reasons might exist to spend money. This particular conflict is inherent in the problem of reducing the federal budget, where one school of thought says, "Spend money to stimulate the economy," while the other says "Reduce federal spending to cut the deficit."

Different Alternatives

With different alternatives, we're forced to choose between two options which are not opposite conditions, but which, for some reason, we're not able to have at the same time. This kind of conflict is inherently a *resource shortage,* which is usually time, money, equipment, or manpower, or a combination. For example, "We have only so much money. We can do either A or B, but we can't do both." This is a classic conflict condition: the choice between equally desirable alternatives that we can't do at the same time.

AN INDICATION OF HIDDEN CONFLICT

One of the prime indicators of an underlying, hidden conflict is a sense of stagnation: We've got a problem. We've tried several times to solve it, but despite our best efforts, we haven't been able to make any headway on it. This kind of situation virtually begs the question, "What's keeping us from solving this problem?" In many cases, competing forces might be stalemating progress.

Are all stagnant situations the result of a conflict? Not necessarily. Maybe the only reason we can't resolve our problem is that we just don't understand what the root causes are, and if we did, we'd fix them immediately. However, if it's a serious, nagging problem that knowledgeable people have tried unsuccessfully to solve, there's a good chance that a conflict is perpetuating the problem. If inadequate knowledge was really the roadblock, good minds and better intentions should have overcome this obstacle and solved the problem already.

One way to know for sure whether the problem is perpetuated by a conflict or inadequate knowledge is to try to build a conflict resolution diagram. If the problem does result from conflict, the conflict resolution diagram can reveal it quickly.

TRADITIONAL WAYS TO RESOLVE CONFLICT

Historically, most opposing sides have resolved conflicts between them in one of two ways: an imposed solution by one side or the other or a compromise.

Win-Lose

The imposed solution is often referred to as a *win-lose* outcome, because one side gets just about everything it wants while the other side might get nothing. Except in games of chance, win-lose outcomes are usually a function of the overwhelming power of the winning side over the loser. The Persian Gulf War is an excellent example of a win-lose conflict. The outcome was never really in doubt, only the magnitude of the casualties on each side. Decisive power enabled the coalition, operating with the approval of the United Nations, to conduct the war on their own terms and ultimately impose the solution on Iraq.

However, win-lose solutions have a downside, too. Inevitably, the losing side in an imposed resolution feels resentful, perhaps cheated. Lingering resentment may discourage the losers from actively cooperating with the winners, and if further negotiations are needed between the two sides later, the losers might be much less cooperative, maybe even intransigent. At the very least, any semblance of trust is completely destroyed by a win-lose solution.

Consider labor negotiations, for example. The union breaks off contract negotiations because management won't budge from its position. A power struggle ensues. The union calls a strike and resorts to picketing to keep people and raw materials from entering the plant, and finished products from leaving. Union leadership might even try to leverage support of other unions in a bid to solidify their power over management.

The employees' union might elicit the cooperation of the truckers' union in keeping delivery trucks from crossing the picket line.

Management, in turn, locks out the union employees, encourages nonunion workers to cross the picket line, assigns management people to fulfill workers' duties, and generally does whatever it can to keep the plant in operation in an attempt to outwait the union. Eventually, one of the two sides caves in, negotiations are reopened, and concessions are reluctantly given up. The strike is over, and the employees are back at work. But both management and the union resent each other's intransigence. And trust? Forget about it! The next time the union and management have to sit down together, for whatever reason, it will be like the Korean armistice sessions across the table at Panmunjom, each side wondering what kind of trick the other will pull next.

Compromise

Everybody wants to win; nobody likes to lose. But sometimes the distribution of power isn't unilateral enough to permit one side to impose a solution on the other. The balance of power between America and the Soviet Union kept the uneasy peace we referred to as the cold war for over 40 years. When two sides of roughly equivalent power have to resolve a conflict, an imposed solution isn't even a consideration. Inevitably, the two sides revert to compromise: each side gives up something it wants in order to protect something else it wants even more. A compromise usually means that neither side gets everything it wants.

From the perspective of all parties, a compromise is better than an imposed solution, but it's been said in jest that a good compromise leaves everybody mad. The lingering animosity inherent in a win-lose outcome might not be there, but subsequent relations between the sides might not be much improved. Each party will approach relations with the other warily at best, perhaps with some mutual respect, but probably not with unqualified trust.

Moreover, there are some situations, especially those where the vital interests of one or both sides are at stake, in which no amicable compromise is possible. In such cases, a stalemate might result, or negotiations might drag on interminably. What can we do when an imposed solution isn't possible, but a compromise isn't acceptable?

THE WIN-WIN ALTERNATIVE

In recent years, the term *win-win* has become popular. It's a shorthand way of describing a third alternative for resolving conflict: both sides get what they want. The solution constitutes a win for each side.

Think about the implications of a win-win resolution for a moment. Both sides aren't just mollified, they're actually pleased, because they got what they really needed. The afterglow of such a solution leaves both sides in a positive frame of mind about one another. Subsequent negotiations aren't dreaded, they're welcomed. Trust between the sides is enhanced, not destroyed, leading to better prospects for cooperation in the future.

Obviously, a win-win solution is desirable, but how practical is it? Most people have a hard time seeing how they can reach agreement with an opponent without having to compromise. In truth, real win-win solutions have historically been somewhat rare, primarily because most people don't know how to structure one. The conflict resolution diagram offers the potential to routinely structure win-win solutions, and the key to that structure is the assumptions underlying each side.

THE CONFLICT RESOLUTION DIAGRAM

What is this conflict resolution diagram? Also sometimes referred to as an *evaporating cloud* (so named by Dr. Eliyahu M. Goldratt because of its potential to evaporate conflict), the conflict resolution diagram is the second of five logical tools designed to help people improve systems. (Figure 6.1). It identifies and displays the relationship between the key elements of a conflict situation and suggests ways to resolve it. The diagram includes the system objective, necessary-but-not-sufficient requirements that lead to it, and the prerequisites—usually the outward indications of the conflict—needed to satisfy them. Conflict resolution diagrams allow us to surface hidden assumptions that, though currently accepted as valid, are really questionable. If we can invalidate one or more of these assumptions, we might be able to render the conflict moot. Often, just identifying the invalid assumptions suggests ideas for solutions to complex problems.

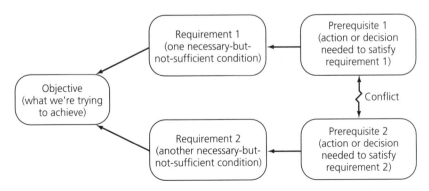

FIGURE 6.1   Conflict resolution diagram.

The conflict resolution diagram is intended to achieve the following purposes:[1]

• Confirm that conflict actually exists
• Identify the conflict perpetuating a major problem
• Identify all assumptions underlying the problems and conflicting relationships
• Explain in depth why a problem exists
• Create solutions in which both sides win
• Create new, breakthrough solutions to problems
• Resolve conflict
• Avoid compromise

Conflict can have serious performance implications for organizations of any kind. Problems exist because strong competing forces perpetuate them. Healthy competition is not necessarily bad, as long as it doesn't degrade the success of the whole system. But carried too far, competition at some point becomes conflict, and conflict within a system is an indication of suboptimization, which, as we already know, is detrimental to the system as a whole.

STRUCTURING HIDDEN CONFLICT

In chapter 1, we also saw that for a company to achieve its goal, it usually must satisfy more than one necessary condition. These necessary conditions can be considered requirements, each essential, but not sufficient alone to result in goal attainment.

For example, a company's profitability (the goal) might depend on how well it satisfies its customers (a necessary condition) and how successfully it can compete with other contenders for a share of the same market (another necessary condition). Both of these requirements are necessary, but neither is sufficient alone (Figure 6.2).

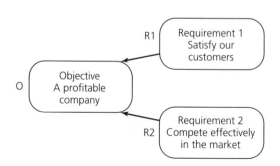

FIGURE 6.2 Requirements: necessary conditions for goal attainment.

These requirements are not in conflict with one another. Theoretically, there is nothing inherent in either one that precludes the achievement of the other. But requirements demand that we *do something* to satisfy them, and often the actions we feel compelled to do conflict with one another. In our conflict resolution diagrams, we'll refer to these actions as *prerequisites*. In the example described above, the two requirements for profitability are (1) satisfied customers and (2) compete effectively in the market. The action we might feel obligated to do to satisfy customers could be to spend more money on product improvements (Figure 6.3). However, this seems to conflict directly with the action needed to keep our prices low enough to remain competitive, which would be to reduce company expenditures. Obviously, we can't spend more and reduce expenditures at the same time, so apparently we have a conflict.

THE CRITICAL ROLE OF ASSUMPTIONS

Since assumptions are the key to breaking any conflict, it's important to understand what they are. The dictionary defines *assume* as *to take for granted or without proof.*[2] By extension, then, an *assumption* would be a conclusion of factuality or truth without verification. How many times have we taken something for granted that we later discovered to be wrong? It happens quite frequently. Sometimes it's referred to as jumping to conclusions.

When we find that something we thought was true or valid turns out not to be, the entire complexion of a situation can change. Avenues that didn't exist previously seem to open before us. Our horizons are often dramatically expanded, and new possibilities occur to us. Let's say it's Friday. We're burdened with too many things to do before we go back to work on Monday, and there is not enough time to do them. Naturally, we feel stressed—we'll never get everything completed. But in reaching that conclusion, we *assumed* we'd have to go back to work on Monday. We

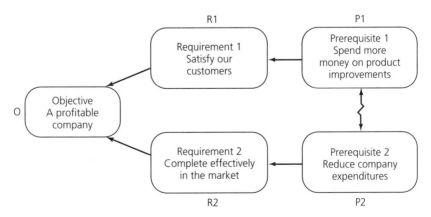

FIGURE 6.3 Completed conflict resolution diagram: What obstructs profitability?

took for granted it was a workday. Then we check the calendar and find that Monday is actually a holiday. We don't have to go back to work until Tuesday! Suddenly, new possibilities open up: not only can we get everything done before we go back to work, there will even be some time left over to do some of the important things, like fishing, playing golf, or spending time with our family! Surfacing the invalid assumption—that Monday would be a normal workday—opened up new possibilities. We've broken through the stalemate to reach a win-win outcome: our obligations are fulfilled, and we can still set aside some leisure time for ourselves.

Recognizing and verifying the underlying assumptions we make about our situation empower us to break, or invalidate, one or more of them, thus creating a breakthrough opportunity to reach a win-win solution.

The key to resolving our conflicts lies in the assumptions—usually unspoken, and sometimes subconscious—that we make about the relationships between our necessary conditions, or requirements, and the prerequisites we believe we must fulfill to satisfy them. But what's the connection between conflict and undesirable effects that grew out of our current reality tree?

In chapter 5, we saw that the visible undesirable effects we experience are traceable through an unbroken chain of cause and effect back to a few root causes, or, in the best of circumstances, a single core problem. In many cases, we probably weren't aware that these root causes were producing the undesirable effects. But now that we know the root causes—*what* we want to change—our obvious next step is to fix them.

As long as we know what to change, how to proceed, and can do so without opposition, we don't really need a conflict resolution diagram. However, if there's any chance of resistance, active or passive, or if we aren't sure what kind of change to make to the root cause, a conflict resolution diagram is an easy next step to ensure a smooth transition to an effective solution of a problem.

THE INFORMATION SYSTEMS PROBLEM: AN EXAMPLE

For the sake of argument, let's assume that the core problem we've identified in a current reality tree is entrenched because of an inherent conflict. What makes the entrenchment even more difficult is that it's rooted in human organizational behavior, one of the most difficult things to change.

The core problem seems to be a constraint to the company's throughput posed by the operations department's inability to obtain timely data processing services. Existing company policy gives the head of the information systems department sole control over the schedule and priority of the data processing jobs completed by his department, and because the director is evaluated on the efficiency of his department, suboptimization is a very dangerous possibility. The company is highly dependent on these data for the success of its operations, so the director of the information systems department wields a great deal of power.

The workload in data processing is intense. The customers of data processing vie with one another to have their jobs done first. After all, *their* departmental efficiencies are on the line, too! Favors are often exchanged to obtain a better position in the queue. Also, the information systems director enjoys the power he exercises.

Our current reality tree has indicated that the company's problems with on-time delivery to external customers (an undesirable effect) are directly traceable to delays in operations' data processing support. The operations manager has the solution: he wants the authority to establish the information processing priorities. Obviously, this is an idea that will make the late delivery problems go away, but the operations manager is at the same organizational level as the information systems director (roughly equivalent status and power), so he can't impose his solution on the director. The information systems director isn't about to countenance a raid on his rice bowl, so we have a conflict. It's not overt, because the operations manager hasn't broached the idea to the information systems director yet. But we can certainly anticipate what his reaction will be!

Moreover, this issue isn't the whole war, it's only one battle. Over the long haul, we'll still have to work with the information systems director, and it would be nice if we could do so on friendly, cooperative terms. This tends to discourage us from seeking an imposed solution from the president of the company. But how do we fashion a win for both the information systems director and the operations manager? What should the shape of the solution be?

BUILDING THE CONFLICT RESOLUTION DIAGRAM

Our first challenge is to structure the conflict so clearly that both sides can plainly see the conflict and the problems it produces. We can do this by building a conflict resolution diagram. Once the diagram is completed, we can begin to expose the underlying assumptions and create ideas to break them.

1. *Articulate the Conflict.* The first step is to articulate the conflicting positions as best we can. We know that on the one hand, the information systems director wants to retain control of the work assignment priority, but on the other hand, the operations manager wants to be able to put his jobs at the top of the priority list. We have to express these opposing positions in simple statements (Figure 6.4). For example, the information system director's position might be phrased, "Information systems director sets data processing priorities," which is what current company policy calls for. The operations manager would like to see something different happen: "Operations manager sets data processing priorities."

We shouldn't worry too much about perfection in wording these conflict statements. Inevitably, they'll have to be adjusted once the diagram is finished. For now, take a solid shot at stating each conflicting position

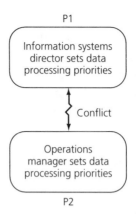

FIGURE 6.4 Articulate the conflict.

in as short and simple a sentence as possible, and connect the two statements with a zigzag arrow. Label the top statement *P1* and the bottom
one *P2*.

It doesn't really matter which side of the conflict is on the top. From
a persuasion standpoint, it might be more favorable to acknowledge the
importance of the other party's position by placing it on top, but there's
no hard-and-fast rule.

2. *Determine the Requirements.* The second step is to identify the
immediate need each side is trying to fulfill in defending its position. In
other words, each side *wants* something it believes necessary to satisfy
some immediate requirement short of the overall objective.

The Information Systems Manager. Why does the information systems
director want to set the data processing priorities? The issue of power
is undoubtedly a factor, but the negative impression conveyed by
empire building means that the information systems director is unlikely
to base his justification on that alone. And in reality, there was probably
some rational reason, thought to be beneficial to the organization, for
the director to have that authority in the first place. If asked, that's the
reason the information systems director would undoubtedly cite.

Support of operations is clearly very important to the company's
success, but there are other functions that depend on data processing
as well. These departments can't be ignored, either. So the organizational requirement the director is probably trying to satisfy is to fulfill
company-wide data processing needs effectively and efficiently. Figure
6.5 shows how the prerequisites (P1 and P2) lead to the requirements
(R1 and R2).

The Operations Manager. What need is the operations manager trying
to fulfill? It's probably safe to say that many operations people consider
information systems support a necessary evil. They know they depend on
it, but if they didn't have to, they'd be much more content. Their focus is
on the job that operations is assigned to do, which is to produce the company's product or service. So it's probably safe to say that the operations
manager's desire for some control over data processing is centered on his
need to complete production operations effectively and efficiently.

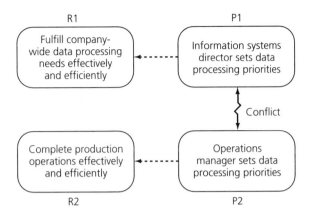

FIGURE 6.5 Determine the requirements.

It might help to visualize the relationship between the requirements and the prerequisites another way. Because they're considered necessary-but-not-sufficient conditions for attaining the overall objective, the requirements can be treated as *nonnegotiable needs.* Both of them must be satisfied in order to achieve an overall objective. The prerequisites, on the other hand, can be considered *wants,* rather than needs. They're the things we feel compelled to do in order to satisfy the nonnegotiable need for which we're responsible.

It's possible that some of these wants might actually be codified in policies, lending them an aura of requirement. The information systems director undoubtedly has a policy somewhere that gives him the authority to establish data procession priorities. However, being a written policy doesn't make it any more of a requirement (a necessary condition) for achieving the objective. It's still something discretionary that we do within the organization to satisfy some higher purpose, and if doing it compromises some other higher purpose (R2, for example), then the policy becomes a candidate for reconsideration.

There is another compelling reason for defining the requirements and prerequisites as needs and wants: the basis is formed for resolving the conflict as a win for both sides. Instead of focusing directly on the conflict itself (P1 and P2), we can redirect attention to the truly important needs of both sides that must be fulfilled for the ultimate success of everyone. If each side acknowledges that the other has a legitimate nonnegotiable need that doesn't conflict with its own, both parties are likely to be more open to new ways to satisfy those needs without having what they're demanding now.

Once we've formulated requirement statements, we place them to the left of their related prerequisites (P1 and P2) and label them *R1* and *R2,* respectively (Figure 6.5).

3. *Identify the Objective.* Now that the conflict has been articulated and the needs of both sides determined, we must connect the needs to a common objective. Since we said that the requirements are necessary (but not conflicting) conditions for achieving some larger purpose, we must now say what that purpose, or objective, is.

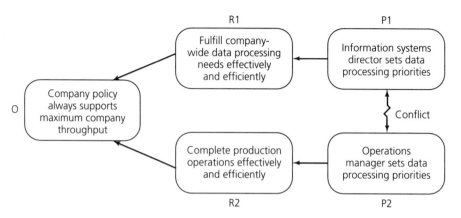

FIGURE 6.6 Completed conflict resolution diagram (first attempt).

Let's go back to the information systems example to see how we might determine that objective. Remember that we started with a current reality tree, which gave us our core problem: Data processing priorities are suboptimized for the efficiency of the information systems department. Ideally, the objective of our conflict resolution diagram should be something diametrically opposite, not just Data processing priorities *don't* suboptimize. . . .

The question we must answer is, "What objective embodies the best possible circumstances opposite from the core problem, while maintaining a necessary condition relationship with both requirements?" This means the statement of our objective must specifically address the importance of operations' needs *and* those of the information systems department. One way to incorporate all of these characteristics might be to say, "Company policy always supports maximum company throughput." (Figure 6.6).

Notice that this wording is not simply the opposite of the core problem statement. It's the best possible condition we could hope for that is diametrically opposed to suboptimization. Also, it leaves plenty of room to accept both operations' and information systems' requirements (R1 and R2) as necessary conditions leading to its achievement. Write the objective statement to the left of the two requirements, connect it to them with arrows, and label it *O.*

4. *Polish the Diagram.* Now that we've completed our first attempt at the conflict resolution diagram, we have to take off the rough edges. It's time to see if it sounds right. This means we have to read it aloud, from left to right, rather than the way we built it (right to left). Unlike the current reality tree, which we read in an If . . . then. . . format, the way we read the conflict resolution diagram is, In order to . . . we must. . . .

Starting with the objective, read the diagram first across the top axis, then start over again across the bottom axis. For example:

In order for company policy to always support maximum company throughput (O), the information systems department must fulfill company-wide data processing needs effectively and efficiently (R1).

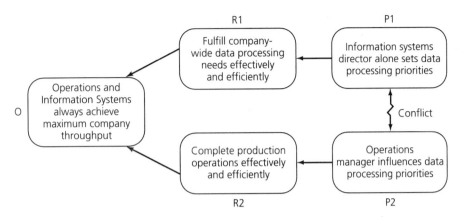

FIGURE 6.7 Conflict resolution diagram (final form).

> *And in order to fulfill company-wide data processing needs effectively and efficiently (R1), the information systems director must set data processing priorities (P1).*
>
> *In order for company policy to always support maximum company through-put (O), operations must complete production effectively and efficiently (R2).*
>
> *And in order to fulfill company-wide data processing needs effectively and efficiently (R1), the operations manager must set data processing priorities (P2).*

Doesn't sound quite right, does it? The upper limb of the diagram seems pretty solid. But when we read the lower limb, the connection between R2 and O seems a little shaky, and the wording of P2, while most assuredly the diametric opposite of P1, seems unrealistic. Of course the operations manager wants some leverage over the policy to ensure his needs are met, because operations is the reason the company is in business. But does the operations manager *really* want to spend part of his day establishing data processing priorities for all the users outside his domain? Of course not. So the first order of business is to restructure the wording of P2.

The words in P2 have two duties to perform. First, they must reflect the perception that P2 must be done in order to satisfy the need stated in R2. It must also be crystal clear that P2 directly conflicts with P1. Therefore, any change to the wording must embody both those characteristics.

Here's a possible alternative for P2: Operations manager influences data processing priorities. It relates well to R1, but the conflict between P2 and P1 is not as distinct as it could be. So let's tweak the wording of P1 a little by adding one word: "Information systems director *alone* sets data processing priorities. This still seems to support R1 well, but it more clearly defines the conflict between the two prerequisites (Figure 6.7).

Now let's look at the connection between R2 and O (Figure 6.6): In order for company policy to always support maximum company through-put (O), operations must complete production effectively and efficiently (R2). This doesn't seem quite right either. Logically, operations doesn't support policy. If anything, it would seem to be the other way around. One of these two statements needs adjusting, and since we've accurately defined the motivating need behind the operations manager (R2), we should probably look first at the wording of the objective (O).

The objective must be worded in such a way that the requirements 1 and 2 are clearly both necessary conditions for achieving it. At this point it's not clear that R2, as worded, is necessary to achieve O. Here's a modified objective statement:

> *Operations and information systems always achieve maximum company throughput.*

Notice the difference. *Company policy* has been replaced by *operations* and *information systems*. This statement is still definitely the diametric opposite of the core problem (Data processing priorities are suboptimized for the efficiency of the information systems department), yet it still seems to be at a higher level than each of the necessary conditions that support it. Figure 6.7 shows the conflict resolution diagram in its final form.

5. *Expose the Assumptions and Identify the Invalid Ones.* As we discussed earlier, the key to breaking conflict is to find the erroneous (invalid) assumptions each side makes that cause them to take their respective conflicting positions. In our information systems example, what makes the information systems director believe *sole* authority is required to set data processing priorities? Something must be making the director think so, and that something is an assumption he is making about the connection between sole authority and effective data processing service.

Likewise, something makes the operations manager think that his influence over data processing priorities is necessary to completing production effectively. Whatever that reason might be, it's an assumption the operations manager is making about the connection between P2 and R2. Let's look at some possible reasons for each side (Figure 6.8).

As you can see, there are several assumptions underlying each side of the conflict. We improve our chances of finding invalid assumptions, or ones that we can *invalidate,* if we list as many as possible. We do this by continually asking *why* we need the prerequisite to satisfy the requirement, until our knowledge well is dry. Once we have a complete list for both sides of the conflict, we're ready to determine which ones are invalid, or can be made so.

Figure 6.8 shows six assumptions underlying the arrow between P1 and R1, and five between P2 and R2. In the upper half of the figure, assumptions 2 through 5 are probably valid at face value. Only the first and the sixth fairly beg to be challenged. However, on closer examination, we can see that while numbers 3 and 4 are probably valid, we might be able to come up with ideas about how to make them invalid. For example, if we could persuade top management that evaluating and rewarding people based on local efficiencies was detrimental to the

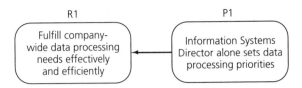

In order to fulfill company-wide data processing needs effectively and efficiently (R1), the information systems director alone must set data processing priorities (P1), because.... (Why?)

1. Only the information systems director (IS director) knows how to do it.
2. Effective and efficient data processing are possible only with unity of control.
3. Effectiveness and efficiency of data processing services are critical to the IS director's performance appraisal.
4. The IS director doesn't trust anyone else with influence that could affect his/her performance appraisal.
5. There are many departments that need data processing support.
6. No department is more important than any other.

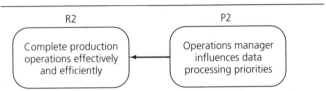

In order to complete production operations effectively and efficiently (R2), the operations manager must influence data processing priorities (P2), because... (Why?)

7. Operations will never get the data processing priority it needs without the operations manager's influence.
8. The IS director doesn't understand the importance of operations' data processing needs.
9. The IS director doesn't appreciate the importance of operations' success to company throughout.
10. Operations can't complete production without timely data processing support.
11. Operations is more important to company throughput than any other department.

FIGURE 6.8 Assumptions.

company, they'd probably change the appraisal and reward system. That would immediately invalidate number 3 and render number 4 meaningless in this case. So there are really four of the six assumptions on this side that are invalid, or could be made so.

In the lower half of Figure 6.8, assumptions 8 through 10 are probably valid, but number 7 and 11 are certainly questionable. However, with some tactful dialogue between the operations manager and the information systems director, numbers 8 and 9 could probably be invalidated. Interestingly enough, the same idea that invalidated assumptions 3 and 4 (in the upper half) would probably have the same effect on number 7 as well. The operations manager's need to influence priorities would probably go away once the information systems director's appraisal and rewards became dependent on something other than local efficiencies—something like improved company throughput.

6. *Create Injections to Replace One or Both Prerequisites.* What's an *injection?* It's a condition, circumstance, or action that doesn't exist now. It's something new that we have to *inject* into existing reality. We have to create it, or make it happen. Another way to define an injection is *an idea for a solution.* It's important to distinguish between ideas and solutions. Solutions are *implemented* ideas. The problem can't be considered solved until after we can measure some positive difference in reality, and that can't happen until after implementation. But at this point, we're more concerned with generating ideas than implementing them.

Whatever the injection might be, it is bound to take the place of one, or both, of the conflicting prerequisites. It allows both requirements to be satisfied without needing at least one of the contentious positions that produce the conflict in the first place. For example, if the information systems director's appraisal and rewards are based on overall company success, rather than the efficiency of his own department, he will naturally look for ways to contribute more to company success. That search will inevitably lead the director to a new appreciation for the role of operations. It's possible that an additional injection might be needed to accelerate this search, perhaps a dedicated effort to educate the director about how the company produces throughput. In Figure 6.9, we see the two injections, or ideas, positioned beside the arrows representing the assumptions to be broken.

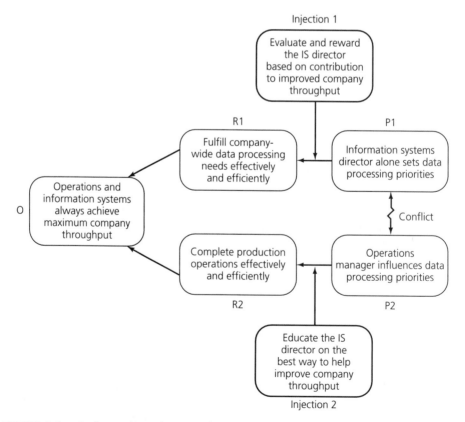

FIGURE 6.9 Conflict resolution diagram with injections.

BREAKTHROUGH SOLUTIONS

One of the most important benefits of the conflict resolution diagram is its capacity to expand our thinking beyond the confines that tradition or common practice invariably construct around us. Everyone has heard the two standard phrases that identify the presence of such boundaries: "That's not the way we do things around here," and "We've always done it this way so why change now?" But the reality of today's world poses new and complex problems, which demand new ways of thinking to overcome them. As Albert Einstein once said, "The problems we face today cannot be overcome at the same level of thinking we were at when we created them." The following is a simple example.

Your task is to connect the nine dots in Figure 6.10, using only four straight lines. Typically, we look for ways to draw our lines around the outer edges, hoping for a way to pick up the dot in the center. That's the result of traditional thinking, which drives us to make unwarranted assumptions about our environment. These assumptions chain us to the old ways of looking at the world, rather than encouraging us to challenge the bonds of tradition. As soon as someone points out a new way to connect the nine dots (Figure 6.11), the inevitable response is, "Oh, you didn't tell us we could go outside the box!" That's traditional thinking constraining our search for solutions. Guess what? The real world is like that, too. Our boxes, though, are the *policies* we assume are immutable. But complex problems usually require us to think outside the box. And the conflict resolution diagram is a superior tool to stimulate such thinking.

Here's how it works. Let's say you've constructed a good conflict resolution diagram. Everybody who looks at it says, "Boy, you've hit the problem on the head. That's definitely what's causing it." It's been said that a well-defined problem is more than half solved. But the actual solving part is often the most troublesome. How can we think outside the box to achieve a breakthrough solution?

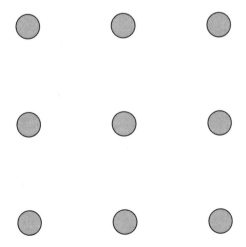

FIGURE 6.10   Connect the nine dots using four continuous straight lines.

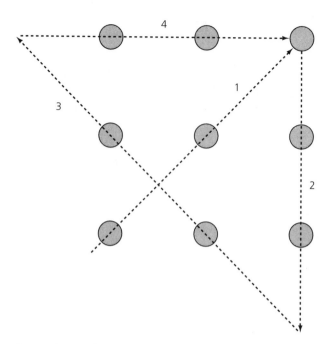

FIGURE 6.11 Connect the nine dots: one solution.

One technique is called an *alternative environment*. You begin by taking one part of the conflict resolution diagram only: a requirement and its connected prerequisite. Ask yourself, "How can I satisfy this requirement *without needing* this prerequisite?" For example, let's say your requirement is to eat. (Figure 6.12). Most people would assume that the prerequisite would be money. We'd read this part of the diagram this way: In order to eat, I must have money. But is having money the only way to eat? Look at all the other ways we can eat without needing to have money.

Now translate that concept to your conflict. Think of all the ways you can satisfy the requirement without needing the prerequisite. In our information systems problem, we saw a relationship between R2 and P2 that looked like Figure 6.13. When we ask "how we can have effective, efficient production operations without the operations manager having to set data processing priorities a number of other alternatives come quickly to mind. After we complete this task for one side of the conflict, we do the same with the other side. The net result can be a wealth of options we might never have considered before. This is how we begin to think outside the box.

Another very effective method for generating breakthrough ideas is called TRIZ (pronounced trees—but not to be confused with logic trees). This strange word (all capitalized) is an acronym for the Russian words meaning *theory of inventive problem solving*.[3]

The TRIZ of the 1990s has been evolving and maturing even longer than the theory of constraints. Conceived in the late 1940s by Genrich Altshuller and refined over the next 40 years by Altshuller, Boris Zlotin, and Alla Zusman, TRIZ was specifically designed to do the apparently impossible: structure creativity. Although its objective was *breakthrough*

I don't need money to eat; I can...

- Beg
- Work for food
- Go "dumpster diving"
- Hunt
- Fish
- Grow my own food

- Steal food
- Get arrested (go to jail)
- Join the military
- Barter
- Go to Salvation Army soup kitchen

FIGURE 6.12   Alternative environment.

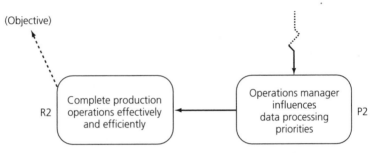

We don't need the operations manager to be
involved in setting data processing priorities; we can...

- Educate the IS director on the criticality of operations priorities for company profitability

- Educate the IS director on the best ways to improve company throughput

FIGURE 6.13   Alternative environment (information systems example).

solutions to engineering problems, there are indications that TRIZ can be effectively applied to nontechnical policy problems, too. As an injection generator, TRIZ may prove to be without equal.[4]

THE SILVER BULLET FALLACY

There's a natural tendency for people to look for a single idea to solve the problem completely, a silver bullet that will make the conflict and the resulting undesirable effects go away. Happy endings like that usually happen only in the movies. In the real world, we're not as likely to find one single, all-powerful solution. It's much more likely that we'll need to make several changes, in combination, to achieve our desired effect.[‡]

[‡]Professor James Holt, Washington State University, likens challenging of traditional assumptions to a *silver wedge*—a way to exploit a crack in an otherwise impenetrable wall. A breakthrough idea, while perhaps not sufficient alone, provides the wedge with which to tap lightly on a crack in the wall—an invalid assumption—splitting the wall to admit new opportunities.

In the information systems example, we could have changed the appraisal and reward system alone, leaving the director to discover independently what it would take for him to increase company through-put. But rather than leave that to chance, we elected to educate the director, and perhaps others throughout the company as well, on the actions and decisions needed to improve system throughput. That was our second injection.

CONFLICT RESOLUTION IN PROJECT MANAGEMENT

If there is one environment that seems to have been tailor-made for the conflict resolution diagram, it's project management. Just ask any experienced project manager. They'll tell you that life in project management is a series of compromises and trade-offs. They trade off cost for schedule or performance, or they sacrifice some of the schedule to ensure better performance. In many situations, they fail to achieve any of the three. But what are compromises and trade-offs except the two less desirable ways to resolve a conflict? Yet in a project environment, it's almost natural to resort to them immediately, instead of really looking for the win-win solution.

My project management students have told me that the conflict resolution diagram is the one tool of any kind that they see the most possible applications for in project or program environments. Here's an example of how one project manager resolved what seemed like an impossible conflict concerning his project.

The senior management of the company, responding to profitability pressures from the board of directors, directed all project managers to adhere to their project budgets. No more money would be available to cover unforeseen events. Moreover, each project was expected to produce the forecasted profit for the company. Project managers' feet would be held to the fire on this one.

The project in question was a research and development effort for an external customer. Several other competitors were also doing the same kind of project for the same customer. Once the project hardware was delivered, the customer would assess the success of each competing design and award a lucrative long-term production contract to the best one that met the delivery schedule. Because the development project was done under a firm fixed price contract, there would be no additional money from the customer to accommodate the unforeseen. The company would have to cover any overruns from its own funds.

The project manager's company was reasonably sure their concept would qualify as the winning design, but unforeseen problems with vendors and subcontractors threatened late delivery. Only additional funds would permit the project to be completed on time. The project manager constructed a conflict resolution diagram (Figure 6.14). The conflict—spend more money versus don't spend more money—

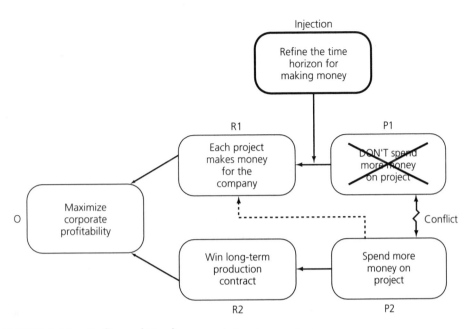

FIGURE 6.14 Conflict resolution diagram project management.

appeared unresolvable. However, in examining the assumptions underlying P1 to R1, the project manager found an invalid one made by senior management when they mandated budget adherence. The assumption was that bringing all projects in within budget is the *only* way the company can make money.

Once the project manager was able to redefine *making money* to include the medium and long term, instead of just the next quarterly statement, the foolishness of sacrificing a chance to win a long-term production contract just to help a quarterly financial statement became apparent to senior management. In this particular instance, they withdrew their mandate (P1), realizing that P2 would, in fact, satisfy both requirements, while insisting on P1 would probably ruin any hope of achieving R2. The project manager subsequently credited his success in making his case to the simplicity and logic of the conflict resolution diagram.

CONFLICT RESOLUTION IN DEVELOPMENT AND PRODUCTION

The conflict resolution diagram can be just as easily applied to a production environment. Take, for example, a company that made electronic components for the 800-pound gorilla in the telecommunications business, AT&T. Let's put ourselves in their shoes for a moment.

Our company makes a wide variety of these components: resistors, switches, potentiometers, capacitors, and so on, all requiring high-quality electronic microcircuitry for reliability.

AT&T has dealt with our company in the past specifically because of our reputation for reliability—they like our quality. Now they come to us

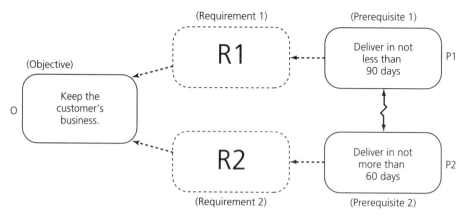

FIGURE 6.15 The production conflict: 60 days or 90 days?

with an offer to place a very large order for a new kind of electronic switch. They tell us that they need the first delivery of 10,000 of these switches in 60 days—and the switch hasn't even been designed yet! Upon hearing this, our director of engineering throws up his hands. "We can't possibly design, certify, and produce this switch in less than 90 days!"

"And by the way," says AT&T, "several of your competitors have already said they can deliver in 60 days, so if you can't do it, we'll find one who can."

This is a real dilemma. They want it in 60 days, and we can't do it in less than 90 days. Let's see how it looks in a conflict resolution diagram (Figure 6.15).

The objective (O) is clear: we want to keep AT&T's business. Who wouldn't? On the one hand (P1), our engineering department says, "Deliver in no less than 90 days." On the other hand (P2), AT&T says, "Deliver in no more than 60 days." This is starting to come together quickly. All we need to do is figure out what the nonnegotiable requirements (R1 and R2) are. So we ask.

Our engineering department says, "We need 75 days just to do the design, testing, and certification. It'll take another 15 days to get the production process set up." Okay, we know that, but what *need* are we trying to satisfy with this 75 days of engineering work? It's not rocket science, just a switch. It turns out that the testing and certification are quality assurance requirements. AT&T has acknowledged that they have come to us in the past because of our proven quality. That's why they've come back to us again. So R1 becomes, *Satisfy the customer's quality requirement.*

Now what about the other prerequisite. Why does AT&T want delivery in 60 days? The answer is fairly clear. They have a schedule of their own to meet, and our switch is just one part of a much more complicated orchestration to ramp up their production. So R2 becomes, *Meet the customer's production schedule.* The conflict resolution diagram is now complete (Figure 6.16). All we have to do is come up with a way to

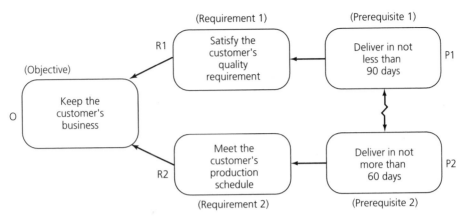

FIGURE 6.16 The production conflict: Completed diagram.

satisfy both requirements without needing one or both prerequisites. Determining the assumptions on each side requires playing "twenty questions" with both our engineers and the AT&T people—their production engineers, not just their purchasing department. We are able to do that, and both groups even help us identify the invalid ones. (It's amazing how quickly this can be done when both sides *want* to see the conflict resolved!) Figure 6.17 shows the assumptions, with the invalid ones highlighted, and the injections we developed to break them are indicated in the center.

Notice that of assumptions 1 through 5, we thought only number 3 completely valid. As we verbally question the other four, some of our bright engineers offer alternative ideas. By subcontracting some of the testing, we find that assumptions 3 and 4 are rendered invalid. By doing some testing in parallel, we invalidate numbers 1 and 2. Also, by setting up a pilot line while testing was going on, we invalidate number 5. The net result was that we find the capability to produce a short run of 500 switches by the 65th day, and the remaining 9500 by the 70th day.

Unfortunately, that isn't enough to meet the 60-day delivery date. But just how firm is that deadline? Our industrial engineers talk with the AT&T engineers and discover that the real date the switches are needed is day 68, but AT&T's industrial engineers had specified an earlier date to purchasing as insurance. Even at the 68th day, they need only enough switches to ramp-up and test their own production line, which will then be shut down for a few days while the output of the pilot run is evaluated and set-up adjustments are made. Full production isn't scheduled to start until the 75th day.

Our engineers negotiate a 65-day delivery for the 500 switches our pilot line will be able to produce, with the remaining 9500 coming on the 70th day. Based on prior working relationships, the customer has confidence in our engineers' promises to meet the revised delivery dates. We win the contract, snapping victory from the jaws of defeat, and our relationship with the customer is strengthened.

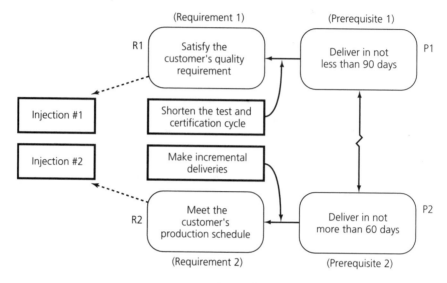

Assumptions
- 1. Testing and certification can never be done in less than 75 days
- 2. Nothing in design, test, and certification can be done in parallel
- 3. Test equipment is not always instantly available
- 4. Only we (internally) can do the required testing
- 5. There is no way to shorten manufacturing ramp-up

(Requirement 1)   (Prerequisite 1)

R1 — Satisfy the customer's quality requirement   Deliver in not less than 90 days — P1

Injection #1

Shorten the test and certification cycle

Injection #2

Make incremental deliveries

R2 — Meet the customer's production schedule   Deliver in not more than 60 days — P2

(Requirement 2)   (Prerequisite 2)

Assumptions
- 6. The customer's production starts on the 60th day
- 7. There is no "pad" in the customer's production schedule
- 8. The customer needs the FULL 10,000 on the 60th day
- 9. The customer doesn't have their own ramp-up schedule to full production

FIGURE 6.17 The production conflict: Assumptions and injections.

ALUMINATOR WIRE COMPANY

Aluminator Wire[††] is a multifacility company providing insulated wire to the automotive and appliance industries. Aluminator's plant in northeast Arkansas generates $53.5 million in sales per year. One particular customer accounts for almost $1.3 million of that total. After cutting Aluminator's wire to fixed, specific short lengths, this customer uses the wire in electrical connections. However, before the short lengths of wire can be used, a measured amount of the insulation Aluminator applies to the wire is stripped from each end. Aluminator's customer has machines that do this stripping automatically.

The customer's stripping machines use a very low level stripping force to peel off the insulation from the ends of the wire. Because the natural friction of the insulation against the wire exceeds this stripping

---

[††]*Aluminator* is a pseudonym for a real company. The author is indebted to Jack Middleton, quality engineer for Aluminator, for the information used in this case.

force substantially, Aluminator lubricates the wire before applying the insulation, thus reducing the force required to strip the wire ends to the level specified by the customer.

However, for well over a year the customer had been complaining about Aluminator's wire. The cut pieces were stripping improperly. The stripping machines removed too much or too little insulation, or displaced the entire insulation jacket from its desired position on the wire. For over a year, Aluminator had been replacing wire damaged in the customer's stripping machines at an average cost exceeding $4500 per month.

Aluminator's management formed a technical team to address the problem. For nearly two months, the team struggled with the problem, using traditional problem solving methods such as brainstorming, Ishikawa diagrams, and failure modes effects analysis. These efforts indicated a correlation between the inconsistencies in stripping force required to remove the insulation at the customer's sites and the application of the lubricant to the wire before insulation was applied. Aluminator found it impossible to apply the lubricant evenly enough to sustain consistently low stripping forces without causing the insulation to be displaced on the wire during stripping.

After two months of fruitless effort to solve the problem of uneven lubrication, Jack Middleton, Aluminator's quality engineer, led the technical team in constructing a current reality tree (CRT) to clearly trace the cause-and-effect relationships inherent in the problem. They identified the core problem of the CRT as the low stripping force specification for the wire. It was this force specification that prompted Aluminator's use of a lubricant in the first place.

The team then constructed a conflict resolution diagram (CRD) to try to find a solution to the problem (Figure 6.18). The conflict was simple:

P1: Lubricate the wire versus P2: Don't lubricate the wire

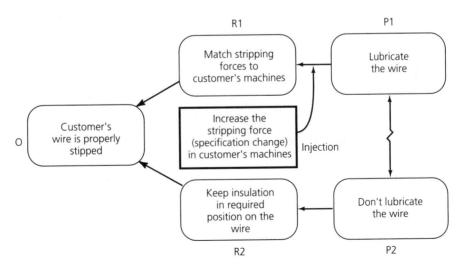

FIGURE 6.18   Aluminator wire's conflict resolution diagram.

Lubricating the wire (P1) was perceived to be necessary to reduce stripping forces to a level that the customer's stripping machines could handle (R1). Not lubricating the wire (P2) was perceived to be necessary to preclude the entire insulation jacket from displacing during the stripping operation (R2). The ultimate objective was a properly stripped piece of wire (O) coming out of the customer's machines.

After identifying the assumptions underlying each side of the conflict, Jack Middleton and the team settled on one major injection to break the conflict: Increase the stripping force in the customer's stripping machines. This injection would replace P1 (lubricate the wire) without conflicting with P2 (don't lubricate the wire). Both requirements would be satisfied, and the objective would be attained.

However, there was an obstacle: convincing the customer to revise their stripping force specification upward. Using the CRT to substantiate the problem and a future reality tree to demonstrate the effectiveness of the proposed injection, Aluminator was able to persuade the customer to test the unlubricated wire with a higher stripping force set into its machine. The test was successful, and no adverse effects of the higher stripping force were noted in the customer's process. Aluminator began producing wire without the spray (a variable cost reduction, so throughput increases). In the three months following the change, stripping failures and customer complaints went to zero, and Aluminator's process capability (CP_K) improved from 0.51 to 2.06.

After previously struggling without success for two months, by using the thinking process, the total time to develop and test this solution, persuade the customer, and deploy the solution at seven separate customer plants was just over four weeks.

The financial benefits were noteworthy. Aluminator reduced the cost of production by eliminating the lubrication part of the process. They avoided future warranty replacement costs of over $54,000 a year. And the retention of the customer's goodwill led directly to an additional $360,000 of new business during the year that followed.

SUMMARY

The conflict resolution diagram is a simple, effective way to peel away the distractions surrounding a conflict, reduce it to its essential elements and create breakthrough ideas to overcome it. So far, all of our examples have centered on industrial cases, and those have been tactical rather than strategic. But the conflict diagram applies to the strategic policy level, too, and not just in the manufacturing or for-profit sectors. Consider Figure 6.19. This is hardly manufacturing, and it certainly isn't small scale. But is there any valid reason why the same *principles* can't be applied to the larger societal problems we face?

Assumptions

1. A bankrupt government is unstable
2. A bankrupt government can't provide even minimal service to its people
3. A balanced budget provides for critical services (e.g., defense, justice, etc.)
4. Critical nonentitlement federal programs (e.g., defense, justice, etc.) will be unfunded
5. Entitlements are 51% of the federal budget and increasing
6. Entitlement spending is increasing the budget deficit
7. Increased entitlement spending will overwhelm any cuts in discretionary spending by 2012
8. Entitlements for 76 million baby boomers will break the government financially by 2012
9. Entitlements will consume 100% of federal government revenues by 2030
10. Little room is left for cutting discretionary funding without compromising critical nonentitlement programs
11. Anticipated new revenues from taxes can't increase fast enough to make up the difference.

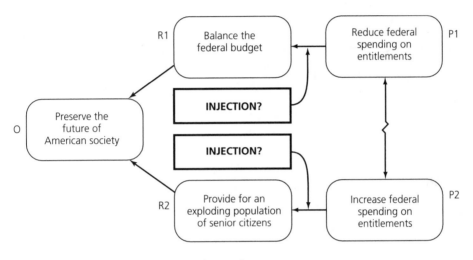

Assumptions

12. America has a tradition of providing assistance to those who truly need it
13. America has a moral obligation to provide assistance to those who truly need it
14. The baby boom generation will increase the numbers entitled to social security and medicare by 76 million by 2012
15. Failure to fulfill entitlement obligations will promote discontent and unrest to those entitled
16. A growing elderly population will require more medical care
17. More people than ever before will need government financial support
18. People will be living longer than before
19. Entitled citizens will be collecting entitlements longer than ever before
20. Federal obligations to entitled citizens will increase beyond the capability of any current or anticipated discretionary budget cuts to offset
21. The federal budget is the only possible source of funding for entitlements

FIGURE 6.19   *Federal entitlements (Social Security, Medicare). This conflict resolution diagram created by Melissa A. Dettmer. Used with permission*

In Appendix D, the Vector One case study continues with a conflict resolution diagram. Now might be a good time to take a look at it.

I'm looking for a lot of men with an infinite capacity for not knowing what can't be done.

—*Henry Ford*

NOTES

1. H. William Dettmer, *Goldratt's Theory of Constraints: A System's Approach to Continuous Improvement* (Milwaukee, Wis.: Quality Press, 1996), ch. 4.
2. *Webster's New Universal Unabridged Dictionary* (New York: Barnes and Noble, 1989), 91.
3. John Terninko, Alla Zusman, and Boris Zlotin, *STEP-by-STEP TRIZ: Creating Innovative Solutions Concepts* (Florida: St. Lucie Press, 1998).
4. Unfortunately, most of the source documents on TRIZ are in Russian only. For more on TRIZ in the English language, in addition to the Terninko, Zusman, Zlotin book, consult the following:

   Genrich S. Altshuller, *Creativity as an Exact Science* (New York: Gordon and Breach, 1988).

   H. Altov, (pen name of Altshuller), *And Suddenly The Inventor Appeared* (Auburn, Mass.: Technical Innovation Center, 1994), (translated by Lev Schuylak).

   Stan Kaplan, *An Introduction to TRIZ: The Russian Theory of Inventive Problem Solving* (Southfield, Mich.: Ideation International, 1996).

Chapter 7
DESIGNING TOMORROW'S SYSTEMS:
The Future Reality Tree

It is a simple thing to make things complex, but a complex task to make them simple.

—Meyer's law

How do you know your idea will work? Who among us hasn't heard—or asked—that question? You've more likely heard it expressed as disbelief: "Yeah, that idea will work—*when pigs fly!*" Most of us have been faced with this kind of skepticism at one time or another, and we've dearly wished to be able to respond with more than, "It will *too* work!"

If we lived in a bipolar world, where everything was either black or white, zero or one, challenges like this would be much easier to address. Unfortunately, in life, very few questions are reducible to one of two choices. In most cases, we have a wide range of options from which to choose. How can we tell which choice is the best? Decision analysis is a complete field of study unto itself, and it offers a variety of tools and methodologies that can be very useful in reaching decisions.

The problem with many decision tools is that they're confined to situations that can be mathematically modeled—important factors can be quantified in financial or other measurable terms. Or probabilities can be assigned to certain aspects of the future. Cost-benefit analysis is an example of the former, and decision trees are an example of the latter. Unfortunately, many of the problems we're faced with don't reduce to numbers very well, and attempts to do so can dangerously misrepresent both the problem and the viability of the solution. Some problems can't even be quantified at all. Take, for example, the question of what the president of the United States should do about a political situation halfway around the world that is moving swiftly toward open conflict, or how leaders can deal with sagging morale. Such situations are virtually impossible to quantify. How does one numerically express, for example, the political intentions of a head of state half a world away, or the motivation of individuals on a team?

MODELING BUSINESS DECISIONS

Many business decisions are difficult to apply numbers to as well, or at least their most important aspects are. For example, a chief financial officer can analyze the costs associated with a particular course of action and can predict cash flows and revenues *if* certain assumptions are made about how future events will unfold. The results of such an analysis will always be expressed in dollars and cents, inevitably leading to decisions based on financial considerations alone, and usually short-term ones, at that. However, some of the most important decisions are less concerned with money, or any other measurable criterion, than they are with the qualitative outcomes of the decision. Who could say, for instance, what the future cost might be of a decision *not* to enter into a new technology development, perhaps leaving that potentially fertile field for one's competitors to till alone? About the best one can do is say, "That would be bad, or *very* bad. Or even disastrous."

Moreover, there's not a mathematical model in the world that can completely replicate a real-world business environment. Because so much is neither quantifiable nor predictable, all such models come with preconceived assumptions locked into them—assumptions that might not be valid for the circumstances in which they're used. Some aspects of reality are deliberately left out of such models because they pose unmanageable combinations and permutations of outcomes. Reality's sharp corners are often rounded off to make the modeling job doable. These round-offs vary from one set of circumstances to another, but their effect is the same. They pull models away from accurate depictions of reality to varying degrees, and the big unknown is *how far removed from reality are they?*

It's a fact of life that, when deciding what course of action to take, we're forced to act under conditions of imperfect information. If our information were perfect all the time, we'd always know what the right decision should be. But that virtually never happens. So what can we do about situations that can't be mathematically quantified or modeled effectively, or situations in which we don't have full (perfect) information?

DESIRED RESULTS AND ADVERSE EFFECTS

In the absence of perfect information at decision time, there are two questions to which executives and managers should always have good answers if they're to maximize their probability of success: (1) Will this option produce the results we desire and (2) Will the option produce any devastating new effects of its own?

Obviously, it would really be wonderful if we could depend on our options to produce highly desirable outcomes. However, sometimes it's not practical to achieve the results we'd really like to have—the truly positive ones. Sometimes we must be satisfied with turning an undesirable situation into a neutral one. Even in that situation, we'd like to be sure that what we propose to do will, in fact, make the situation better, even if better really means less bad. What's just as important is the need to be sure that we don't create more, or worse, problems for ourselves with the solutions we decide on.

Goldratt conceived the future reality tree as the means to answer those two key questions. The future reality tree is akin to a bench test, or a field test, or perhaps a computer simulation model. It begins with the idea we've developed, by whatever means, to solve the problem, and it examines the logical cause and effect that unfolds from that decision, in light of whatever situation we're experiencing at present. Unfolding future reality enables us to determine whether there really is a logical connection between what we propose to do and the results we hope to achieve. Strange as it might seem, not all great ideas lead to useful solutions.

While we're testing the workability of the solution, however, we don't want to ignore the possibility that we could win the battle but lose the war. Our brilliant brainstorm might lead to other consequences we couldn't possibly stand. If this is the case, we're faced with another decision: Does the proposed solution offer such great potential for overall improvement that we're willing to search for ways to prevent the new negative side effects from happening? Or are we willing to live with those side effects, if preventing them isn't practical? In the worst case, the cure might prove worse than the disease. If the new side effects are so devastating—and unresolvable—it would be better to reject the idea to begin with. A component of the future reality tree known as a *negative branch* can help identify such unfavorable outcomes and suggest ways to deal with them.

Wouldn't it be nice to know all these things, with some degree of assurance, *before* embarking on implementation? The future reality tree and the negative branch can help with decisions like this. The following is a real-world example.

CASE STUDY: BMG NORTH AMERICA

In 1992, BMG North America, Ltd., a Canadian supplier of auto parts, was offered an ultimatum by its primary customer, General Motors: enter into a long-term preferred supplier contract with the automotive giant, or lose their existing business. On the surface, most companies would consider it a privilege to be invited into such a deal with an important customer. But for BMG, this was a tough choice because the long-term contract carried with it some very onerous terms. Among these was that BMG had to promise consistent price reductions over time, with no guarantee of additional business volume above their current levels.

BMG's chief executive officer, Jim Robinson, discussed the conundrum with the other members of the industry association to which he belonged. All were unanimous in their opinion that the preferred supplier contract was a bad deal for BMG. Jim was faced with an agonizing decision: opt out of the long-term agreement and lose 60 percent of the business of the company's largest division, or take the long-term contract under what appeared to be impossible terms and slowly hemorrhage red ink until the company eventually went bankrupt. It was a case of do *this* and die now, or do *that* and die later, albeit more slowly, but die, nonetheless.

Jim and his corporate brain trust resolved to cut this Gordian knot with a future reality tree, or, more precisely, with *two* future reality trees. They developed the first tree from the decision: "BMG does *not* enter into a long-term contract with GM (Figure 7.1). As expected, all the outcomes were bad. Not one desirable effect could be found. Two very undesirable effects of the loss of GM's business constituted a fatal wound from which the company would quickly bleed out.

The second future reality tree unfolded to a slightly different outcome from the decision: BMG *does* enter into a long-term contract with GM (Figure 7.2). There were still many undesirable effects, but from this tree, there were a few potentially *desirable* effects as well. Compared with the other option, BMG had no choice but to see if the decision to take the long-term agreement could be made to work.

Over the next several months, Jim Robinson and his staff figured out ways to trim all those negative branches off the second future reality tree, leaving only the desirable effects of the long-term agreement. They turned some of the undesirable effects to merely bearable. They were able to eliminate others completely. Their execution of the plan wasn't easy, but it *was* doable, and with cooperation from everyone—and some creative ideas—they made it happen.

BMG used a future reality tree to snatch victory from the jaws of defeat. They were one of only two companies in their industry association to accept GM's long-term agreement, and they made money by doing so, when others said they couldn't.

THE READY-FIRE-AIM SYNDROME

Most people can probably think of at least one great idea that died aborning. It was supposed to be the company's salvation, but instead it drove the final nail into the coffin. Why does something like this happen? The answer is probably *incomplete solution testing*. People and organizations often rush off to implement ideas that look like a million dollars, but in reality haven't been well thought out. Some critical aspect of the idea has been ignored or overlooked. The risk in doing so is failure to achieve the planned objectives and the creation of unanticipated new problems.

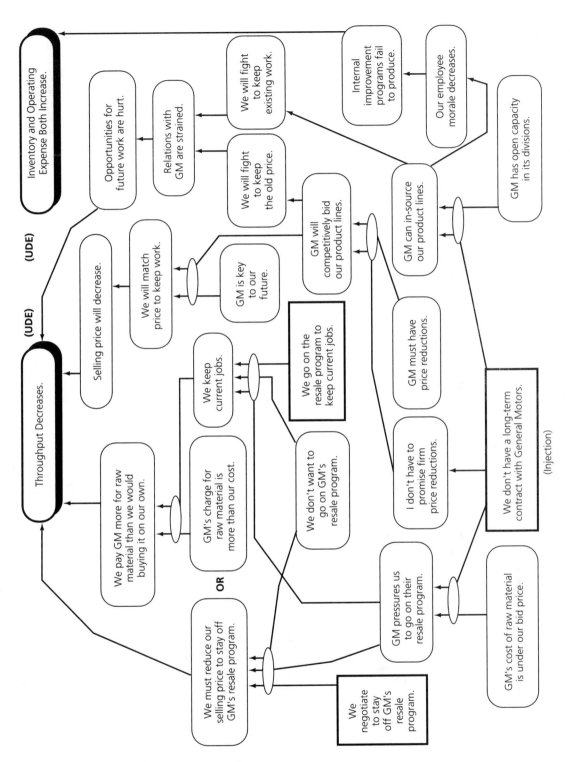

FIGURE 7.1 Future reality tree 1: BMG North America.

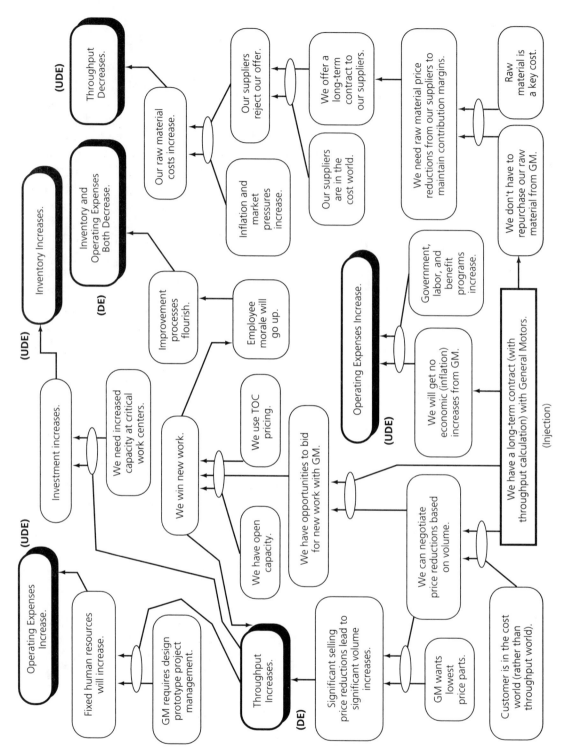

FIGURE 7.2   Future reality tree 2: BMG North America.

THE NORTH AMERICAN FREE TRADE AGREEMENT (NAFTA)

If there was one thing during his first term of office that President Clinton and the Republicans in Congress agreed upon, it was that the North American Free Trade Agreement (NAFTA) would be a good thing for the United States. It would lead to the creation of new jobs and increased business for U.S. companies by opening new markets for their products in Mexico.

NAFTA has never realized its promise. In other words, its desired effects have not been achieved. NAFTA was sold to the American people based on the purported benefits to the U.S. economy. In fact, the preamble to the agreement listed 15 specific effects NAFTA was supposed to achieve.[1] Figure 7.3 shows seven of the most significant ones, but it also shows nine major undesirable effects that are directly at odds with the purposes stated in the NAFTA preamble. While the objectives of the agreement might have been realized, the benefits have been decidedly one-sided, and *not* in favor of the United States. Could this problem have been anticipated at the time that the president and Congress were considering NAFTA? Mexico's economic, political, cultural, and social conditions weren't a national secret. The warning signs were there, for those who knew where (or cared) to look. With a structured, logical way of examining the outcome of approving NAFTA (that is, developing a future reality tree), this outcome could have been anticipated. Figure 7.3 doesn't show all the logic of how the path to the desired effects petered out. Determining why the agreement didn't pan out would require much deeper analysis. However, there are people with the knowledge to flesh out a complete future reality tree on the subject.

The problems of failing to test the solution don't end there. At an even more practical level, the failure of the administration to consider the adverse side effects of key provisions of the agreement could have proved disastrous. One such problem surfaced in December 1995, just before the provision was to take effect.

This provision allows large trucks from one country to pass freely, literally and figuratively, between Mexico and the United States. At the time NAFTA was concluded and approved by the U.S. Congress, the consequences of this and other less visible provisions were not foreseen. These consequences are addressed later in this chapter.

With a little help, the concerns that subsequently arose could easily have been anticipated, but none of the people involved knew anything about future reality trees, or negative branches, which are discussed in more detail later in this chapter and in chapter 8.

THE FUTURE REALITY TREE CONCEPT

The concept behind the future reality tree is relatively simple. We start with *injections*—the changes we would like to initiate. To those, we add elements of existing reality, producing new effects not currently existing.

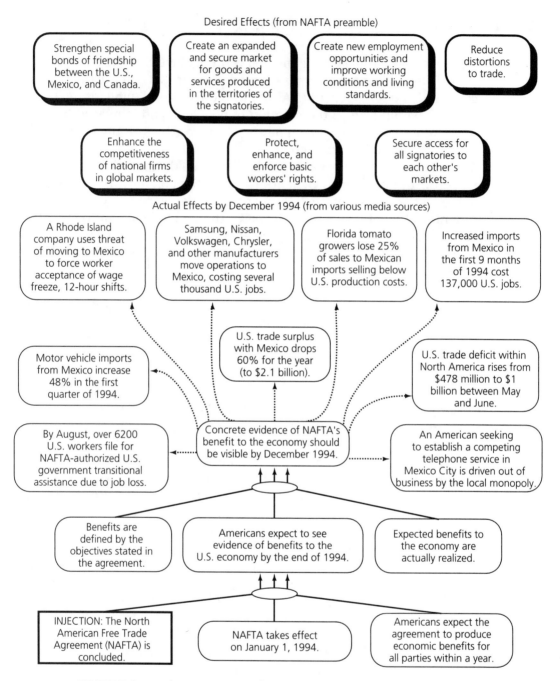

FIGURE 7.3 North American Free Trade Agreement: Did it do what the American people expected?

To the new effects, we add other injections as required to advance the chain of cause and effect progressively toward our ultimate objective—our desired effects.

As we develop the future reality tree, we learn the answers to two very important questions about our proposed idea. First, will it really get us closer to our desired effects, or, are we, like NAFTA, doomed to mill around aimlessly? Second, what are the weaknesses of the basic idea we want to try? In other words, what additional changes (injections) will be required to sustain progress toward the desired effects? Knowing the answer to the first tells us whether our new idea is worth continuing with in the first place. Knowing the answer to the second gives us some idea of the other factors we'll need to consider to make the basic idea work.

The future reality tree, unlike the current reality tree, is built from the bottom up. Instead of working downward from the desired effects to the injection, we work upward *from* the injection.

As long as we understand the categories of legitimate reservation (chapter 4) and how to apply them, the future reality tree is actually easier to build than the current reality tree. There are two reasons for this. First, when we built the current reality tree, we started from scratch, with nothing but the undesirable effects, to build a detailed picture of existing reality. When we begin the future reality tree, if we've previously constructed a current reality tree, we already have a fairly clear picture of the existing reality and its interdependencies. This makes it much easier to visualize the shape of future reality that will unfold from our actions.

Second, almost anything is easier to build when you already have the important building blocks in place to start with. In building a future reality tree, we start with more known elements. In the current reality tree, we've already identified the undesirable effects. The future reality tree's desired effects are usually no more than the *diametric opposite* of these undesirable effects. For example, if one undesirable effect was, Sales are too low, it's diametric opposite desired effect might be, We have all the demand we can possibly handle.

Therefore, by reversing the undesirable effects, we establish the very top of our future reality tree. With our basic injection, we have the very bottom of the tree. If we constructed a conflict resolution diagram, some elements of that will also be usable in the future reality tree, specifically, the objective from the CRD and at least one requirement—maybe both. These would lie somewhere in the lower part of the tree, between the injection and the desired effects. It's probable, too, that many elements of existing reality from the current reality tree would be usable in the future reality tree as well, since not all current reality will change when the future is designed. Figure 7.4 shows how these existing building blocks might be arrayed to start a future reality tree. Thus, building the tree becomes an exercise in *interpolation*—filling in the gaps between established milestones—which is why the future reality tree usually comes together much more quickly. Of course, this presumes that you've already constructed the current reality tree and the conflict resolution diagram. If you haven't, the future reality tree might require a little more skull sweat, but it can still be done.

NEGATIVE BRANCHES

Recall that earlier we said the future reality tree served two purposes: to verify that our proposed change will actually produce the results we want and to ensure that we can anticipate and avoid any devastating new

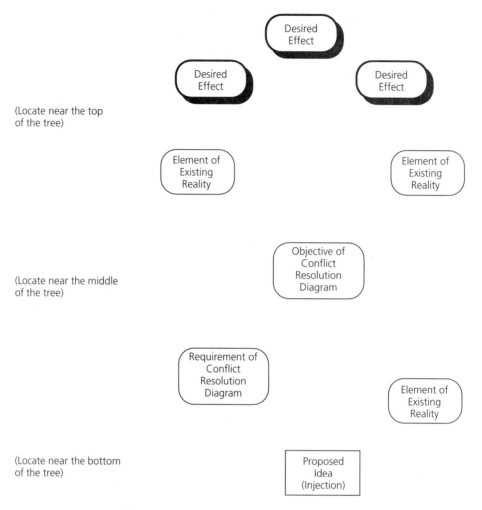

FIGURE 7.4 Future reality tree: Typical starting layout.

effects from the same change. We've seen how to verify the capability of our injection to produce our desired effects. The second part of the purpose, avoiding devastating new effects, is the job of the negative branch.

Once we've completed the future reality tree and satisfied ourselves that the basic idea for change will work, we must find out whether that new idea will cause us more problems than it solves, or even as few as one serious problem that we can't afford to have happen. Starting with each injection individually, we look for what could possibly go wrong if we go ahead with it.

Remember that one person's *improvement* is somebody else's *change.* And not everybody views change as a positive thing, even if it's ultimately beneficial to the system. So when evaluating the possible negative outcomes of a proposed change, it's a good idea to keep two questions in mind. First, is the possible negative outcome really the *system's* outcome, or does it just seem to affect a department or an individual? Maybe such an effect is significant enough at the department level that it will have some overall impact on the system. If so, however, this effect should be revealed in the negative branch. Second, is there a realistic probability that the negative effect will actually happen? For example, if your change will intensify the probability of damage from a lightning strike, but the probability of lightning striking in the first place is infinitesimal, it's probably not worth considering that negative outcome as an obstacle to your original idea.

Remember, too, that not every injection is likely to produce a bad negative effect, so don't be surprised if you have some injections that don't seem to produce negative branches. But inevitably, some injections *will* have them. Some will probably jump out at you; others you might overlook completely. Each of us has our own blind spots, and we can usually overcome them by having different people look at our future reality tree with critical eyes.

The negative branch is built much like the future reality tree itself. Once we realize where the negative effects in it appear, we have a decision to make: Is the potential value of the original idea (that is, the benefits we expect to achieve) enough to warrant efforts to try to keep the negative effects from happening? Or is the negative effect so bad and so difficult to overcome that we'd be better off going back to the conflict resolution diagram and working out a new idea? If the original idea *is* worth saving, we're now faced with the next question: Where and how do we act to eliminate the negative branch, or, in other words, how do we trim it from our future reality tree? The answer to this question will be found in chapter 8, which shows how to use negative branches, both as part of a future reality tree and as a stand-alone tool for evaluating decisions.

Figures 7.5, 7.6, and 7.7 are a set of three negative branches showing the adverse outcomes of NAFTA that resulted from incomplete solution testing, which a future reality tree *could* have averted. Fortunately, the impending disaster was recognized at the last possible moment, and execution of this provision of the agreement was indefinitely suspended until repairs could be effected. Why did this have to happen in the first place? One reason is that no effective tool for anticipating negative outcomes was available to the architects of the agreement.

This NAFTA case is a particularly effective example of the capability of the TOC thinking process to deal with policy problems and other non-quantifiable issues. A relatively few knowledgeable people with an understanding of how to construct a future reality tree and negative branches could have identified all the places where this agreement would fail to meet expectations. Even more important, they could have prevented untold aggravation and heartache from unanticipated adverse effects.

ALL CIRCUITS ARE BUSY. . .

Let's look at a recent situation that gained national attention. In late 1996, America OnLine® (AOL), the superpower among Internet service providers, decided it would be a good idea to change its pricing structure.

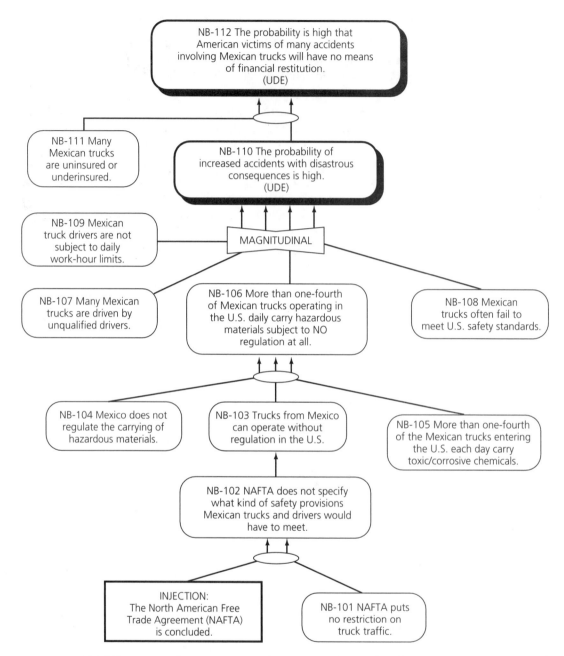

FIGURE 7.5 North American Free Trade Agreement: Negative branch 1.

AOL's management thought this would be a great way to build its customer base even higher than its industry-leading 8 million subscribers. Their chosen injection for doing so was a flat rate: $19.95 per month per subscriber for unlimited access time. Previously, AOL's pricing structure had been $9.95 for the first five hours in any month, and about $3.00 for each hour of on-line time over the basic five. The rate went into effect on December 1, 1996.

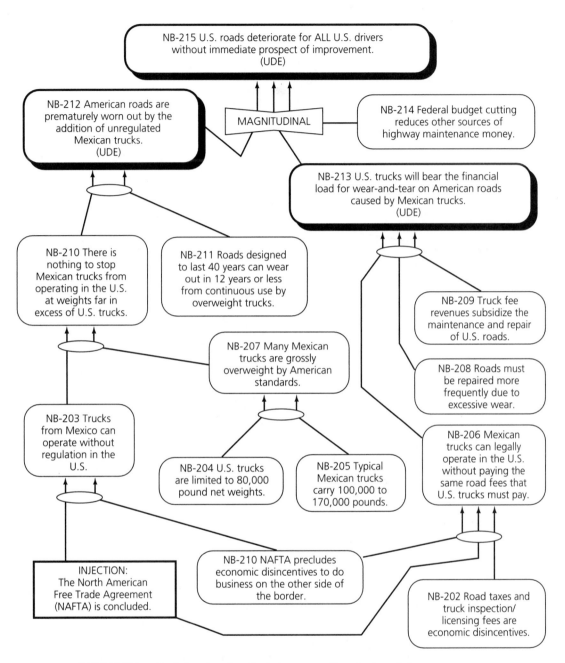

FIGURE 7.6 North American Free Trade Agreement: Negative branch 2.

By early January, AOL was in deep trouble. Existing subscribers found it nearly impossible to log into the system. Complaints soared. Some subscribers defected to other services, which wasted no time advertising that they weren't as clogged as AOL. New subscribers, who signed with AOL in response to the service's advertising campaign touting the flat rate, were frustrated and angry when they encountered busy signals

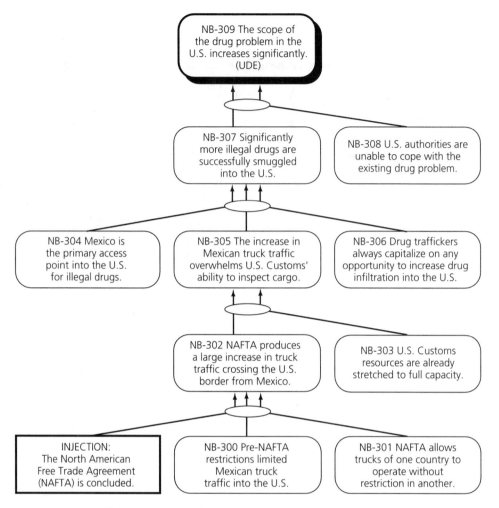

FIGURE 7.7 North American Free Trade Agreement: Negative branch 3

instead of expeditious connections.[‡2] What AOL had overlooked was, in essence, a combination of a capacity constraint and the predisposition of people to take their time on-line when they don't have to worry about time limits. AOL's 260,000 telephone lines, while adequate when timed rates encouraged short on-line durations, were completely unequal to the task of serving up to 8 million people who felt free to log on and "set a while". The access problem became so bad that the attorneys general of 36 states filed legal motions charging AOL with selling services it knew it couldn't provide and requiring refunds to customers unable to obtain access they had paid for.[3] What seemed like a good idea had turned into a disaster.

---

‡In January 1997, AOL's call failure rate—the proportion of members who received busy signals or were otherwise unable to connect with AOL's host computer—was 80.2 percent during prime evening hours. SOURCE: Inverse Network Technology, Sunnyvale, CA.

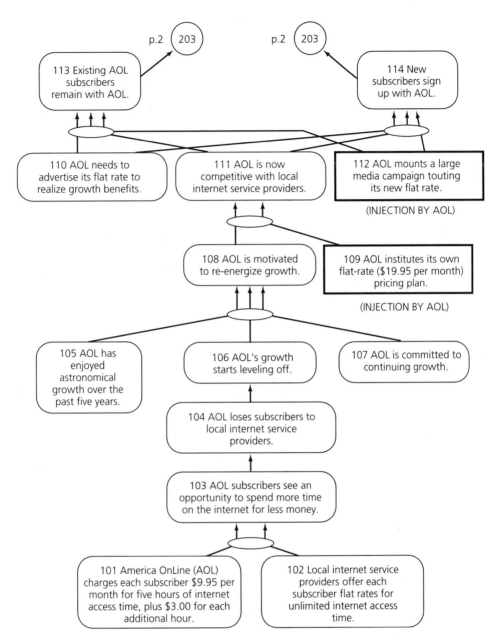

FIGURE 7.8.1 AOL Future reality tree: "All circuits are busy . . ."

How could this have happened? What AOL ignored was the need to *verify* that the idea (a flat rate) would actually deliver the results they expected. Clearly, it did not. AOL could have benefitted from a future reality tree (FRT). Had AOL built a future reality tree to validate its decision, that tree might have looked like Figure 7.8, and it would have been clear that AOL's desired effects would not be achievable by the way they planned to proceed. As we'll see later in chapters 9 and 10, had AOL had the future reality tree in Figure 7.8, their plan would still have been salvageable, and without the headaches they subsequently endured.

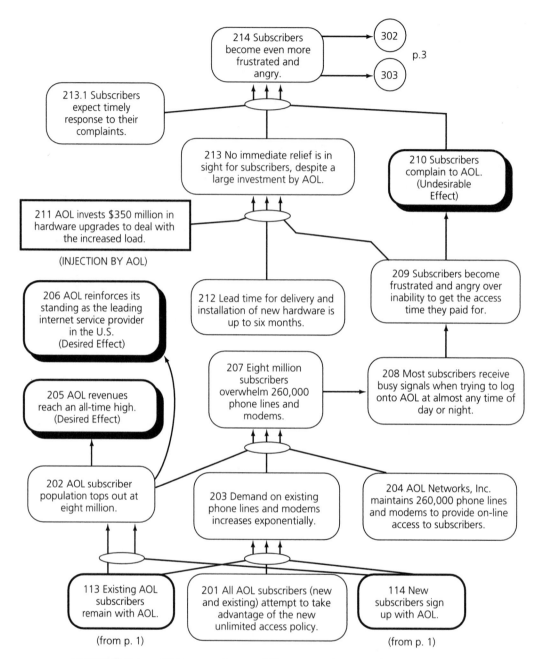

FIGURE 7.8.2 AOL Future reality tree: "All circuits are busy . . ."

POSITIVE REINFORCING LOOPS

The best solution is one that not only overcomes a problem, but keeps working afterward without constant attention or correction. Once the future reality tree is completed and the negative branches identified and trimmed, we can turn our attention to what might be done to make the new solution self-sustaining. The means for doing this is called a positive reinforcing loop.

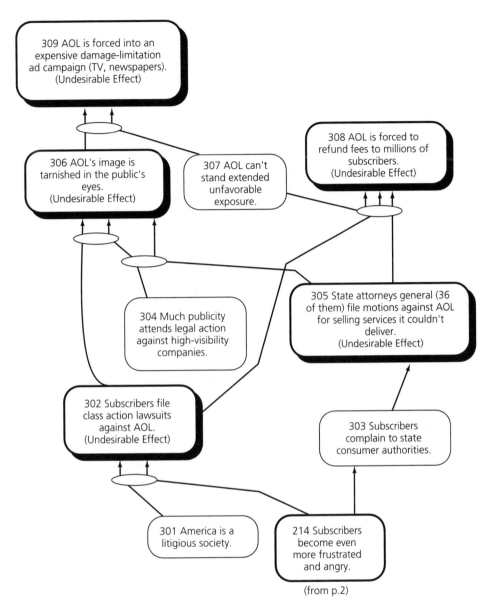

FIGURE 7.8.3   AOL Future reality tree: "All circuits are busy . . . "

You might recall, in our examination of current reality trees, we saw the destructive effect of negative reinforcing loops (refer to Figure 5.3). These occurred where undesirable effects looped back down, reentering lower in the tree to amplify the original cause of the undesirable effect. Naturally, this kind of loop reinforces the undesirable effect as well. A positive reinforcing loop is no more than the opposite of the negative one. Rather than making things continually worse, the positive loop makes effects better. Figure 7.9 shows an example of a positive reinforcing loop that is part of a larger future reality tree.

Positive loops sometimes occur naturally, but not very often. So if we want the desired effects of our future reality to be self-sustaining, we

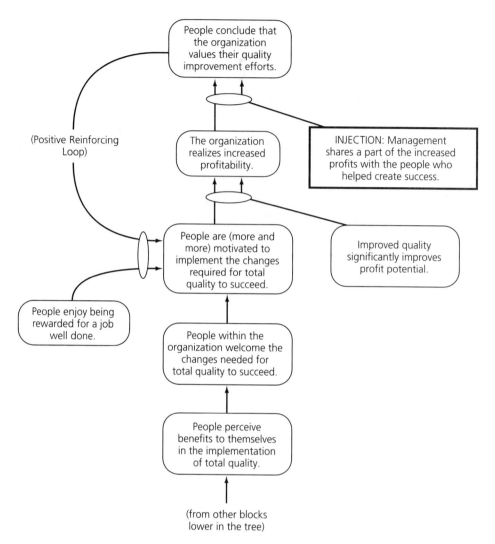

FIGURE 7.9 Positive reinforcing loop example.

usually have to make a special effort to build them into the tree. The steps for building a future reality tree that follow include guidance on how to do this.

BUILDING A FUTURE REALITY TREE

1. *Determine the Desired Effects of the Injection (proposed change)*. If you have a current reality tree to start from, you can make the desired effects the *diametric opposites* of your current reality tree's undesirable effects (Figure 7.10). If you're starting your future reality tree from scratch, you'll have to decide what positive effects you want from your proposed injection.

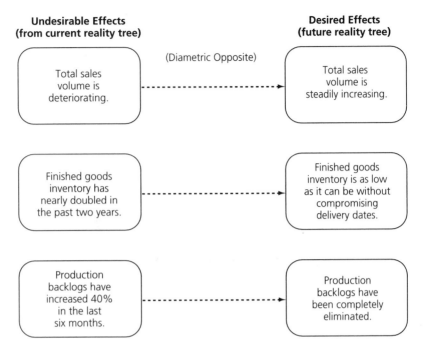

Undesirable Effects
(from current reality tree)

Desired Effects
(future reality tree)

(Diametric Opposite)

Total sales
volume is
deteriorating.

Total sales
volume is
steadily increasing.

Finished goods
inventory has
nearly doubled in
the past two years.

Finished goods
inventory is as low
as it can be without
compromising
delivery dates.

Production
backlogs have
increased 40%
in the last
six months.

Production
backlogs have
been completely
eliminated.

FIGURE 7.10   Determine the desired effect of the injection: Step 1.

In either case, state the desired effects in complete, simple sentences. Write them on Post-It™ notes, or reduce them to graphic boxes in a computer-based drawing program. Arrange them at the top of a clean sheet of paper.

2. *Formulate the Basic Injection of the Future Reality Tree.* Write the injection in a complete sentence on a different color Post-It™ note, or reduce it to a square-cornered box, to distinguish it from effects or statements about reality (Figure 7.11). Remember that at this point it isn't necessary to know exactly *how* the injection will be executed. For now, we're only concerned with knowing whether it will do the job *if* we do it. Place the injection near the bottom of the page. Leave plenty of space between the injection and the desired effects for intermediate effects and other injections.

3. *Incorporate Any Other Elements Already Developed.* If you started with a current reality tree, look for statements about existing reality that will be pertinent in the future. Transcribe these onto Post-It™ notes and locate them in the future reality tree in the same approximate respective position they occupied in the current reality tree.

If you have a conflict resolution diagram, you already have the injection you developed with it. Transcribe also to Post-It™ notes the objective and the two requirements of the conflict resolution diagram. These will represent milestones enroute to the desired effects. You might not need to indicate *both* CRD requirements in your future reality tree, but you will certainly need *one:* the requirement the injection is intended to

We have a reward/
compensation plan that
links satisfaction of
individual needs with
achievement of the
organization's goal.

(Basic Injection)
Example

FIGURE 7.11   Formulate the basic injection of the FRT: Step 2.

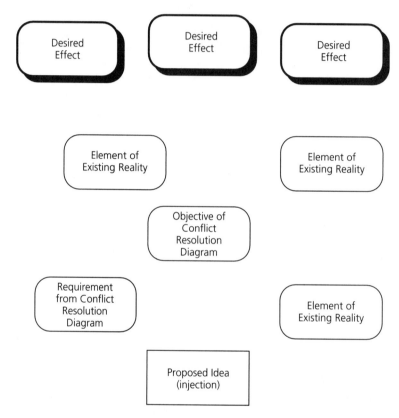

FIGURE 7.12   Incorporate any other element already developed: Step 3.

satisfy. If the injection replaces *both* prerequisites from the conflict diagram, you'll probably need to show both requirements.

Place the objective and the requirement(s) above the injection. Your starting configuration for all of these elements should resemble the layout in Figure 7.12

4. *Start Filling in the Gaps.* Begin with the basic injection. Hypothesize a direct and unavoidable outcome of putting the change into effect. Add blocks to incorporate any statements about existing reality needed to make the causal connection complete (sufficient). Evaluate the connection using the categories of legitimate reservation (refer to chapter 4).

When you're satisfied that the logical connection between the injection and the first effect is sound, assess whether this effect has brought you one step closer to your desired effects. If not, start over, looking for a different effect of the injection. If so, continue.

Determine whether this first effect leads automatically (that is, without any further action on your part) to other effects that move you closer to the requirements or objective from the CRD, or to the desired effects. If so, write those successive effects into the tree above the first-level effect, make the connection, and check it for logical sufficiency. Add other reality statements as necessary.

When you reach the point where your construction no longer has any momentum of its own—in other words, it seems to stop, but short of where you want it to go—consider what *other* injection you might create to keep the cause and effect progressing toward the next milestone.

Repeat this process until you can bridge the gap to the requirements, the objective, and, eventually, the desired effects. Each time your progress seems to be slowing, look for an opportunity to speed it up again by adding injections (Figure 7.13).

Eventually, you'll be able to make the final connection between the most recent effect and the desired effects. At this point, you'll probably have the original injection at the bottom and several others (maybe many, if your tree is complex) between the bottom and the desired effects. Once you make the final connection, read the tree in its entirety, from bottom to top, with a critical eye and the categories of legitimate reservation in mind. When you find intermediate effects missing, add them. When you discover logical deficiencies, correct them (Figure 7.14). When you think you have a logically sound tree, go on to the next step.

5. *Look for Opportunities to Build In Positive Reinforcing Loops.* Remember that the best solution is one that is self-sustaining. Examine the effects nearer the top of the tree. Look for places where one of these effects might loop back down one or more levels to amplify an effect lower in the tree. It's possible that you might need to combine that higher-level effect with a new injection in order to have the sufficiency to improve the lower-level effect. If so, add that injection to the tree, too (Figure 7.15).

6. *Search for Possible Negative Branches.* This is one of the most critical steps of all. You've already verified that you have a potentially effective solution to your problem and that it will give you the results you want. But you must be sure that you're not creating more problems, or worse ones, for yourself in the process of solving the original one.

The construction of negative branches should be done on separate pieces of paper, preferably a different one for each negative branch. Additional injections will be required to trim negative branches as well, and these should be added to your future reality tree after you've verified that they will, in fact, eliminate the negative branch (Figure 7.16). Chapter 8 tells how to build and incorporate negative branches into future reality trees.

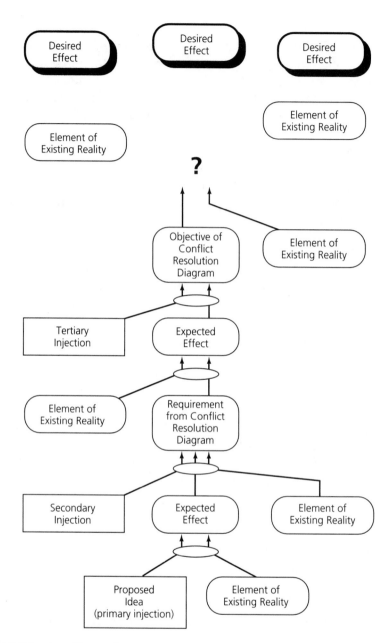

FIGURE 7.13 Start filling in the gaps: Step 4.

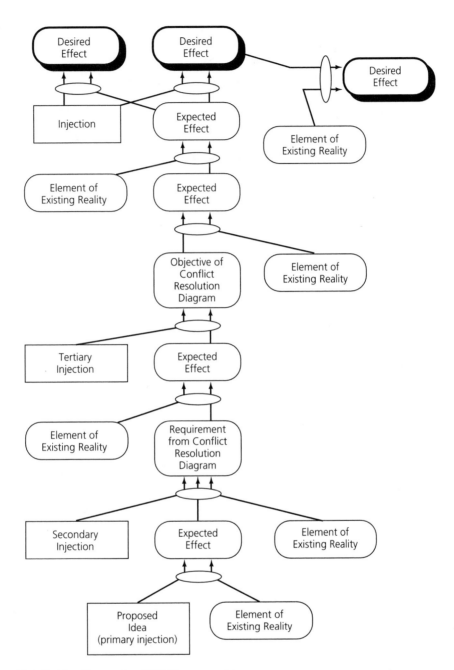

FIGURE 7.14 The completed FRT (first attempt).

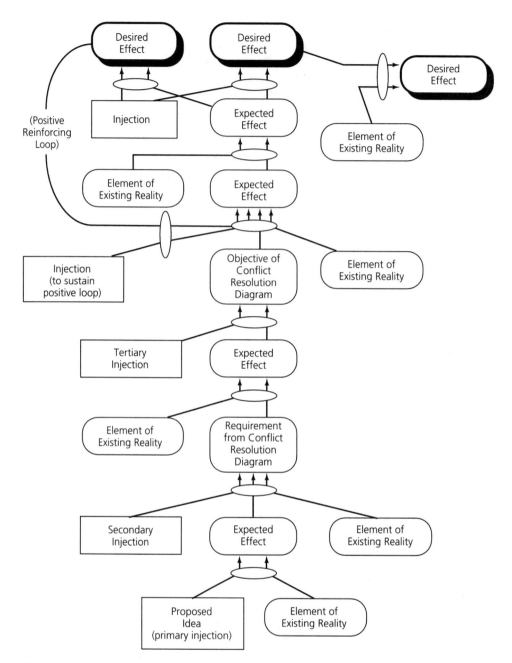

FIGURE 7.15 The completed FRT (positive reinforcing loop built in).

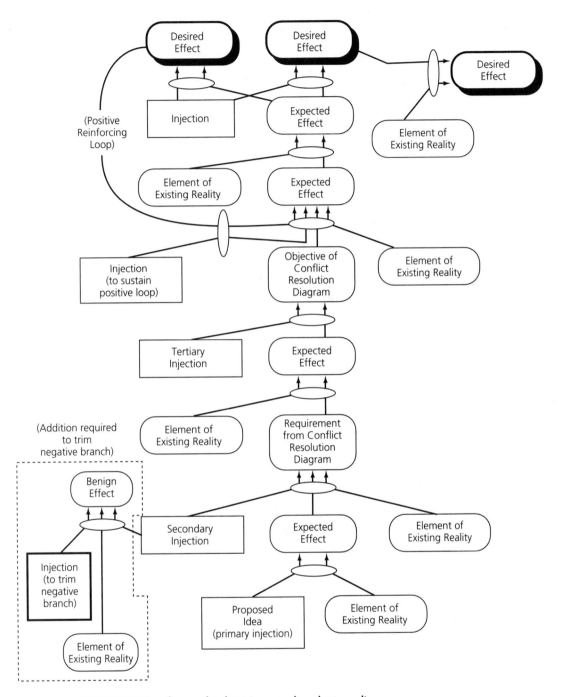

FIGURE 7.16   The completed FRT (negative branch trimmed).

Your final future reality tree should have in it every injection you'll need:

- The original injection
- Additional injections to sustain progress toward the desired effects
- Injections needed to support positive reinforcing loops
- Injections needed to trim negative branches

Identifying these injections is the *real* reason you built a future reality tree in the first place. Collectively, they constitute the road map of actions you'll need to take and conditions you'll need to create in order for your desired effects to become reality. Once you're confident that this road map will take you where you want to go—in other words, your proposed changes have been verified, progress has been reinforced, and all possible adverse effects have been accounted for and neutralized—you're ready to begin implementation. And not a moment before! Chapters 9 and 10 will describe implementation planning in more detail.

Before we go on, it's time to revisit Vector One Corporation (Appendix D) and find out how they're doing with their future reality tree.

If you want to reach your goals, you need to change your vocabulary.
—Unknown

NOTES

1. North American Free Trade Agreement (1993), Preamble.
2. "Speedier Net Connections Boost On-Line Performance," *USA Today* (Thursday, February 5, 1998), 1D.
3. "AOL to Pay Refunds to Its Customers," *Wall Street Journal* (Thursday, January 30, 1997), A3.

Chapter 8
ANTICIPATING DISASTER:
The Negative Branch

A new idea is delicate. It can be killed by a sneer or a yawn; it can be stabbed to death by a quip, and worried to death by a frown on the right person's brow.

—Unknown

The Hippocratic oath sworn by doctors says, in part, "Do no harm." The oath tacitly recognizes that medical practitioners might not, in all cases, be able to do good for their patients, but at the very least, a patient should not suffer more from their actions. A competent doctor, following the Hippocratic oath, will weigh the possible consequences—both good and bad—before deciding on a course of treatment. After all, the old saying that the operation was a success, but the patient died is the ultimate insult to throughput and goal attainment (not to mention gross suboptimization).

In our daily management roles, whether we're managing a corporation or a household, don't most of us have the same concern? We obviously want to do things that will advance our systems toward their goals, but at the very least, we want to avoid *creating* new problems we didn't already have. As we've seen, the future reality tree provides us the capability to evaluate new ideas that involve significant changes. One of the most important features of the future reality tree is the negative branch, which permits us to identify any devastating new effects such changes might create. The key word here is *devastating*. It's rare that a change doesn't produce some kind of negative effect somewhere for somebody. Our challenge is to ensure that the negative effect constitutes no more than a tolerable level of pain for the system while doing as little harm as possible to the people within.

Though originally conceived as a component of a future reality tree, the negative branch is a flexible and potentially valuable tool in its own right. Every day we're faced with decisions, some serious and some not. In how many of these situations do we have the time to construct a complete future reality tree? Probably not many. Moreover, a complete future reality tree probably isn't necessary for most of these decisions. In some cases, any positive outcomes of a decision might not even be relevant for us, but any *negative* ones might.

For example, let's say a department head comes to an executive with a proposal to change the way that department does business. Let's also assume that the change will influence other departments as well (system interdependency). The executive might be personally neutral about the benefits the subordinate department achieves from approving the proposal, but she might see new problems created by the decision to change, problems that the department head never considered. This might be a case of nothing in it for the decision maker but another headache.

However, the decision might not be as easy as saying, Disapproved! Outright refusal could send the wrong message to the department head: the executive doesn't care about their problem, and she isn't receptive to new ideas. Even if that's not true, she could degrade communication and motivation with an arbitrary rejection of an idea that the department head clearly sees as potentially valuable.

In a situation like this, it could be very helpful if the executive had a nonthreatening way to logically develop the cause and effect leading to her concern about the decision and to communicate her reservations to the department head. The negative branch can be an effective tool for doing so, because it can be used independently of a complete future reality tree. In fact, such independent uses are so wide-ranging that the negative branch is equalled only by the conflict resolution diagram in the variety of its applications.

EXAMPLE 1: "MAY I GO TO A ROCK CONCERT?"

Here's a very personal example. A few years ago, my eldest daughter, then a junior in high school, came to me with a brilliant idea: "Dad, Bonnie and I want to go to the Bryan Adams concert in Los Angeles next Friday." Bonnie was my daughter's best friend, and Bryan Adams was their favorite rock-and-roll performer.

"Well," I said, "how do you plan to get there and back?" The arena was some 70 miles from where we lived.

"Bonnie's going to drive," she replied. "She just got her driver's license."

Instantly, I thought to myself, I don't like this. . . . But I was quite conscious of the importance of not arbitrarily rejecting the request out-of-hand without a rational reason, which I hadn't the presence of mind to come up with on the spot. So I said, "Let me think about it."

The negative branch in Figure 8.1 is the result of some thoughtful reflection on my daughter's request. When I was ready to discuss the matter with her, I started from the bottom, as if I had decided to approve her request. Then I traced it through each level of *if-then* to the undesirable effects, which are unarguably undesirable. She was not entirely happy with what she heard, but she understood my concern, because it was plain to her that their safety was clearly at serious risk. This led her directly to the question that I wanted *her* to pose: "But how can we go to the concert without being in danger?"

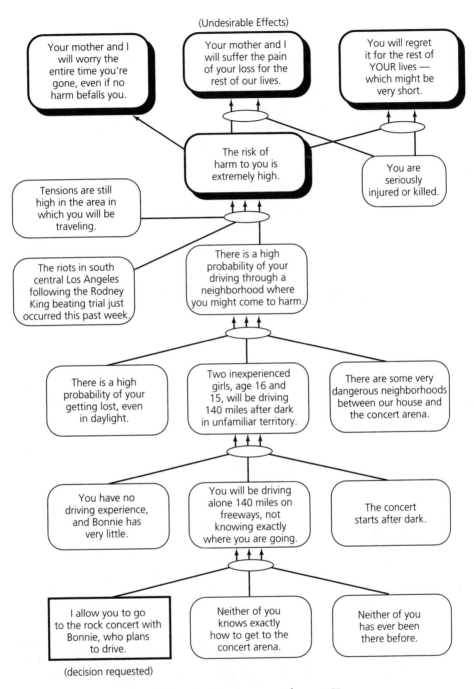

(Undesirable Effects)

Your mother and I will worry the entire time you're gone, even if no harm befalls you.

Your mother and I will suffer the pain of your loss for the rest of our lives.

You will regret it for the rest of YOUR lives — which might be very short.

The risk of harm to you is extremely high.

You are seriously injured or killed.

Tensions are still high in the area in which you will be traveling.

The riots in south central Los Angeles following the Rodney King beating trial just occurred this past week.

There is a high probability of your driving through a neighborhood where you might come to harm.

There is a high probability of your getting lost, even in daylight.

Two inexperienced girls, age 16 and 15, will be driving 140 miles after dark in unfamiliar territory.

There are some very dangerous neighborhoods between our house and the concert arena.

You have no driving experience, and Bonnie has very little.

You will be driving alone 140 miles on freeways, not knowing exactly where you are going.

The concert starts after dark.

I allow you to go to the rock concert with Bonnie, who plans to drive.

Neither of you knows exactly how to get to the concert arena.

Neither of you has ever been there before.

(decision requested)

FIGURE 8.1 Negative branch. Example: "May I go to a rock concert?"

I had already considered ways to trim this negative branch. One was for me to drive them to the concert, wait, and pick them up for the drive home. I could have built an entirely separate negative branch about why *that* would have been a bad idea, based on much the same undesirable effects as the first one! Instead, I offered this alternative: wait until the next time the performer came to town, perhaps at a different location, and her mother and I would chauffeur the two of them to and from the concert, taking in dinner and a movie while they did major damage to their hearing.

Was my daughter completely happy with this counterproposal? Of course not. She was disappointed, but not exceptionally so because she saw the risk to her safety. Any resentment she harbored was not directed toward the disapprover of her idea, but toward the circumstances.

My suggested alternative turned out to be an acceptable way to trim the negative branch. They got to go to the concert they wanted to see about four months later, yet we were assured of their safety. In other words, she gave up on the idea of instant gratification in exchange for a chit redeemable at a later date.

EXAMPLE 2: "IF IT DOES NOT FIT, YOU MUST ACQUIT . . ."

Here's another example. This obviously *didn't* happen, but it could have, and the outcome of *The People v. O. J. Simpson* might have been quite different if a negative branch had been used.

At a critical juncture in the prosecution's case, the district attorney decided to try to nail the door shut on Mr. Simpson with a courtroom demonstration. Two bloody leather gloves had been found by the police, one at the scene of the crime and the other at Mr. Simpson's house. Earlier testimony by a glove expert had substantiated that (a) the two gloves were a matched pair, (b) they were the same size, twelve, as Mr. Simpson's hand, and (c) no more than 200 pairs of these gloves had ever been manufactured in Mr. Simpson's size. Photographic evidence also had been offered to show Mr. Simpson wearing an identical pair of these gloves at a football game prior to the murders for which he was charged. Moreover, a New York department store clerk testified that Mr. Simpson's wife, one of the murder victims, had purchased the gloves. A sales receipt dated prior to the murders supported the contention that Mr. Simpson had, in fact, owned such a pair of gloves.

The district attorney seemed to have a lock on this one. All that remained was for the prosecution to directly connect the gloves the murderer wore with Mr. Simpson. What better way to do this—and very dramatically—than for the prosecution to ask Mr. Simpson to try on the gloves in full view of the jury? This was going to be a slam dunk, the last powerful piece of circumstantial evidence in a very persuasive argument. What could possibly go wrong. . . ?

A prosecution future reality tree wouldn't have been necessary. A negative branch, constructed by the district attorneys with the help of the glove expert would have been more than sufficient to show that this demonstration was a bad idea. Figure 8.2 shows what such a negative branch might have looked like. Notice that the injection at the bottom— "We make Simpson try on the gloves in front of the jury"—is the beginning

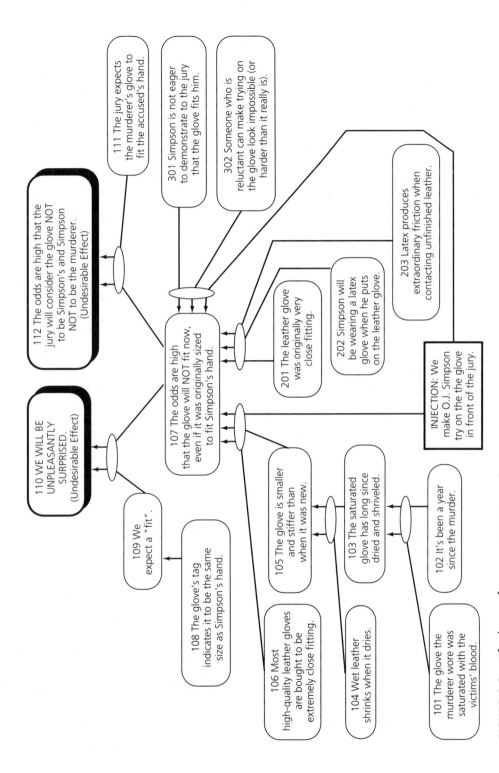

FIGURE 8.2 *"If it does not fit, you must acquit. . . ."*

of the negative branch, the decision we're considering. Combined with other elements of existing reality, this decision starts a chain of dominoes falling that ends with the gloves apparently not fitting Mr. Simpson and the jury possibly concluding that he did not commit the murders—not exactly what the prosecution was trying to prove!

Notice, too, that there's not just *one route* to these undesirable effects. There are *three independent ways* the prosecution could have traced this decision to these effects. Any one of them would have been enough to damage the prosecution's case. One factor was the problem of leather shrinkage due to saturation with blood. Another was the need to preserve the integrity of the evidence by not contaminating the bloody gloves through contact with Mr. Simpson's bare hands, so he would wear a pair of latex gloves when he tried on the leather ones. Finally, Mr. Simpson would have had to have been brain-dead to *want* those gloves to go on easily, whether or not he was really the murderer. In any of these cases, the gloves might not appear to fit, and this risk could easily have been anticipated by building a negative branch. The prosecution could have foregone the demonstration and let the rest of the evidence make its case.

But they didn't. And the rest, as they say, is history. Mr. Cochran, Simpson's attorney, made an emotional and persuasive argument about the gloves in his final summation to the jury: "If it does not fit, you must acquit." And they did, discounting a virtually insurmountable mountain of DNA blood evidence, and buying into the defense's argument that Mr. Simpson was framed by the police. Sometimes the consequences of failing to consider the devastating new effects of a possible decision can be disastrous.

ANTICIPATING THE UNDESIRABLE EFFECTS OF CHANGE

The unspoken assumption about the negative branch is that we can immediately foresee disagreeable consequences of the action, decision, or policy we're about to undertake. Obviously, if we don't see how anything could go wrong with it, we'd never be able to build a negative branch. Each of us has our own blind spots, and these are more likely to exist when the idea or change is our own brainchild. So this is where it often helps to solicit review from someone else.

Goldratt has suggested offering your logic tree for review by your worst enemy, because he or she has a vested interest in finding the weaknesses in your logic. While this approach might be a little extreme, there's no doubt that a neutral party, not emotionally invested in the solution (but one who has content knowledge of the situation), is likely to be in a better position to find the holes in your logic. The fact is, most of us are better at telling others why their ideas *won't* work than we are at creating these ideas in the first place (those who cannot *do,* criticize). So it should be relatively easy to find a third party willing to try to puncture your balloon.

External scrutiny or review is an important factor in developing any of the five logic trees, but it's especially crucial when we get to the point where we're about to take action to change the system. Change often requires the commitment of substantial resources: time, effort, money, or material. The more difficult it would be to back out of the change, the more important it becomes to verify that we aren't creating worse problems than we're curing. As we saw in chapter 7, failure to consider the unintended, but potentially devastating, consequences of the North American Free Trade Agreement almost resulted in disaster. For America OnLine™, it *was* a disaster. Therefore, if you've constructed a future reality tree, get someone else to help you find the negative branches that might result from its injections. Even if you're only contemplating a decision without a future reality tree, consider enlisting help in identifying negative outcomes you might overlook—*especially* if you don't see any yourself.

HOW TO BUILD A NEGATIVE BRANCH

If you already understand the rules of logic (the categories of legitimate reservation), developing a negative branch is fairly easy. Whether the negative branch is part of a larger tree or stands alone, the methodology is essentially the same. As an example of how to develop and eliminate a negative branch, we'll consider the possible outcomes of fertilizing our yard to improve the quality of the grass. We've decided to do this because we're embarrassed about the ragged appearance of our lawn.

1. *Write the Proposed Action, Decision, or Policy.* Assuming we feel uneasy about (or see outright problems with) the action, decision, or policy we're about to undertake, we're ready to start building a negative branch. We begin by stating the change we're contemplating, writing it as the injection (in a box) at the bottom of a page. For the example we've selected, that might be, "I fertilize the entire yard."

2. *List the Possible Outcomes of the Action, Decision, or Policy.* The outcomes of any change can be positive, neutral, or negative. They can also be positive for some people and neutral or negative for others. Presumably, you're considering the change because it seems to have some positive effects associated with it, either for you or for someone else. On a separate piece of paper, list these in one column, and the negatives in a second column.

While the whole purpose of the negative branch is to highlight the possible negative outcomes, the positive ones will serve a useful purpose, too, as we'll see later. The negatives are as much undesirable effects as those in the current reality tree are, even though we're considering a future that hasn't unfolded yet.

In our example, the positive outcome is a thick, consistent, dark green lawn. But weeds also thrive when fertilized, so we also have an undesirable effect: "Weeds take over my yard." Another negative might be,

Contemplated Action

| I fertilize the entire yard. |

Positive Outcomes

1. A thick, consistent, dark green lawn

Negative Outcomes

1. Weeds take over my yard

2. The lawn requires cutting more frequently

FIGURE 8.3   List the possible outcomes.

"The lawn requires cutting at more frequent intervals." Write each of these in the appropriate column on your list of positives and negatives (Figure 8.3).

3. *Build the Negative Branch Upward to the Undesirable Effects.* Using the same techniques for building a future reality tree, we begin unrolling cause and effect into the future, until we reach the undesirable effect we've previously identified.

As we go, we must ensure that our cause-effect connections are logically sound—that is, they are *sufficient*, and they don't require a transoceanic leap in logic from cause to effect. Remember that sufficiency requires a primary cause (our proposed change) to be combined with a contributing cause (perhaps a condition of already existing reality). Also, the effect must be *direct and unavoidable*—the next domino in line, not one that is three or four downstream.

We continue building the negative branch upward until the next direct and unavoidable connection is the undesirable effect (Figure 8.4).

Notice in our example that the contributing causes we include in the negative branch are facts of life—things that are happening now, regardless of the action we plan to take. In Figure 8.4, NB 2, 4, and 5 are examples of such facts of life.

4. *Identify the Turning Point.* When we've connected all the undesirable effects to the branch, we look for the connection (arrow) at which the tone of the tree turns from positive or neutral to decidedly negative. This happens at the first effect we can clearly say we don't like. The turning point might be the first effect after the injection, but more likely it will be several cause-and-effect steps farther along. If we believe the positives (from our list in Step 2) outweigh the undesirable effects, it will usually be worthwhile trying to trim the negative branch. This means we want to complete the action or approve the decision but keep those undesirable effects from ever seeing the light of day. To keep the undesirable effects from happening, we usually have to take an additional step. To ensure that this preventive step won't compromise the beneficial effects we still want, we will usually apply it *at the turning point.*

In our example, it's fairly obvious that NB 3 is the last entity in the negative branch that is clearly positive. At NB 6, the tone turns decidedly negative. The turning point lies between NB 3 and NB 6 (Figure 8.4).

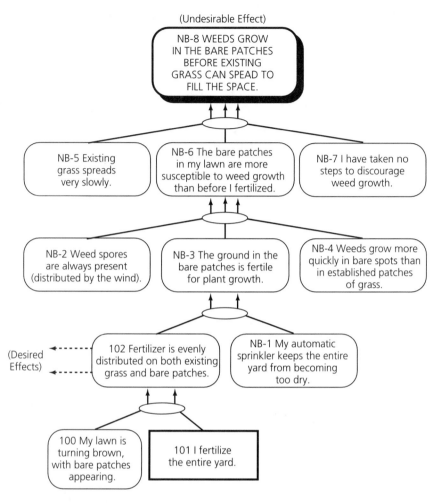

(Undesirable Effect)

NB-8 WEEDS GROW IN THE BARE PATCHES BEFORE EXISTING GRASS CAN SPEAD TO FILL THE SPACE.

NB-5 Existing grass spreads very slowly.

NB-6 The bare patches in my lawn are more susceptible to weed growth than before I fertilized.

NB-7 I have taken no steps to discourage weed growth.

NB-2 Weed spores are always present (distributed by the wind).

NB-3 The ground in the bare patches is fertile for plant growth.

NB-4 Weeds grow more quickly in bare spots than in established patches of grass.

(Desired Effects)

102 Fertilizer is evenly distributed on both existing grass and bare patches.

NB-1 My automatic sprinkler keeps the entire yard from becoming too dry.

100 My lawn is turning brown, with bare patches appearing.

101 I fertilize the entire yard.

FIGURE 8.4 Negative branch: "Weeds Take Over My Yard."

5. *Determine the Underlying Assumptions at the Turning Point.* Remember we said earlier that every arrow in a cause-effect tree implies at least one underlying assumption, maybe several of them. These assumptions are statements about reality (current or future) that we consider valid, whether they really are or not. Sometimes these assumptions are not explicitly stated; other times they might appear as contributing causes (the aforementioned facts of life). For example, NB 2 ("Weed spores are always present") is a typical assumption shown as a contributing cause. It adds clarity and sufficiency, but most of us would probably have assumed its presence, even if it hadn't been explicitly stated. Whether they're explicit or implicit, at this point we must articulate these assumptions. If they're not already a part of the negative branch, write them down beside the arrow to which they apply. These assumptions will give us clues about the kind of action we'll need to take to trim the negative branch at the turning point—to keep the undesirable effect from ever happening.

Two such assumptions associated with the arrow between NB 4 and NB 6 might be that (a) we can't stop the quick growth of weeds, or (b) there's no way we can eliminate the bare spots in the lawn before the weeds grow. Both of these assumptions fairly invite challenge.

6. *Develop an Injection to Break the Assumptions.* This is a creative exercise. It often requires "thinking outside the box." Our challenge is to come up with something else we might do to neutralize one of the assumptions we identified in step 5. For example, we might spray some kind of weed inhibitor on the bare patches, something that would stop or slow germination of the spores. Another option might be to buy some sod and use it to fill in the bare patches. Or we might need both.

7. *Verify That the Chosen Injection Will Effectively Trim the Negative Branch.* We have to be sure that our idea to keep the undesirable effect from happening will actually work. To do this, we write this new idea as an injection and position it at the same level as the *last positive entity.* Then read all the entities at that level (including the new injection) as a *cause sufficiency* leading to a new effect—one that *replaces* the first negative one. For example, Figure 8.5: If weed spores are always present (NB 2), *and* the ground in the bare patches is fertile for growth (NB 3), *and* weeds grow more quickly in bare spots (NB 4), *and* I fill in the bare spots with sod before weeds can germinate (injection), *then* there are no bare patches where weeds can grow quickly (favorable outcome, replacing undesirable effect).

8. *Take Action to Implement the Injection.* If your negative branch grew out of a future reality tree, incorporate the new injection into the FRT, along with that part of the negative branch from the original injection up to the new favorable effect (Figure 8.5). If you built your negative branch as a stand-alone, accomplish both injections.

HANDLING PROPOSALS FROM OTHERS WITH UNDESIRABLE EFFECTS

Earlier we discussed how risky it is to discourage peers or subordinates from offering new ideas. It's really easy to shut down creativity by stomping on somebody's idea for an improvement. But often the undesirable effects of a proposal that has been only partially thought out can be even more devastating. So the question is, How can we point out problems with a proposal without discouraging the proposer?

Here's a simple way to use a negative branch to turn such a potential problem into a win for both sides. Let's say a subordinate comes to you with an idea to significantly change the way your department functions. The subordinate makes a good case for some real benefits that could result. However, you can see a major pitfall in the idea that will create a major problem for your group. Your first step would be to ask for time to consider the proposal. Make an appointment to discuss it with the subordinate later.

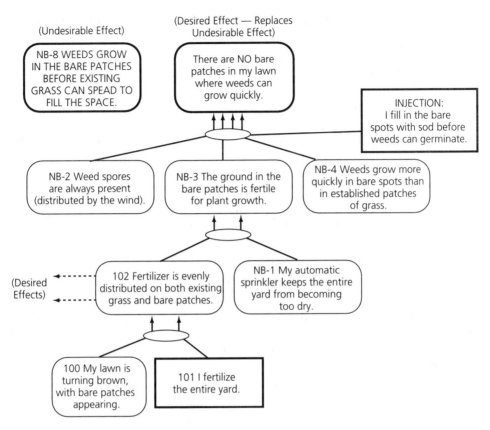

FIGURE 8.5 Negative branch: "Weeds Take Over My Yard" (trimmed).

Then build your negative branch all the way to the undesirable effect. Don't leave anything to chance. Make sure you have *every* successive step in place—*no leaps of logic!* Once you've completed the negative branch, meet with the subordinate again.

Reinforce the subordinate's impression that you're willing to listen to new ideas by letting him or her know you appreciate their initiative in bringing the suggestion to you. Then recite all the potential positives you developed in step 2 of the procedure. In most cases, the subordinate will have already given you many of these in the original proposal. Reiterate them anyway. Then lead the subordinate through the negative branch, starting from the injection, "I approve your proposal." Read the entire negative branch to him or her aloud, pausing after each cause-effect connection to make sure he or she is following your logic: "Are you with me so far?", or "Does that make sense?". Or just look for the non-verbal feedback—a nod of the head, perhaps—that indicates the person accepts your causal connections.

When you finally reach the undesirable effect together, you have two choices. If the original suggestion seems to have merit, you might say, "This is an undesirable outcome, but it doesn't necessarily mean that your idea isn't worth doing. It just means that it needs a little more work. Let's talk about it a bit. Then you take it back and work on a way that we can do what you propose, but keep the undesirable effect from happening." Then dangle the carrot: "If you can do that, I don't see why I shouldn't approve your idea."

It's also possible that the subordinate's proposal is really ill-founded; that if you were to approve it, the undesirable effects would be worse (and more costly to overcome) than the benefits to be realized from it. In that case, when you reach the undesirable effect in your joint review of the negative branch, your response should be, "See why I've got a problem with this idea?" Then *don't say anything more*. This puts the ball back in the subordinate's court, without any encouragement to continue.

The probability is fairly high that subordinates will lose the motivation to continue pursuing the idea at that point. Even if they don't, the worst that will happen is that they'll return later on their own with a new or modified proposal. At this point, it's a new ball game and probably worth your time to evaluate the idea again from the beginning.

It's taken much longer to explain how to build a negative branch than it actually takes to do it. Once you are familiar with the categories of legitimate reservation, you can complete an effective negative branch in about 15 minutes, assuming you know enough about the situation and can readily see the negative outcomes.

We've seen two examples of stand-alone negative branches, and the America OnLine® example in chapter 7 shows another that's part of a larger future reality tree. Appendix D contains a negative branch that developed out of the Vector One future reality tree, and the injection used to trim it.

By the time we've completed a current reality tree, a conflict resolution diagram, a future reality tree, and any pertinent negative branches, we've gone farther than most problem-solving methodologies usually take us. We've identified the problem (the constraint) and the conflict that might be perpetuating it. We've created a breakthrough solution (an injection), and we've tested it for effectiveness, verifying that it will enable us to reach our desired effects. We've also determined that any devastating consequences that might result from this new idea are nipped in the bud. But at this point, all we've got is still just an *idea*—and ideas are not solutions. An effective solution requires implementation, which brings us to the next topic: prerequisite trees.

La madre de fessi e sempre incinta. (The mother of idiots is always pregnant.)
—*Italian proverb*

Chapter 9
OVERCOMING OBSTACLES TO CHANGE:
The Prerequisite Tree

Apathy can only be overcome by enthusiasm, and enthusiasm can only be aroused by two things: first, an idea which takes the imagination by storm, and second, a definite intelligible plan for carrying that ideal into practice.
—Arnold Toynbee

Ideas are relatively easy to come by, but solutions aren't. What's the difference between the two? A solution is an idea that has been completely implemented. Some might add that it has proven effective, too. Unfortunately, many ideas never make it to the solution stage. There can be any number of reasons why this might happen.

In some cases, we know what we want to do, but we aren't sure exactly how to make it happen. Often the magnitude of the task is so disheartening that we find ways to procrastinate on getting started. Other times, unforeseen obstacles frustrate our efforts, or obstacles we might not know how to overcome. The more complex the execution of the idea, the more likely it is that one of these impediments will occur.

ORGANIZATIONAL CHANGE

The ideas that have the greatest impact on a system usually involve considerable organizational change. In any organization involving more than one person, successful change requires the cooperation of others besides the initiator. Because of limits to one person's effective span of control, the larger the organization, the more the that cooperation needs to move from merely nonresistance to active, willing participation.

New ideas are often considered improvements only by their creators and sponsors. In practice, whether one considers an organizational change to be an improvement or not depends largely on whose ox is being gored in the process. People are rightfully skeptical about change, and the human factor in change is inevitably the most difficult to deal with. *Reengineering*, for example, has generated more than a little flak, because in many cases, it has translated into downsizing (or its more benign alias, right-sizing).

Even in organizations where change doesn't usually result in piecemeal or wholesale job losses, repeated change often takes on a flavor-of-the-month quality. People don't take it seriously, or cooperate only half-heartedly. Or worse, they slow-roll the change efforts: *If we only hold our breath long enough, this, too, shall pass. . . .* One wag even coined the term BOHICA—bend over, here it comes again—to characterize the combination of potential risks to job security and the flavor-of-the-month phenomenon.

The net result of this kind of attitude is that good, maybe even great, ideas founder and sink in the execution stage, and the probability of success in each subsequent attempt at change diminishes because each failure squanders precious credibility capital within the organization. Failing to enlist the support of people within the organization can be one of the biggest obstacles to success for any organizational change. Ironically, in many organizations, it's the one obstacle that elicits the least attention.

How can we avoid this pitfall? What can we do to conserve our credibility capital and enlist the willing support of our organization's members? Assuming we've verified that the idea we want to implement is valid and the adverse side effects have been clearly identified and dealt with, the next best thing we can do is complete—on the first attempt—a swift, clean execution without stumbling. But we can't hope to do this unless we know what obstacles to success lie in our path.

Even when the foremost risk in the change isn't internal acceptance, failure to identify and deal with the technical obstacles can sink a change effort. Consider the America OnLine® (AOL) situation we saw in chapter 7. The future reality tree that might have prevented a disaster was never built, so a chance to anticipate and avoid the trap AOL eventually fell into was lost. Even without a future reality tree, AOL might still have succeeded if they had dealt with technical implementation obstacles. However, they never adequately identified the obstacles to a successful flat-rate transition. Had they done so, rational people would have taken steps to avoid them. As we'll see later in this chapter, AOL could have used the thinking process to identify the obstacles to successful implementation and correctly sequence the actions needed to overcome them.

THE PRESCRIPTION FOR SUCCESSFUL CHANGE

What are the minimum requirements for successful change? The prescription is fairly simple:

- Identify and decide how to overcome obstacles to implementation

- Lay out an effective step-by-step plan for execution, including accountabilities and measures of success
- Act with determination and perseverance to execute the plan

The latter requirement is purely a leadership function; neither the principles nor the tools of the theory of constraints (TOC), or any other methodology, can substitute for the will to see the job done. But TOC tools, especially the thinking process, can be particularly useful in the first two requirements. The prerequisite tree was specifically designed to help identify and overcome the obstacles to effecting change, and the transition tree can be a productive execution planning tool. In this chapter, we'll see how the prerequisite tree works, and how it forms the foundation for the transition tree (chapter 10).

STRUCTURE OF THE PREREQUISITE TREE

The prerequisite tree has only three kinds of elements: an ultimate objective, obstacles, and intermediate objectives. There's only one objective. It's the *deliverable* of the effort—a completed project or executed change—and it resides at the very top of the prerequisite tree. Below the objective, the obstacles are arrayed in parallel or in sequence, as the situation dictates. Between each level, or layer, of obstacles are the intermediate objectives needed to overcome each obstacle (Figure 9.1).

Notice that the prerequisite tree's (PRT) appearance is substantially different from current or future reality trees (CRT, FRT). The intermediate objectives are connected to the objective, and to each other, by vertical arrows, each pointing inexorably upward. The obstacles have arrows extending to the midpoints of the arrows issuing from the lower intermediate objective. This indicates which obstacle a particular intermediate objective is supposed to overcome. The upward flow is similar to that in the CRT and FRT, but there the similarity ends. There are no sufficiency ellipses, and most PRTs converge at the top toward a single entity—the objective—while the CRT and FRT often diverge toward various desirable or undesirable effects.

The most significant difference of all, however, is in the logic inherent in the arrows themselves. Remember that the logic behind the current and future reality trees was based on *sufficiency*—that is, identifying all the critical causes of an effect, failing any one of which the effect could not be achieved. The prerequisite tree, on the other hand, identifies only those critical success factors or necessary conditions that we *don't already have* in place, and which must be in place prior to reaching each successive level in the tree.

The following is a clearer example of the difference between sufficiency and minimum necessary conditions (Figure 9.2). Let's say we want to build our own house, not hire some contractor to do it. For the sake of simplicity, we'll assume we've already obtained a lot and had it prepared,

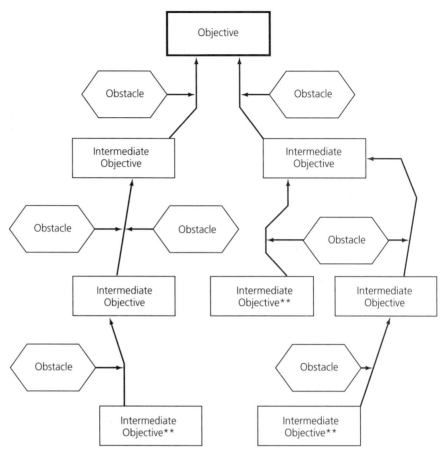

** = No obstacle to attaining this intermediate objective exists

FIGURE 9.1 The prerequisite tree.

received the proper permits, and had utility hookups installed at the lot. From this starting point, what do we need to complete our house?

Obviously, we need materials, tools, plans, and the skills to construct the house. All of these elements are reflected in the sufficiency tree on the left side of Figure 9.2. Remember that we read this kind of tree using *if* and *then*:

If we have the right materials, tools, skills, and adequate plans, Then we can build a house.

We might have learned the carpentry, plumbing, electrical, masonry, drywall, and finishing skills from our father, and we might have obtained adequate plans from a commercially available book or an architect. But for most people, collecting all the right materials and tools is a big challenge. Let's say we *don't* have the materials and tools. While there are four causes that would be considered *sufficient* to build our house, implementation is obstructed by only the two that we *don't* have: the materials and the tools. So while the sufficiency tree at left would indicate everything we'd need to build the house, the necessary condition tree on the right shows only those elements that constitute obstacles to proceeding with construction.

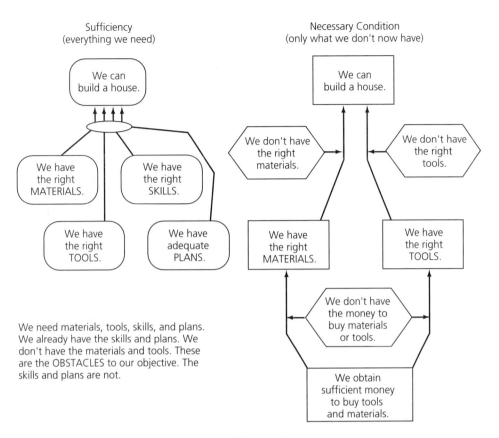

FIGURE 9.2 Sufficiency versus necessary condition.

The prerequisite tree shows only what we need that we don't already have: in this case, the materials and tools. Notice, too, that the PRT in Figure 9.2 has an additional level. The materials and tools needed to build a house are expensive, and we might not have the cash to buy them. This would be an obstacle to obtaining the right materials and tools, and it would require another intermediate objective, lower in the tree, to overcome this obstacle. In this case, that intermediate objective would be to obtain sufficient money to buy materials and tools. We might do this by borrowing from someone or from a bank. That would be another intermediate objective even lower in the tree.

Is the pattern becoming clear? The prerequisite tree deals only with the current obstacles to achieving our objective—anything that we need but do not at this moment have in hand. It also enables us to chronologically sequence these intermediate objectives, showing which ones depend on the prior attainment of others. Note, too, that two intermediate objectives (having the right materials and tools) are obstructed by only one obstacle: lack of money. The single act of overcoming that one obstacle allows us to attain the two intermediate objectives at the next higher level. The structure of a prerequisite tree is regimented only to the extent that alternating layers of obstacles and intermediate objectives occur. The vertical branches are very much free-form, depending on the specifics of a particular situation.

The prerequisite tree is verbalized a little differently than a current or future reality tree. Whereas the CRT and FRT are read using *if* and *then*, the prerequisite tree is read this way:

In order to *be able to build a house*, we must *have the right materials*, because *we don't have any materials now*.

In order to *be able to build a house*, we must *have the right tools*, because *we don't have all the tools we need now*.

In order to *have the right materials and the right tools*, we must *have sufficient money to buy them*, because *we don't have enough money now*.

If this looks somewhat familiar, it's because you've seen it before in chapter 6. We read the conflict resolution diagram (CRD) using essentially the same wording. The CRD employs the same kind of *necessary condition* structure. Like the requirements and prerequisites in a CRD, the intermediate objectives in a PRT are *necessary, but not sufficient alone*.

PROJECTS: A SPECIAL KIND OF IDEA IMPLEMENTATION

A classic example of complex idea implementation is a project. These days, the term *project* is carelessly used to characterize a wide variety of activities, many of which are closer to production than projects. Production activities are largely repetitive, even though the distinct character of the output might change. No one would entertain the idea that building an automobile is a project, even though two consecutively delivered automobiles might be very different from one another. The same types of activities, done the same way each time, produced both.

Projects, on the other hand, are usually distinguished by their *lack of repetitiveness*. They're usually onetime efforts. The output of a project is usually a deliverable of one. Size or scope of the deliverable has no bearing on whether an effort is a project or production. Boeing builds airliners costing in the hundreds of millions of dollars, each requiring months to assemble. Some might consider each one to be a project in and of itself, but it really isn't. The project part of the effort was starting from scratch to design, develop, and test the prototype, proving both the design and the procedures to build subsequent airplanes at the same time. When we reach the point of repetition, the activity has metamorphosed from project to production.

Almost any significant change in any organization has the onetime characteristic of a project, rather than a repetitive production effort. By the very nature of their onetime characteristic, projects present different challenges than repetitive production. Uncertainty in performance, cost, and schedule are all usually much higher in projects than in production.

Prerequisite trees offer a particularly useful capability to project planners. Any complex project begins with the structuring of the task or activity network. Once a project is begun, some activities are accomplished in parallel, some in sequence. The more parallelism in a project—

and the less sequential dependence—the faster the project is likely to be completed, but the complexity of the coordination effort increases proportionately.

Many project sponsors, managers, and team members focus very heavily on the project schedule as a means of controlling both performance and cost parameters. While other important factors contribute to success in realizing both performance and cost objectives, schedule seems to worry project people as much or more than anything else. A variety of techniques, some more effective than others, is available for managing a project's schedule, but all of them depend on one crucial prerequisite: the prior establishment of an effective activity network. For example, both the program evaluation and review technique (PERT) and the critical path method (CPM) assume that such a network has already been determined. So does the *critical chain* approach favored by Goldratt.[1] However, the formation of such a network is not easy, especially for complex projects, yet the success of any of the previously mentioned schedule control methods invariably depends on it.

The prerequisite tree can be an effective tool in devising the activity network, providing the maximum in parallelism while ensuring that truly sequential dependencies are not overlooked. Figure 9.3 shows how the structure of a prerequisite tree very closely resembles a typical PERT diagram. The numbered nodes on the PERT diagram correspond to the intermediate objectives in the prerequisite tree. All that's missing are the computations of earliest and latest start times and the expected time for each PERT segment. While the structure in this illustration is very simple, both the prerequisite tree and the PERT activity network could be considerably more complex if the project so warranted.[†]

What makes the prerequisite tree such an effective aid in preparing a project activity network is the logical rigor provided by the thinking process to validate the connections. This logical rigor, discussed in detail later, (Figure 9.7 Verifying Obstacles and Intermediate Objectives) ensures that all required activities are accounted for and are *really* necessary. Logical rigor can close many potential loopholes before they turn into a major *oops!* during project execution.

AMERICA ONLINE®: A CONTINUING EXAMPLE

Remember that in chapter 7 we saw a future reality tree concerning America OnLine® (AOL) (see Figure 7.8). The critical juncture in that tree was the place where the negative branch departed from the main trunk of the tree, leading to the desired effects. In chapter 8, we saw that the trimming

---

[†]One of my graduate students at the University of Southern California related that Northrop's PERT diagram for the B-2 bomber contained over 180,000 nodes in multiple levels.

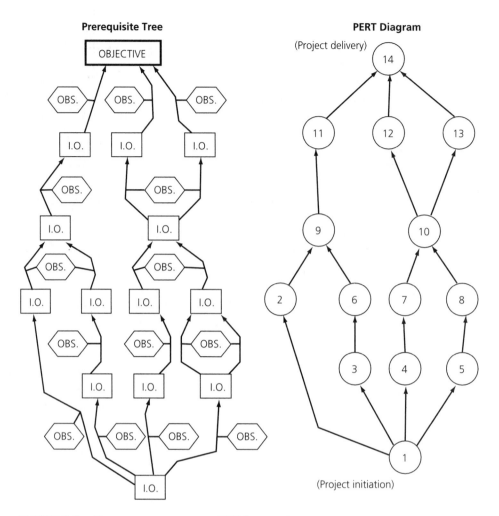

FIGURE 9.3 The prerequisite tree versus PERT diagram: A comparison.

of negative branches should be done at the point where the progress of future reality turns from positive or neutral to decidedly negative. Figure 9.4 replicates this part of AOL's hypothetical future reality tree.

In the original tree (bottom of the diagram), it's easy to see where the branch turns negative. There's nothing inherently bad about an increased demand on existing phone lines and modems, nor is the fact that AOL maintained only 260,000 phone lines and modems at the time necessarily bad. Also, having 8 million subscribers is definitely nothing to complain about. But the combination of those three produce the word *overwhelm* in block 207, and that's definitely not good! So the turning point in this part of the tree occurs in the arrows leading into block 207.

If we follow the procedure described in chapter 8 for trimming negative branches, we'd want to keep 207 from happening. This means we have to replace one of the causes leading into it with some new entity, something that doesn't exist now, something we have to *make* happen: an injection. That new injection, combined with the previously existing

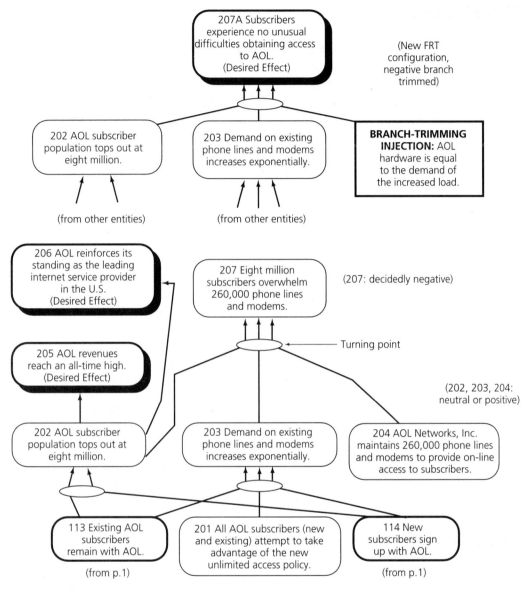

FIGURE 9.4 Future reality tree: "All circuits are busy. . . ."

effects of our new flat-rate policy (202 and 203), should give us a new 207 (we'll call it 207A) that might read:

Subscribers experience no unusual difficulties in obtaining access to AOL.

What might that injection be? Since we're working here at a decidedly *macro* level, the injection should be worded as a fairly complex condition of future reality:

AOL hardware is equal to the demand of the increased load.

In reviewing the causal relationship between this injection and the new effect (the upper part of Figure 9.4), we can see that the injection we've chosen effectively eliminates all the undesirable effects that might have proceeded from the original untrimmed negative branch. However, that injection is clearly no easy thing to do. Remember, AOL actually thought they had this one under control. It wasn't until everything began to unravel that it became clear the implementation hadn't been completely thought out. So how on earth will we make that happen?

Remember in chapter 7 we said that the purpose of the future reality tree was not implementation, but rather *verification.* People have a natural tendency to look at what needs to be done and become discouraged because it seems so complex, or they don't really know how to proceed. Some skeptics might even say, "We'll never be able to do that until pigs fly." At the future reality tree stage, this is a dangerous tendency, because it might drive us to discard truly breakthrough ideas. The *how* should be left to the implementation stage: the prerequisite and transition trees. If we can control our natural anxiety at the future reality tree stage and press on with the prerequisite tree, we might be surprised at how easily those pigs become airborne!

In the AOL example, our prerequisite tree will have as its objective this branch-trimming injection: "AOL hardware is equal to the demand of the increased load." *This* is the pig we have to make fly. Figure 9.5 shows how the AOL prerequisite tree might look.

Notice that the prerequisite tree culminates with the objective, but the numbers of the obstacles and intermediate objectives *start* there and work downward to the bottom of the tree. This reflects the way the tree was constructed (from top to bottom, much like a current reality tree). As you can also see, the entities that are shown in this tree don't by any means constitute everything there is to do in order for the objective to be attained. Only those conditions that haven't been achieved yet are shown, but they *are* in the sequence that they should take place.[‡‡]

The last intermediate objective (103) before the final objective (100) is the rate change implementation. This has to occur before the increased load mentioned in the objective happens. However, before (below) that, the tree branches into two parallel paths. The one on the left addresses the acquisition and installation of the new hardware. The branch on the right deals with the creation of the increased demand. The branches then converge again at blocks 200 and 201. These entities represent the contracting of the new hardware capability, which has to take place before either the advertising campaign or installation occurs. Following the tree down to its lowest level, we can see that it diverges again into two branches, one for the quantification of modems and the other for telephone lines.

[‡‡]Keep in mind that, like the future reality tree, this is strictly a notional prerequisite tree. None of the America OnLine® trees are offered as accurate depictions of reality. The only source of information consulted for any of these AOL trees was the mainstream media. America OnLine® was not asked to provide any information to comprise the content of the trees. Any divergence between reality and what is represented here is the author's responsibility alone. The trees are offered exclusively as examples of how the thinking process might have been used to create and implement change effectively the first time in a complex business situation.

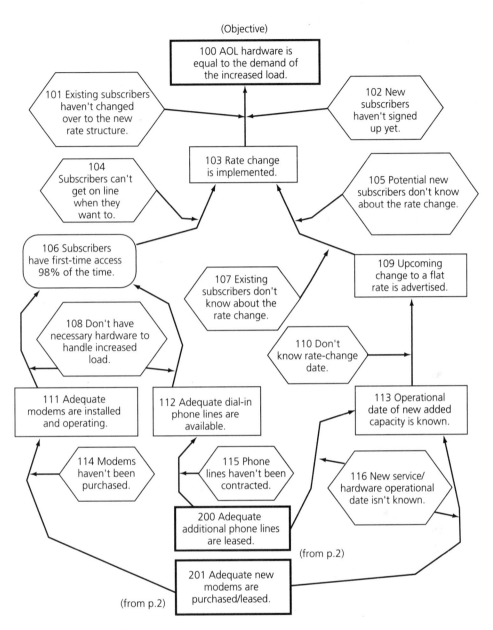

(Objective)

100 AOL hardware is equal to the demand of the increased load.

101 Existing subscribers haven't changed over to the new rate structure.

102 New subscribers haven't signed up yet.

103 Rate change is implemented.

104 Subscribers can't get on line when they want to.

105 Potential new subscribers don't know about the rate change.

106 Subscribers have first-time access 98% of the time.

107 Existing subscribers don't know about the rate change.

109 Upcoming change to a flat rate is advertised.

108 Don't have necessary hardware to handle increased load.

110 Don't know rate-change date.

111 Adequate modems are installed and operating.

112 Adequate dial-in phone lines are available.

113 Operational date of new added capacity is known.

114 Modems haven't been purchased.

115 Phone lines haven't been contracted.

116 New service/ hardware operational date isn't known.

200 Adequate additional phone lines are leased.

(from p.2)

201 Adequate new modems are purchased/leased.

(from p.2)

FIGURE 9.5.1 Handling the load of AOL's new flat rate.

Both of these branches again converge at block 211, the determination of access demand, which must occur before hardware can be contracted. This tree should probably continue several layers below 214 and 215, because this is a very uncertain area (and, not coincidentally, the one where AOL apparently miscalculated to begin with). Even though this example stops here, it could just as easily have been extended into the data gathering area. For example, market research firms could have been employed to survey users of local Internet service providers to establish an average on-line session time for other flat-rate services. However, this example adequately demonstrates the capability of the prerequisite tree.

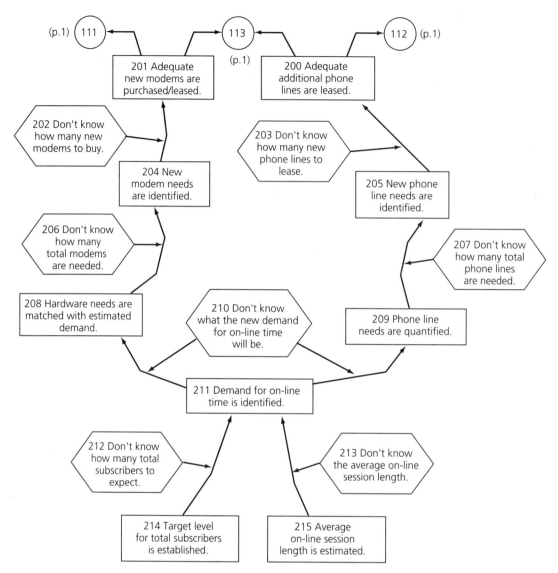

FIGURE 9.5.2 Handling the load of AOL's new flat rate.

BUILDING THE PREREQUISITE TREE

Now that we have a good idea of what the prerequisite tree is and how it works, it's time to see how a PRT is constructed. This is a tree that is usually easier to complete in a small group. While the other trees also can be built in groups, with the PRT it's actually advisable to do so. Why? Because in the same way that developing injections for a conflict resolution diagram or future reality tree is a creative effort, some degree of creativity is required to surface all the possible obstacles to implementation. Since each of us has our own blind spots, working in concert is very likely to produce a more complete list of obstacles more quickly.

Objective: AOL hardware is equal to the demand of the increased load.

Obstacles	Intermediate Objectives
1. Don't know how many modems are needed	1. Hardware needs are matched with estimated demand.
2. Potential new subscribers don't know about the rate change.	2. Upcoming change to a flat rate is advertised.
3. Don't know when the rate change will be effective.	3. Operational date of new capacity is known.
4. New service/hardware operational date not known.	4a. Adequate additional phone lines are leased. 4b. Adequate new modems are leased/purchased.
5. Don't know what the new demand for on-line time will be.	5. Demand for on-line time is identified.
6. Don't know how many new subscribers to expect.	6. Target level for new subscribers is estimated.
7. Modems haven't been purchased.	4b. Adequate new modems are leased/purchased.
8. New phone lines haven't been contracted.	4a. Adequate additional phone lines are leased.

☐ Obstacles are brainstormed, listed in random order

☐ Intermediate objectives 4a and 4b are used to overcome three different obstacles

FIGURE 9.6 Objective, obstacles, and intermediate objectives (list).

1. *Formulate the Objective.* The first step is to decide what the objective of the prerequisite tree is. This is usually the change we want to put into effect. In many cases, it will be an injection from the future reality tree. The PRT's objective should be stated as a *satisfied condition* (Figure 9.6). In other words, when reading the objective statement, it should sound like it's already a *fait accompli*. Recall the AOL objective from Figure 9.5: AOL hardware is equal to the demand of the increased load. That sounds like it's already happened, but what we're doing is verbalizing the way we'd like things to be when the PRT is completely executed. Corporate vision statements often use this kind of wording.

2. *Identify the Obstacles and Intermediate Objectives.* What will stand in the way of our achieving the objective? Begin brainstorming as many obstacles as you can possibly conceive. This is where the help of others can make the job easier. Write the obstacles on a piece of paper in a single column. When you've accounted for every obstacle you (and anyone else) can think of, start with the obstacle at the top of your list and brainstorm *ways around* the obstacle—intermediate objectives (Figure 9.6). Remember that obstacles need not be obliterated. You need only get around them somehow. For example, if the obstacle is a corporate policy, it might not be necessary to eliminate or change it. To execute the change, it might be enough to obtain a waiver or a more flexible interpretation.

Obstacle	Intermediate Objectives
4. New service/hardware operational date not known	4a. Adequate additional phone lines are leased 4b. Adequate new modems are leased/purchased

1. Does the primary obstacle really exist?   ANS: YES

2. Does the primary obstacle really block us from our objective?   ANS: YES

3. Does the intermediate objective really overcome the obstacle?   ANS: PART OF IT (4a only)

4. Is the intermediate objective alone enough to overcome the primary obstacle?
   ANS: NOT COMPLETELY (Need 4b)

5. Is there a secondary obstacle that might also block us from the same objective?   ANS: NO

6. Will the same intermediate objective overcome the secondary obstacle, or is another intermediate objective needed?   ANS: NOT APPLICABLE

FIGURE 9.7   Verifying obstacles and intermediate objectives.

Continue down the list of obstacles, developing intermediate objectives for each one, until you have at least one remedial action for each obstacle. Keep in mind that in some cases, the same intermediate objective might be used to overcome more than one obstacle. Conversely, it might require more than one intermediate objective to overcome a single obstacle. There's no set rule about this. Let your circumstances dictate the tactics here.

3. *Verify the Obstacles and Intermediate Objectives.* This is the step that ensures your prerequisite tree will be logically sound. You verify each obstacle-intermediate objective pair two ways:

- Does the obstacle *really* keep us from attaining our objective? What we're trying to do is to filter out *perceived* obstacles from real ones.

- Does the intermediate objective *really* overcome the obstacle? We want to be sure our chosen intermediate objective will be effective. It's at this point that we sometimes find that two intermediate objectives might be necessary (Figure 9.7).

The outcome of this step should be a scrubbed list of obstacles and intermediate objectives—the building blocks for our prerequisite tree.

4. *Begin Constructing the Prerequisite Tree.* At this step, we make the transition from a list to a graphical structure. The tree itself can be constructed using Post-it® notes on paper, or by computer with a flow-charting or graphic program. For simplicity, we'll assume that we're using Post-it® notes.

We transfer the obstacles and intermediate objectives from the master list we created in step 2 to Post-it® notes. We write the obstacles first. Then, as we write the intermediate objectives, we tack them onto the obstacles that they overcome. The obstacles and intermediate objectives can now be moved and rearranged as joined pairs (Figure 9.8).

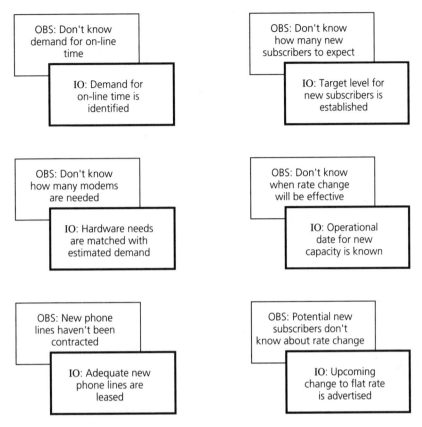

FIGURE 9.8 Transfer obstacles and intermediate objectives to Post-It® notes.

Once the Post-it® notes are completed and paired, begin assembling them into the proper time sequence. Based on their content, group the ones that need to be done later, and put them closer to the top of the paper. The ones that need to be done earlier should be put closer to the bottom of the page (Figure 9.9). For example, in the AOL prerequisite tree, the obstacles and intermediate objectives relating to the advertising and implementing of the rate change clearly occur *closer in time* to the increase in load upon the system hardware. That's why these obstacle-intermediate objective pairs are located nearer the top. The obstacles and intermediate objectives concerning data gathering and demand projections obviously happen near the beginning of the process, and hardware acquisition falls somewhere in between.

5. *Connect the Intermediate Objectives.* Now we look for obstacle-intermediate objective pairs that are clearly consecutive. Place the later pair above the earlier pair, and connect the intermediate objectives with an arrow pointing to the upper one. This part of the process is much like assembling a jigsaw puzzle.

It's also probable that sometime during this part of the effort, you'll find some obstacle-intermediate objective pairs that don't appear to connect directly with one another—something seems to be missing. Very

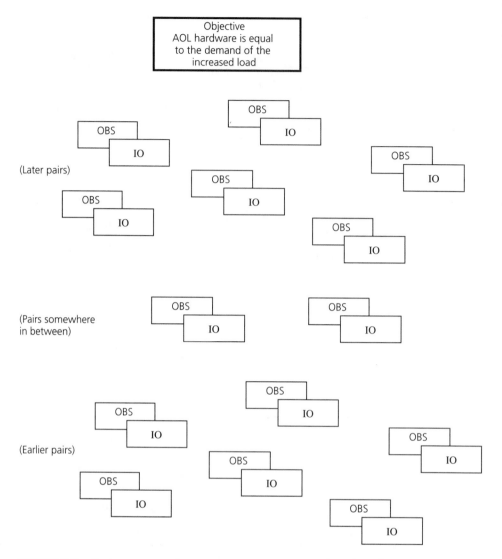

FIGURE 9.9 Begin to structure the prerequisite tree (group pairs chronologically).

often the reason is an obstacle that hasn't been previously identified intervenes. If this happens, this is when you'll normally discover it. Fill in such gaps as necessary, and connect all the intermediate objectives with one another, or with the final objective (Figure 9.10).

6. *Review the Completed Tree.* Once the final connections are made, review the tree in its entirety, looking for obvious gaps or erroneous connections. If you constructed the tree by yourself, now would be the time to have others with knowledge of the situation scrutinize it carefully for you.

At this point, your prerequisite tree is complete—temporarily. Very few implementations ever go exactly according to plan. Despite our best efforts, unforeseen contingencies still occur. However, they don't necessarily invalidate the work originally done on the prerequisite tree. As Will Rogers once observed, "Plans get you into things, but you've got to work your own way out."

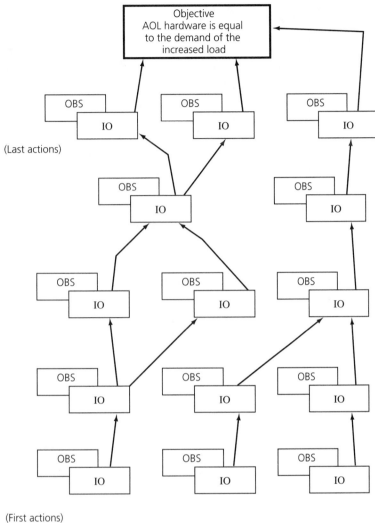

FIGURE 9.10 Finalize arrangement of pairs: Connect intermediate objectives.

If something unexpected occurs, review the prerequisite tree immediately. It should be apparent where in the chronological flow the intervening event has cropped up. It's relatively straightforward adding this obstacle, creating intermediate objectives to overcome it, and modifying the rest of the tree as required to accommodate the change. Remember, *all* of these logic trees are designed to be dynamic, not static. In the same way that business and strategic plans require periodic update, so, too, do logic trees as the environment changes. The original trees are built on the foundation of certain specific underlying assumptions (that's what the arrows represent). As reality changes in unexpected ways, assumptions are often voided or changed, generating a need to review the tree for continuing relevance. This is especially likely during implementation, but, fortunately, updating the prerequisite and transition trees is easy to do.

PROJECT PLANNING REVISITED

Recall that earlier we discussed the application of prerequisite trees to project planning. We saw that the PRT could be a valuable tool in determining the parallel and sequential activity network required to deliver a project in the shortest time feasible. Figure 9.11 shows how the completed prerequisite tree from Figure 9.10 might be converted into a PERT diagram. First, the obstacles are all dropped out, leaving just the intermediate objectives. Then, the intermediate objectives are all reviewed to be sure they're worded as completed tasks. They might even be numbered sequentially at this point. Finally, a project initiation block (sometimes referred to as authority to proceed) is added to the chart and connected to the first task completion nodes. The diagram is now ready for schedule calculation and resource allocation.

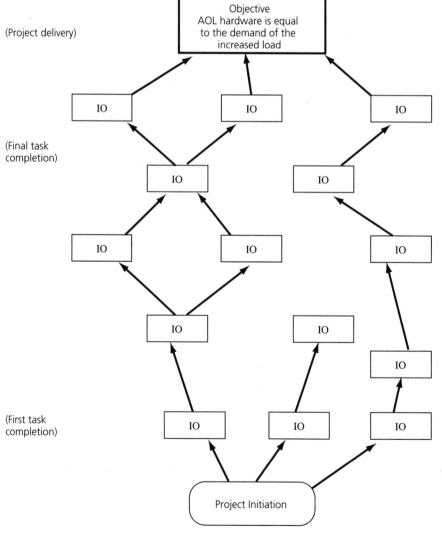

FIGURE 9.11 Prerequisite tree becomes project activity network: Converting to a PERT diagram.

HARRIS SEMICONDUCTOR — MOUNTAINTOP, PENNSYLVANIA[2]

In December 1988, Harris Semiconductor Corporation bought a semiconductor wafer fabrication plant from General Electric/RCA/Intersil. The Mountaintop, Pennsylvania, plant manufactured discrete power semiconductors for the automotive industry and power control applications. This is a commodity market, in which price is the prime determinant of competitive advantage.

By 1991, the Mountaintop plant was losing money and facing shutdown. Over the preceding 10 years, the work force had shrunk from 3,100 to 500. However, within five years the Mountaintop plant had successfully executed a $50 million turnaround, posting a five-fold increase in net income. Nearly all of that increase accrued between 1994 and 1996.

What happened to precipitate such a dramatic turnaround? The desperate situation in 1991 certainly played a part. Raymond Ford, director of Harris's plant operations in Mountaintop, observed that even marginal success at Mountaintop would probably have dampened any enthusiasm for change. Martin Wentz, Mountaintop's manager of training and organizational development, cites three factors in Harris's success at Mountaintop: an improved market, a team foundation emphasizing quality and customer focus, and manufacturing improvements that included total productive maintenance (TPM), synchronous flow manufacturing (SFM), and integrated yield management (IYM).

Beginning in 1992, the Mountaintop plant re-invented itself as a completely team-oriented operation. Using a variety of quality and production management tools including statistical process control, design of experiments, failure mode and effects analysis, synchronous flow manufacturing, and total productive maintenance, Mountaintop's people changed their entire business paradigm.

Among the most significant transformations was the replacement of a traditional cost accounting management approach with the throughput-based approach developed by Goldratt.

The throughput-based approach rejects traditional fascination with gross margins, standard costs, allocation of fixed costs, and consideration of inventory as an asset. It disavows the importance of local machine and labor efficiencies, and the primacy of reducing operating costs. Instead, it emphasizes the importance of increasing system throughput and focusing attention on the system constraint as a way of doing so. Embracing constraint management and throughput as a primary measure of success enabled Mountaintop to concentrate on the "critical few" success elements, rather than the "trivial many". Robert Murphy and Puneet Saxeena summed it up this way: "Cost world statements belong in the company's tax returns and SEC filings. They have little place in real-world production management."[3]

Harris Mountaintop discovered the fallacy of the "balanced line"- the idea that equalizing the capacity of every step in a manufacturing process improves the productivity of the entire line. (See discussion of Variation and Dependence, Ch. 1.) Most of the semiconductor industry still operates this way, however. Now all wafer fabrication facilities at Mountaintop operate on a "balanced flow" concept, rather than striving for high labor and machine efficiencies at every step of the process.

A critical key to Harris Semiconductor's success at Mountaintop was its senior management. The leaders at Mountaintop recognized the validity and value in synchronous flow manufacturing. They believed in it and spared no effort in communicating that belief to all Mountaintop employees, along with their commitment to make it work. They "walked their talk" through their embrace of throughput, inventory, and operating expense as the chosen measures of merit for operational decision making. Their visible support of SFM provided the psychological reinforcement needed to make the new paradigm succeed. William Levinson, staff engineer and industrial statistician at Mountaintop, credits the theory of constraints for the huge increases in overall plant productivity.

SUMMARY

Remember that the primary purpose of a prerequisite tree is to highlight the obstacles that stand in our way—the things we don't already have an answer to—and to help us develop ways to overcome them. In doing so, it naturally sequences the means of overcoming the obstacles in the order in which they must be done. In some situations, it might be possible to implement a plan directly from a prerequisite tree, but the circumstance would have to be so simple that we could hold everything else needed in our heads. Once we get past that point, however, it's advisable to have a step-by-step action plan. That's the function of the transition tree, which we'll see in chapter 10.

However, before we do that, it might be a good time to see how Vector One used a prerequisite tree to identify and sequence its obstacles to a major organizational culture shift. Appendix D has both the prerequisite tree and the story behind it.

If you encounter difficulty, don't change your decision to go. Change your direction to get there.

—Unknown

NOTES

1. Eliyahu M. Goldratt, *Critical Chain* (Great Barrington, Mass.: North River Press, 1997).
2. Levinson, William A. (Ed.), Leading the Way to Competitive Excellence: The Harris Mountaintop Case Study. Milwaukee, WI: ASQ Quality Press, 1998.
3. Ibid., Chapter 9, "Synchronous Flow Manufacturing".

Chapter 10
ASSIGNMENT AND ACCOUNTABILITY:
The Transition Tree

Action may not always bring happiness; but there is no happiness without action.

—Benjamin Disraeli

Great ideas are still only ideas. It's effective execution that turns them into solutions. In chapter 9, we saw the importance of identifying and overcoming obstacles to successful execution of breakthrough ideas. Clearing obstacles is certainly important, but it's not enough by itself to guarantee success. At best, the intermediate objectives we need to overcome obstacles are no more than milestones along the road to the objective. In between lie the details, and as we've all seen at one time or another, the devil is in the details.

TURNING IDEAS INTO RESULTS

At the strategic level, it's sufficient to establish what must be accomplished and when it should happen in a general way at the system level. A strategic plan usually addresses large-scale, broad systemic goals and objectives, such as opening a new market, completing a merger or acquisition, or developing a new product line. It might even establish a time horizon for these achievements and specify which divisions have overall responsibility for them. However, at the tactical level, considerably more detail is required. An effective tactical plan defines all of the component short-term tasks and activities, tells the players who's responsible for each one, allocates resources to do the job, establishes a completion schedule, and specifies the procedures, policies, and reporting requirements to be followed. Armed with such a plan, individuals or groups usually know what's expected of them, though they might not always have big-picture visibility or know precisely why they're doing what they are.

THE IMPORTANCE OF DETAILED EXECUTION PLANNING

Logically sound cause and effect is like a series of dominoes stood on end and spaced closely enough that one falling naturally knocks over the next. Several years ago, much public attention was focused on people who would set up thousands of such dominoes and make them drop in an impressive chain reaction. Such arrangements would branch and converge in creative patterns, often several times, between the first and last dominoes. Often it would take these dominoes 15 minutes or more to fall, but the chain reaction would be the inevitable result of tipping a single domino at the beginning.

Execution planning—whether for an organizational change or for a formal project—is much like setting up and knocking down such complex domino formations. A comprehensive, well-executed plan allows an executive to tip that first domino, then stand back and watch all the tasks and activities interact to complete the project. Unfortunately, the domino analogy isn't a completely faithful representation of the real world. The required tasks and activities might happen, but they're far from automatic. We know that the first step in successful execution is identifying and overcoming obstacles in the right order. The prerequisite tree helped us do that. It provided us a framework, or outline, from which to flesh out the details that make for a comprehensive—if possible, airtight—plan. The transition tree will help us develop that detail with cause-and-effect logic.

A word of caution is in order, however. While people have executed change from a transition tree alone, it's not always a smart idea to forego a formal, written plan, especially when the change or project is complex or requires coordination among many different parties. However, developing a transition tree can be a good start for a more detailed plan, and including transition trees as exhibits in the written plan can aid in communicating the plan to everyone involved.

TRANSITION TREE CONCEPT

The transition tree looks much like a future reality tree. In fact, it *is* a type of future reality tree, because what it contains is a series of causes and effects that don't exist yet (Figure 10.1). Like the future reality tree described in chapter 7, it contains injections that must be accomplished, but while the injections in a future reality tree are largely *conditions* that must be realized, those in a transition tree are all specific, discrete actions. In fact, once completed, all of the transition tree's cause and effect could be deleted except for these actions, and what would remain would be a step-by-step checklist of actions to be accomplished.

The distinction between a transition tree and a future reality tree is more than just cosmetic. Their purposes are significantly different. The purpose of the future reality tree is test and validation only—will the

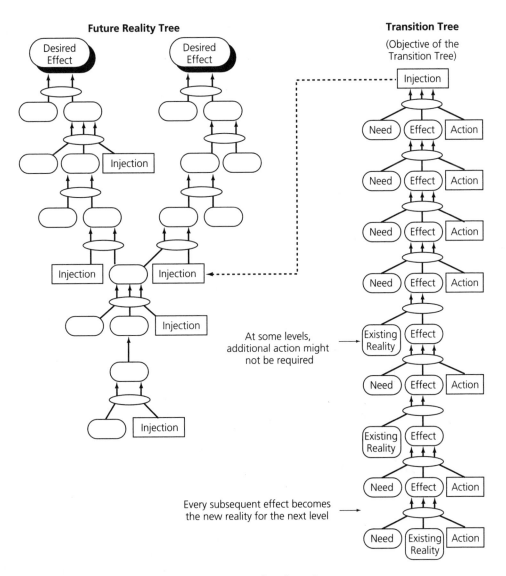

FIGURE 10.1   Future reality and transition trees: The relationship.

idea produce the results we desire, and will it create any adverse new effects that we can't stand? The purpose of the transition tree is step-by-step implementation. This is why the level of detail is so important in a transition tree; it can't be effective without it.

Notice something else implied in Figure 10.1. The future reality tree is made up of many injections that are conditions: outcomes of complex activities. The transition tree is the delineation of the details of those activities. While a future reality tree with very few injections (maybe only one or two) might be implemented with a single transition tree that incorporates all FRT injections as desired effects, more complex future reality trees might require a separate transition tree for each injection. In fact, constructing transition trees in this manner makes it easy to parcel out task responsibility to different people or departments for implementation.

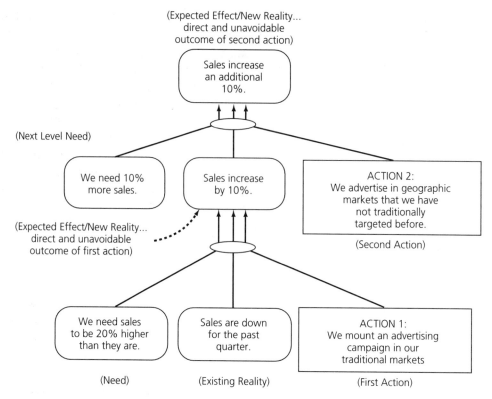

FIGURE 10.2 Structure of the transition tree.

STRUCTURE OF THE TRANSITION TREE

The transition tree is different from the future reality tree in another key respect. While the future reality tree is very much free-form in nature, the transition tree has a repetitive structure embedded within it. That structure is composed of four basic elements: a statement about existing reality, a statement of need, and a specific action, all of which lead to an expected effect‡ (Figure 10.2).

The causality represented by an existing state of affairs, a need for change, and an action to initiate that change must have logical sufficiency to produce the new expected effect:

> If we *need* sales to be 20 percent higher than they are, and sales *are down* for the past quarter, and we *mount an advertising campaign* in our traditional markets, then sales increase by 10 percent.

We needed a 20 percent increase and achieved only 10 percent, so we're closer to our objective, but not quite there yet. This expected effect becomes our new reality. Now we also have a new need for 10 percent

---

‡Some people use a fifth element: a rationale for the next-level need. That variant of the transition tree is omitted here because it adds complexity to the transition tree, which is not necessary in many cases.

more. This might prompt us to a second action: We advertise in geographic markets that we have not traditionally targeted before. These three second-level elements together should be sufficient to produce the additional 10 percent, possibly more. If it's not clear that they will, another action and need might be added, creating an added level of causality.

The basic structure (need, reality, and action leading to a new effect) basically repeats all the way up the tree until the objective is reached. Note that the first effect may not be the final objective, but it *does* constitute progress. Each layer of the transition tree brings us closer to the final objective—usually an injection in a future reality tree—until, at some point, a final action is sufficient to produce the FRT injection as an effect.

THE TRANSITION TREE AND THE PREREQUISITE TREE

The transition tree in Figure 10.1 looks like a stovepipe. It's simply a single vertical column of cause and effect. Not all situations are so straightforward that a single sequential line of dominoes will accurately portray what must be done. In many cases, execution actions branch and converge on their way to the objective.

Remember the prerequisite tree in Figure 9.3? It looked much like a project PERT diagram. Earlier we said that the intermediate objectives in a prerequisite tree could provide the framework of milestones that would make a transition tree easier to build. Since the prerequisite tree addresses only obstacles—things we don't already have—we must depend on the transition tree to integrate what we already *do* have with the intermediate objectives that overcome the obstacles. The detailed actions in the transition tree will also provide the step-by-step guidance needed to overcome the obstacles. Figure 10.3 shows how a transition tree might look if built upon a skeleton comprised of a prerequisite tree.

PERSUADING WHILE DIRECTING

One of the principal benefits of using a transition tree to execute a change is its capacity to explain *why* the directed actions are needed in the sequence they're presented. The increasingly complex work environments we see today require more capable, intelligent people who can think for themselves. The trend toward employee empowerment, in particular, gives rise to a work force that is no longer willing to blindly accept directions without seeing a need for them—and that need had better relate directly to the organization's goal and objectives.

Unfortunately, management doesn't always take time to explain the big picture to employees. Often, they just say, "Do this!" When there is little or no variation possible in the outcomes of following such directives,

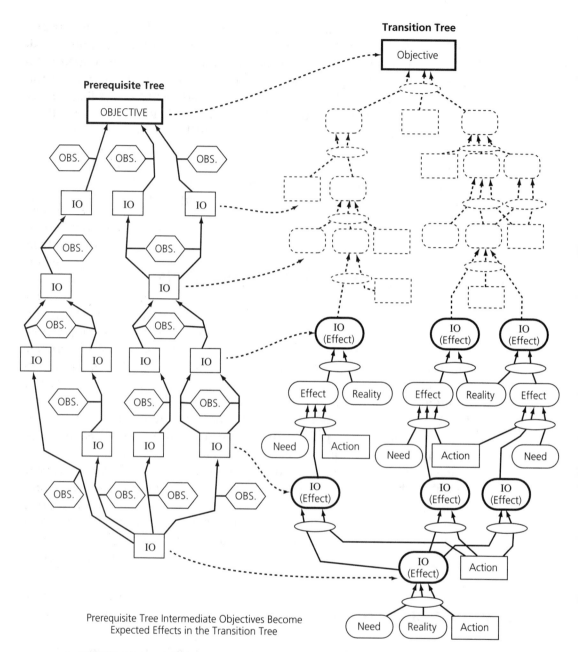

Prerequisite Tree Intermediate Objectives Become
Expected Effects in the Transition Tree

FIGURE 10.3 Prerequisite tree to transition tree: An evolution.

saying, "Do this!" is probably enough. But without an explanation of what the directed action is expected to achieve, employees aren't likely to detect results that don't fit management's expectations. Moreover, there's much less likelihood that employees will take any initiative on their own if they don't understand the ultimate objective.

The transition tree has such explanations embedded in it in a very logical form. The needs, realities, and effects that are parts of the tree explain what to do and why in a simple, progressive way. Employees then have no trouble following the rationale for why management is asking them to do certain things. And there at the top of the tree lies the objective of these actions, for all to see. If, halfway through the transition tree, the employees find the actions are no longer producing the expected effects, they're better able to act on their own to achieve the objective or to raise problems to management's attention. The transition tree is an excellent communication tool.

AMERICA ONLINE®

Let's look at a practical example of a transition tree. In chapter 9, we saw a prerequisite tree showing the obstacles America OnLine® needed to overcome to successfully implement a flat-rate pricing plan on the first attempt. Figure 10.4 shows how that prerequisite tree might be fleshed out into a transition tree.

Note that there are 15 discrete actions in this tree. Each one is combined with a statement about existing reality and a need to produce a new effect. Sometimes that effect is one of the intermediate objectives from the AOL prerequisite tree. Other times, it's merely an effect that gets people closer to their ultimate objective. As they read it from bottom to top, those who will be charged with executing this transition tree clearly see why the designated actions are the right ones at the right time. The existing realities, new effects, and needs provide the rationale for these actions. In other words, the tree communicates its own justification.

There is one feature missing from this transition tree (Figure 10.4) that should be included: *accountability.* None of the actions provide any indication about who should be responsible for them. It's usually a good idea to include this responsibility. Take the first two actions, for example. A better way to have phrased them might be:

> Action 1: *The executive steering committee establishes* an entry-level ceiling for total subscribers.
> Action 2: *The vice-president for marketing hires* a market-research firm to gather session length and frequency data from providers already on flat-rate billing.

This makes it unmistakably clear who's responsible for doing what.[‡‡]

Once the transition tree is completed, it may be retained intact for communicating the plan of attack to everyone on the team, or it can be reduced to a flowchart or checklist of the actions alone that individuals

---

[‡‡]Accountability was not included in the actions for this transition tree because it was created as a notional example of how AOL might have used the thinking process. Since the author has no personal knowledge of the internal structure and responsibilities at AOL, the accountability was omitted from this particular tree. However, whenever possible, the person or office responsible for the action should be identified in the action statement.

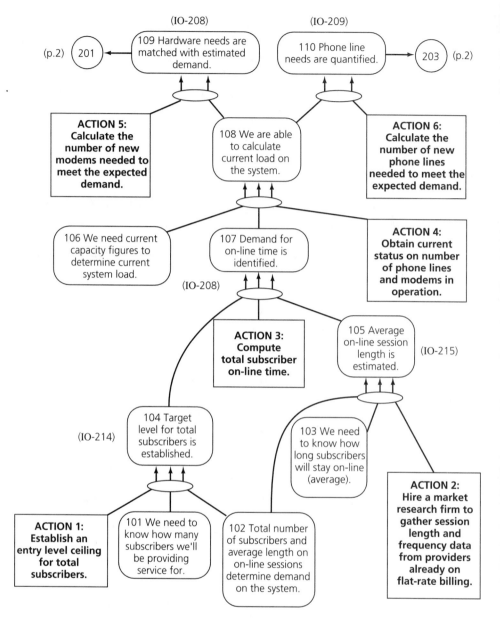

FIGURE 10.4.1 Transition tree: America OnLine® avoids disaster.

can refer to as they discharge their responsibilities. Completion deadlines can be assigned as well. Figure 10.5 shows an example of such a reduction, with some notional completion dates included. Whether these dates are realistic or not, let's assume that they are. AOL would have had to decide to initiate this change sometime in early February 1996. If it's already later than that, the changeover to the flat rate would have to be slipped commensurately in order to complete all the actions needed to avoid saturation of hardware capacity.

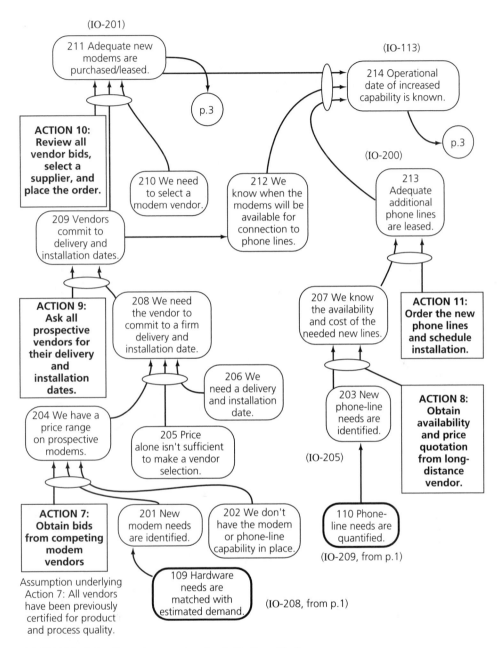

FIGURE 10.4.2 Transition tree: America OnLine® avoids disaster.

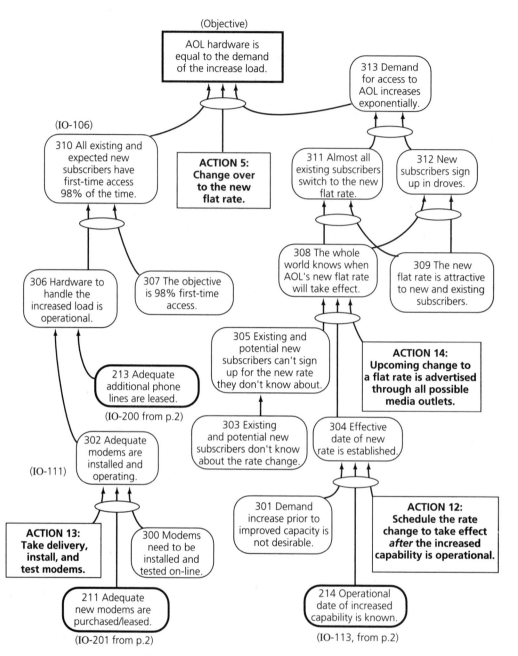

FIGURE 10.4.3 Transition tree: America OnLine® avoids disaster.

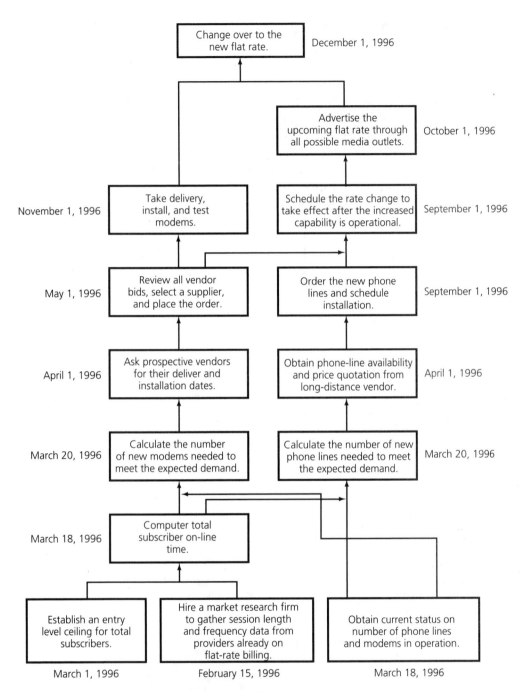

FIGURE 10.5 A transition tree reduced to a flow chart.

BUILDING THE TRANSITION TREE

Constructing a transition tree is similar to building a future reality tree. We start at the bottom, with an initial action, and build upward toward a predetermined objective. Along the way, we touch base at the intermediate objectives required to overcome obstacles. This means we begin the process with some elements already in place. The first step, then, is to put the objective and intermediate objectives from the prerequisite tree onto Post-it® notes and arrange them approximately in the same relative positions on a clean sheet of paper (Figure 10.6).

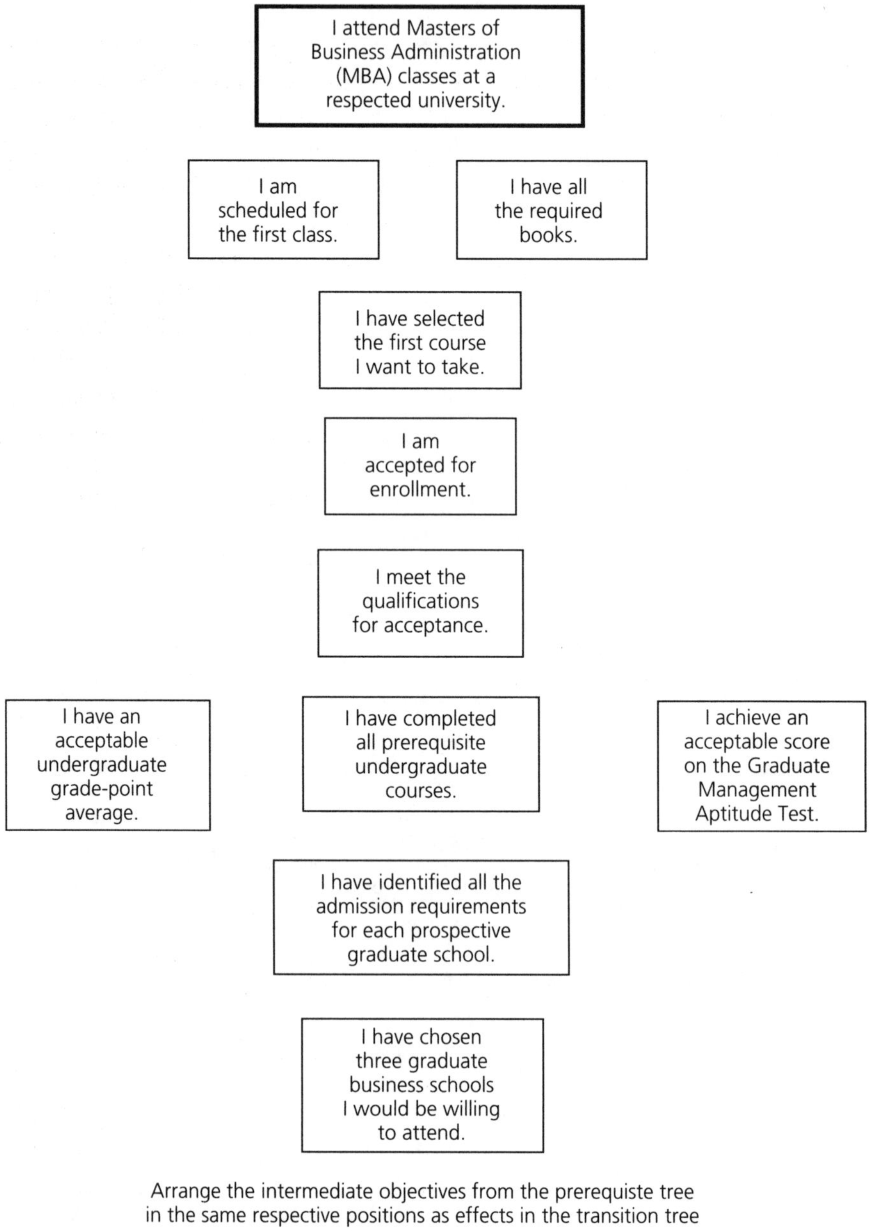

Arrange the intermediate objectives from the prerequiste tree
in the same respective positions as effects in the transition tree

FIGURE 10.6   Building a transition tree: Step 1.

The second step is to focus exclusively on the lowermost intermediate objective and determine what need, reality, and action would be necessary to produce that intermediate objective as an effect. Remember that this will be a cause-effect connection, and it must satisfy all of the categories of legitimate reservation (Figure 10.7).

The third step is to evaluate this proposed action: are we able to initiate it right now, or must some other conditions be in place first? If there are obvious preliminary steps we must take *before* we can accomplish the action we've put on paper, these steps must be appended *in the correct sequence* below it (Figure 10.8). Our transition tree must begin with a straightforward action that we already know how—or are able—to do.

Once we are certain that we have really identified the very bottom of the transition tree (the first, simplest level of causality), we can continue building upward from the effect that constitutes the first intermediate objective to the prerequisite tree. We keep building toward successive intermediate objectives until the last logical connection with the transition tree's ultimate objective is made.

From here on, there is no hard-and-fast rule about how many layers of cause and effect might lie between intermediate objectives. There could be as few as one, or very many. Also, it's not absolutely necessary that each layer include an action. Sometimes several layers of cause and effect can unfold on their own without additional effort on our part. The only criteria for each subsequent effect are that (1) each one brings us closer to the ultimate objective than the previous one and (2) all causal connections represent the very next domino in line. There is no restriction

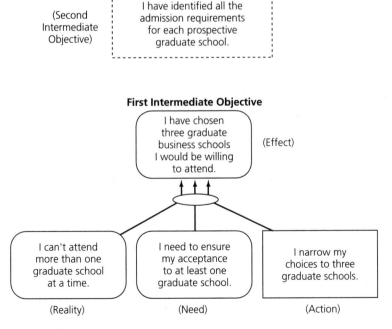

FIGURE 10.7 Building a transition tree: Step 2.

on how many times the tree might diverge into different branches and converge again. The nature of the circumstances will determine this.

When completed, our ideal transition tree will be so logically sound that no further explanation is necessary; anyone who reads it will immediately see the sense in the action sequence and the reasons why each action is necessary. A transition tree that achieves this ideal is a superior instrument of communication and persuasion. Figure 10.9 shows the

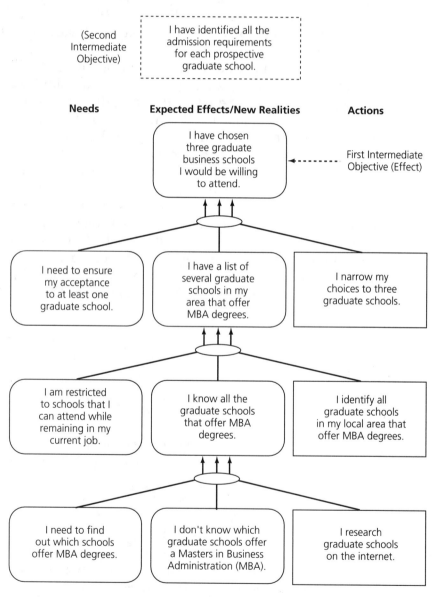

FIGURE 10.8 Building a transition tree: Step 3.

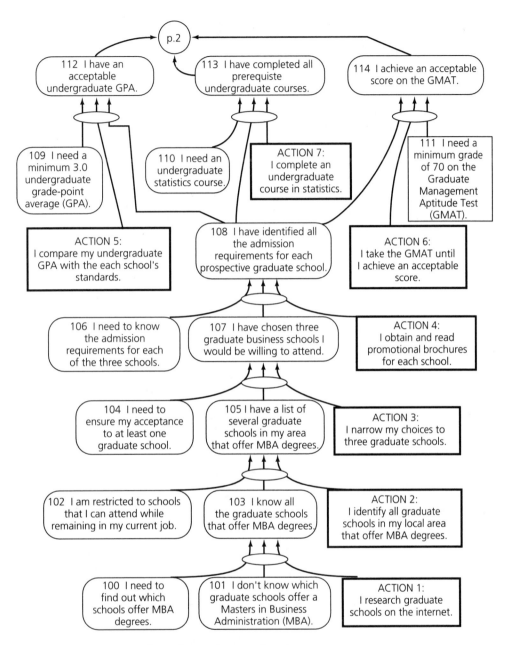

FIGURE 10.9.1 Completing the transition tree: Step 4.

completion of the example begun in Figure 10.6. Notice that the actions, needs, and effects have all been numbered for quick reference.

Remember that a complex change will usually require a future reality tree with many injections. It's possible that many, if not all, of these injections will require transition trees for effective execution. So while we might have only one future reality tree, many transition trees could be required to execute it. Sounds like too much trouble? Compare it to the cost of failure, in terms of both money and squandered management

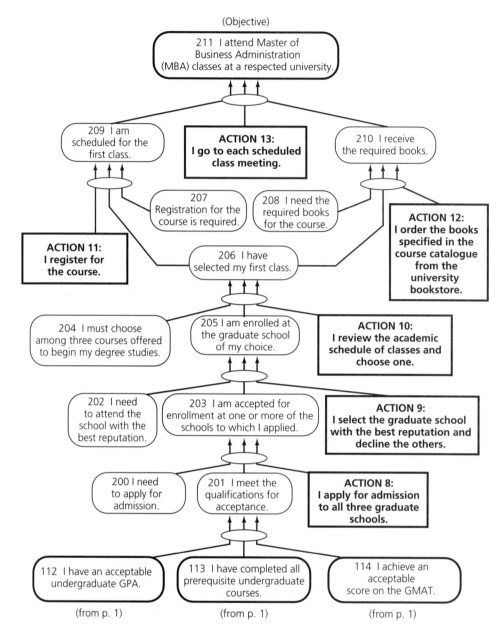

FIGURE 10.9.2 Completing the transition tree: Step 4.

credibility. As with anything newly learned, we develop skill through repetition. As our skill improves, we become both better and faster at the task—that's the learning-curve phenomenon (Figure 10.10). After you practice building these trees a few times, you'll find that it doesn't really take very long to assemble a complete set.

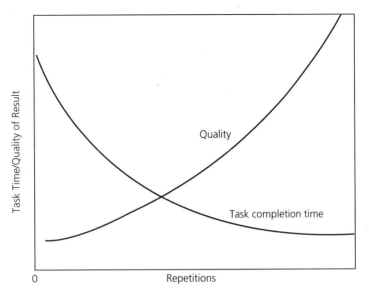

As the number of repetitions increase, the quality of results
increases, and the completion time decreases

FIGURE 10.10 The learning curve.

SUMMARY

We've seen now how all six components of the thinking process work together, or independently, to help us manage the complexity of change in an uncertain, largely qualitative world.

The transition tree—how to *conclude* change—is the culmination of everything that preceded it:

- Current reality tree (*what* to change)
- Conflict resolution diagram (what to change *to*)
- Future reality tree (what to change *to*)
- Negative branch (what to *avoid*)
- Prerequisite tree (how to *begin* the change)

In chapter 11, we'll see how the thinking process might be used to address the human issues associated with change. However, before going on to the next chapter, now would be a good time to review the progress of Vector One's management in completing their transition tree.

Deliberation is the work of many men; action of one alone.
—Charles DeGaulle

Chapter 11
THE HUMAN SIDE OF LOGIC

> *The most effective leaders are those who satisfy the psychological needs of their followers.*
>
> *—David Ogilvy*

We've navigated through all five logic trees now: current reality tree, conflict resolution diagram, future reality tree (with negative branch), prerequisite tree, and transition tree. These are the logical tools that constitute the thinking process that Goldratt created. Their utility in logical analysis and solution of complex system problems is great indeed, primarily because of their unique capability to treat organizations as systems, not just a collection of discrete processes.

In chapter 4, we discussed Deming's concept of *profound knowledge.*[1] Deming suggested that real understanding of any system depended on how much we knew about four basic interdependent disciplines: understanding of systems, the theory of knowledge, psychology, and variation. The theory of constraints and the logical thinking process directly improve our understanding in three of these four areas.

UNDERSTANDING SYSTEMS

Because TOC is based on the interactive nature of systems—a holistic view—it helps us focus on the interfaces, or linkages, between system components, rather than on the components alone. This naturally forces us to consider organizational success as a system function, not an additive process function. The thinking process is currently the only set of tools that performs two functions: (1) graphically depicts the interactions and interdependencies of the entire system, not just adjacent parts, and (2) provides the rigor of the categories of legitimate reservation to prove the logic in each cause-effect connection. As we saw in chapter 4, good cause-effect logic applied to subject matter knowledge moves us well along the continuum toward certainty. Decisions based on logic are consistently better, over the long haul, than those based on gut feeling alone.

THEORY OF KNOWLEDGE

How do we know *what* we know? The field of epistemology is dedicated to answering this question. Clearly, information is a key element. If we don't have an information base of facts or empirical data, we might as well be firing blank cartridges from a gun. But information is no more than the powder and the bullet in this analogy. To turn these into a projectile requires a fully functioning gun to act on the powder and bullet. The principles of TOC and the thinking process provide the gun—the systemic structure, principles, and logic to turn mere information into replicable knowledge. It is knowledge, not information that empowers us to

- Know when a particular set of rules applies and when it doesn't
- Recognize when we're seeing merely correlation, rather than true cause and effect
- Understand the difference between indications of problems and their underlying root causes
- Make rational decisions, confident of the outcome
- Derive our own effective rules of thumb, rather than depending on some rote repetition of a cookbook nature

Philip R. Elder once made the observation that the TOC thinking process "is like a giant pegboard upon which we can hang, arrange, and connect knowledge."[†] This is an excellent analogy. The thinking process permits us to arrange our discrete pieces of knowledge in a way that enables us to see the interactions and logical connections—what causes what. This capability increases the power of our knowledge dramatically.

UNDERSTANDING PSYCHOLOGY

People are the most difficult element of any system for management to deal with. Because of a human's capacity for independent thought and action, the door is open to wide variability in system performance. Sometimes people seem to be rational, other times not. Sometimes they seem emotional, other times logical. Nobody is completely consistent and predictable all the time. In the old *Star Trek* television series, Mr. Spock continually complained that humans weren't logical. What he meant was that human *behavior* wasn't logical.

But Spock was wrong. Human behavior is eminently logical. It follows repetitive patterns, and some prediction of behavior is, in fact, possible. If it were not, the psychologists and psychiatrists of the world would be

---

[†]In a conversation with the author, November 1995.

out of business. The difference between the actual logic of human behavior and its frequent illogical manifestation lies not with the human doing the behaving, but with our *understanding of psychology*. In the same way that some fields of scientific research are poorly understood (that is, still developing), so, too, is human psychology a continually evolving and maturing discipline. Engineers and physicists might say that the study of human behavior isn't yet developed enough to be considered a science, but it is certainly a mature enough field that certain rules and principles can be inferred and consistently applied in a large majority of circumstances. Much of the inaccuracy inherent in predicting human behavior is undoubtedly due to our inability to completely identify all the relevant variables in any given situation.

Since we might never be able to identify all the variables, psychology may never achieve the level of scientific precision of mathematics or physics. However, that doesn't mean that we can't apply some logical rigor to the area of human behavior, especially in organizations. Anyone who has ever been in a group work environment for any length of time would probably disagree with Spock: human behavior *is* logical to a significant degree. That it may appear illogical is more the result of our failure to understand the psychology behind it. The logical thinking process can be a particularly useful tool in managing the unmanageable—the human element—as we'll see in a moment.

By now it's relatively obvious that the only element of Deming's profound knowledge that we haven't yet addressed is variation. While the principles and tools of TOC—the *drum-buffer-rope* solution for production control, for example—can help deal *implicitly* with variation (by working around it), they aren't designed to address variation directly. The thinking process doesn't deal *explicitly* with variation, however it *can* point out the need to apply other disciplines, such as statistical sampling and statistical process control.

BREAKING CONSTRAINTS, ORGANIZATIONAL CHANGE, AND HUMAN BEHAVIOR

In chapter 1, we talked about systems theory and application, and Figure 1.1 provided a simple view of the mechanics of a complex system interacting with its environment. But there's another, more conceptual system architecture. Virtually all business systems can be characterized as a pie with three major slices[2] (Figure 11.1).

One slice of the pie is *activity*. This encompasses technology: the hardware, facilities, equipment, the nature of the task, and the interactions among these elements as they perform well-defined functions in pursuit of the system's goal. The second slice is *human factors*. This includes the physical, mental, and psychological capabilities and limitations of the people who are part of the system. A third slice might be called *context*,

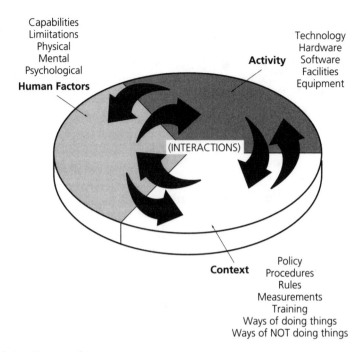

Capabilities
Limiitations
Physical
Mental
Psychological
Human Factors

Activity

Technology
Hardware
Software
Facilities
Equipment

(INTERACTIONS)

Context

Policy
Procedures
Rules
Measurements
Training
Ways of doing things
Ways of NOT doing things

FIGURE 11.1 System architecture.

which is another way of saying the policy, procedures, training, measures of success, or other rules that are established (or not) to regulate the interaction between the other two slices. The individual slices will differ in magnitude within different organizations, but these elements are common to all business systems, whether for-profit or not.

Undesirable effects—those indications that the system's goal or necessary conditions are not being satisfied—can appear in any of these slices. The real system constraint can lie in any one of these areas as well, even if it shows itself through undesirable effects that seem to be in another. If we consider the term *policy* to include traditional ways of doing—or not doing—things, even so-called external constraints (a market constraint, for example) are really rooted *inside* the system, or in our decisions (or lack thereof) to do business in a certain way.

FEASIBILITY OF CHANGE

Our success in reengineering our systems is a function of the *feasibility* of the change we want to make, and feasibility is also three-dimensional.[3] For a change to have a realistic probability of success, it must satisfy three requirements: it must be (1) *technically* feasible, (2) *economically* feasible, and (3) *politically* feasible. A change is technically feasible if we have the skills, hardware, and knowledge to do a job. It's economically feasible if we have the financial resources needed. Finally, it's politically feasible if we can persuade all the *people* whose cooperation is required to go along with

. . . and the possible feasibility obstacles are . . .

If the system problem lies in . . .	Technical (WHAT to change? What to change TO?)	Economic (WHAT to change? What to change TO?)	Political (WHAT to change? What to change TO?)
Activity	MEDIUM (Notes 1,2)	HIGH (Notes 1,2)	HIGH
Context	HIGH	HIGH (Notes 3)	HIGH
Human Factors	HIGH	HIGH	HIGH

. . . then the utility of the thinking process is . . .

Note 1: Other useful TOC tool: "Drum-Buffer-Rope" production control
Note 2: Other useful TOC tool: "Critical Chain" project scheduling
Note 3: Other useful TOC tool: Constraint (throughput) accounting

FIGURE 11.2 Applicability of the thinking process to organizational change.

it. Failure to meet any one of these criteria is enough to sink an idea. Combining the conceptual slices of the system pie with the feasibility criteria, we come up with a cross-interaction matrix that looks like Figure 11.2.

The theory of constraints, and especially the thinking process, functions very well in the technical and economic aspects of problem solving in the *activity* and *context* (policy) slices. It's particularly good for identifying constraints in these areas and constructing logical ideas to break them. But when logical ideas depend upon people for implementation—that is, to turn these ideas into working solutions—problems in political feasibility begin to emerge:

• Individual behavior patterns
• Satisfying personal needs
• Motivating people to active cooperation
• Internal politics
• Emotional resistance

These are just a few of the possible behavioral issues that could derail a good idea, or at least deflate the great expectations for it. What's not commonly realized, however, is that the thinking process can be equally valuable in the *human factors* sector, too, particularly in the area of psychology and human behavior.

Consider the difficulty involved in health-care reform in the United States. Coming up with the ideas for policy changes is the easy part.

Selling the ideas to the U.S. Congress and the public is another story entirely. The ideas might have been completely logical, but their originators did not sufficiently consider how to overcome the emotional and political resistance to the change. As a result, the Medicare reform was dead on arrival in the U.S. Senate and House of Representatives. Could this scenario have been different? Possibly.

A comprehensive current reality tree, conflict resolution diagram, and future reality tree might have clearly identified the root causes of the existing system's failure and provided the blueprint for one that would work—in other words, it would be technically and economically feasible. Negative branches and prerequisite trees could have located and cleared the political and emotional land mines in the road, and transition trees could have laid out the political persuasion steps for implementation as well as the technical and economic ones.

THE LOGIC BEHIND RESISTANCE TO CHANGE

It's not sufficient to construct a technically and economically sound plan for breaking a system constraint. Because the people within an organization are usually the difference between success and failure, the human factor, whether you call it emotional, political, or behavioral, must also be addressed in *any* solution implementation.

Effective organizational improvement requires five elements (Figure 11.3):

- Subject matter knowledge of the system (including technical, economic, and political information)
- The authority to initiate or influence change
- A methodology for defining, designing, and implementing the change
- A desire to see the system improved
- A willingness to accept responsibility for action

Absence of any one of these elements is enough to render any change effort dead in the water. The first three factors reside in the realm of technical feasibility. The last two are unquestionably psychological factors and are inextricably interwoven with political feasibility.

People who have applied the thinking process have traditionally used it to define the problem, design the change, and lay out the technical and economic implementation. But it can also be used to overcome resistance, instill the desire to see the change succeed, and motivate accountability for action.

What might happen if we were to overlay the thinking process—like a template—on top of a comprehensive understanding of organizational psychology? The result would be a powerful tool for addressing the

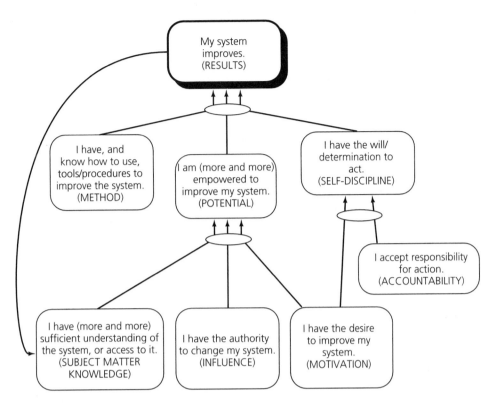

FIGURE 11.3 The route to continuous improvement.

political feasibility of the changes needed to break system constraints. What would this combination look like? Figure 11.4 is a type of current reality tree. While it doesn't address a specific situation, it does show how a known body of psychological knowledge might be arranged to explain the unfavorable outcomes of change efforts. Notice that the root causes in this tree are the change agent's failure to consider the status, authority, security, and satisfaction needs of the people whose cooperation is critical to successful execution. These are psychological needs that can't be satisfied by financial compensation alone.[4‡‡]

Figure 11.4 effectively illustrates the pegboard concept of the thinking process. By hanging known elements of organizational psychology on the thinking process pegboard, we see a more complete picture of our knowledge about resistance to change. Our attention is also drawn immediately to those root causes that must be addressed if our change is to succeed. In terms of Deming's profound knowledge concept, this integration of both psychology *and* the theory of knowledge is most powerful indeed.

---

‡‡The satisfaction of psychological needs is a more powerful motivator of human behavior for many people than the satisfaction of material needs. What person in his or her right mind, for example, would seek the presidency of the United States because of the pay? There isn't enough money in it to compensate most qualified people for the stress they would have to endure in attaining the job and discharging the duties. Clearly, presidential contenders are in the game to satisfy other (psychological) needs.

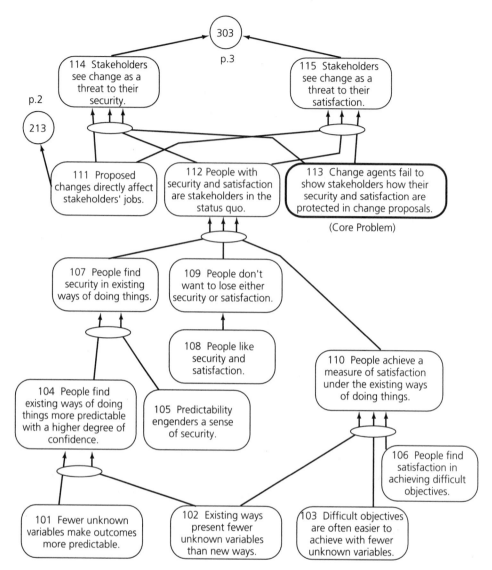

FIGURE 11.4.1 Why stakeholders resist change.

Perhaps the most revealing thing about this tree is that even if we fore-close all stated objections (the excuses shown at the top of Figure 11.4.3) based on logical grounds, all we've done is lull ourselves into a false sense of security, thinking that we've taken care of all the obstacles in our path. We've set ourselves up for a potentially embarrassing—and possi-bly very public—fall later. In fact, all we've done is eliminate the wiggle room for people whose resistance is emotional, but whose circumstances make it politically incorrect to voice objections on that basis. So what do those people do? They quietly resist, and as Gandhi so clearly demon-strated, passive resistance can be a most powerful weapon.

Figure 11.5 is a continuation of the tree begun in Figure 11.4. It begins with the undesirable effect from the first current reality tree. This sec-p.3

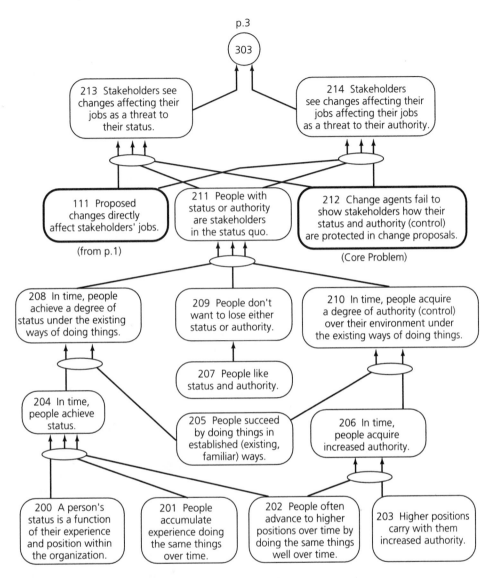

FIGURE 11.4.2 Why stakeholders resist change.

ond tree presumes that the change agents have used this powerful methodology called the thinking process to analyze the system, determine the constraint, and construct a logical solution that is technically and economically feasible. In doing so, they have deliberately developed persuasive responses to any technical or economic objections that anyone could raise. But they've forgotten something important—something *critical* to success. They never considered the political feasibility of the proposal. And so their air tight, logical case for technical and economic feasibility has unwittingly boxed in resisters, whose only refuge now is an emotional objection.

From Figure 11.4, we know that some important players in the execution of the change have serious reservations about it because the

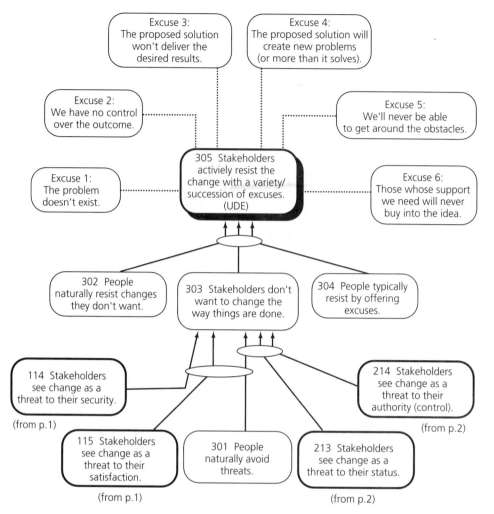

FIGURE 11.4.3 Why stakeholders resist change.

change will have a negative impact on them personally. But it's clearly not good form for them to openly cite personal loss as a reason for objecting to a change that demonstrably benefits the whole organization. Consequently, as the change agents methodically shoot down all the technical objections to the plan, they leave those who will suffer under the change no recourse but to quietly torpedo the improvement effort through passive resistance.

USING THE THINKING PROCESS TO CREATE POLITICAL FEASIBILITY

Figures 11.4 and 11.5 are clearly bad news, but aren't most current reality trees? Yet buried in the bad news is the seed of possible good news later on—the core problem we can attack. In this case, the core problem is clearly identified in Figure 11.4: entities 113/212:

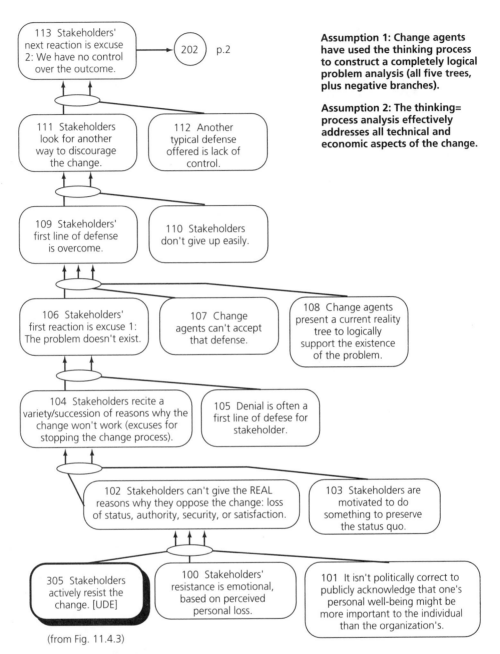

FIGURE 11.5.1 How efforts to force change unfold.

Change agents fail to show stakeholders how their security, satisfaction, status, and authority are protected in change proposals.

We can use the same thinking process that created the change proposal in the first place to solve this political feasibility problem as well.

There might be a potential disaster brewing, but at least we have a good idea where the root of the problem lies. Notice that if we *reverse* the content of entities 113 and 212, none of the subsequent dominoes in either Figure 11.4 or 11.5 fall. The undesirable effects never happen.

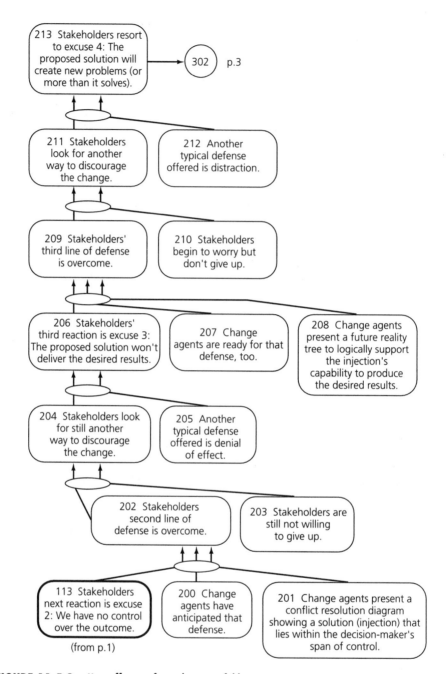

213 Stakeholders resort to excuse 4: The proposed solution will create new problems (or more than it solves).

302   p.3

211 Stakeholders look for another way to discourage the change.

212 Another typical defense offered is distraction.

209 Stakeholders' third line of defense is overcome.

210 Stakeholders begin to worry but don't give up.

206 Stakeholders' third reaction is excuse 3: The proposed solution won't deliver the desired results.

207 Change agents are ready for that defense, too.

208 Change agents present a future reality tree to logically support the injection's capability to produce the desired results.

204 Stakeholders look for still another way to discourage the change.

205 Another typical defense offered is denial of effect.

202 Stakeholders second line of defense is overcome.

203 Stakeholders are still not willing to give up.

113 Stakeholders next reaction is excuse 2: We have no control over the outcome.

200 Change agents have anticipated that defense.

201 Change agents present a conflict resolution diagram showing a solution (injection) that lies within the decision-maker's span of control.

(from p.1)

FIGURE 11.5.2   How efforts to force change unfold.

All we have to do is ensure the security, satisfaction, status, and authority of those whose cooperation we need, and we'll stand a much better chance that those people will support the change. In some situations, all we need do is relieve their concern enough so that their attention turns from their own agenda to the organization's. (And let's not fool ourselves—very few people's personal agendas coincide with the organization's!)

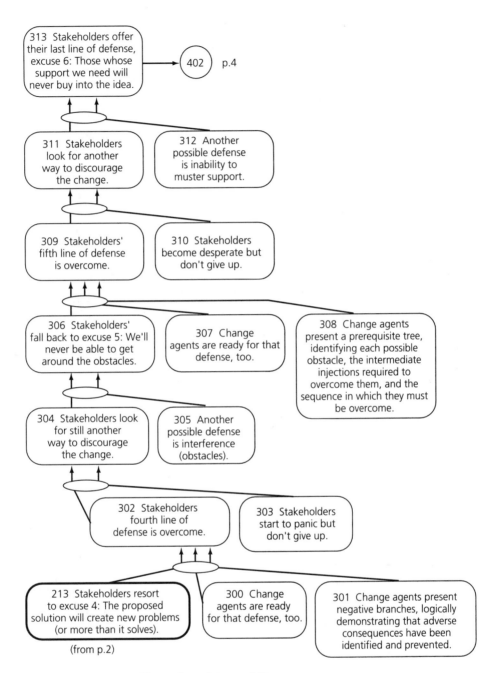

FIGURE 11.5.3 How efforts to force change unfold.

A STRATEGY FOR SELLING THE IDEA OF CHANGE

Now that we have the core problem identified, what do we do next? Normally, we'd see if there was a conflict preventing us from satisfying the psychological needs of the key stakeholders. Then we'd break that conflict with an injection, and test the injection with a future reality tree and negative branches. Lastly, we'd execute that injection with a prerequisite

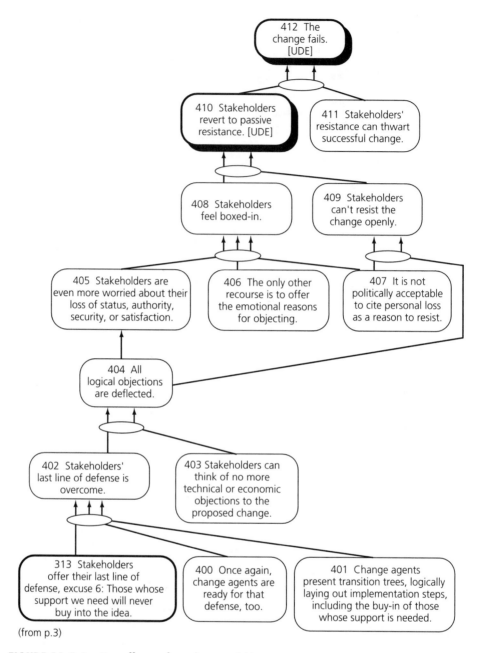

(from p.3)

FIGURE 11.5.4 How efforts to force change unfold.

or transition tree. However, for the purposes of this discussion, let's assume there is no conflict preventing us from accommodating stakeholders psychological needs. Let's assume that doing so will, in fact, elicit their cooperation, so no conflict diagram or future reality tree are needed at this level of the problem.

Instead, let's focus on how we might go about making the change proposal more palatable to the stakeholders. We need a strategy. As a starting point, we might try answering the question, "Whose cooperation is critical to our success?" This will help us define the power groups or influence centers that can make or break the idea. Avoid the temptation to answer, "Everybody's cooperation is critical!" This is rarely true. While realizing the idea's full potential might truly require everyone's motivated effort, a threshold level of success usually demands satisfying only a limited number of necessary conditions, and those conditions are usually under the control or influence of key people or departments.

Goldratt has classified organizational players into one of three categories:[5]

- Outside people: those whose role is so limited as to not affect, or be affected by, the change very much.
- Intimately involved people: those for whom the change poses a significant difference in the way business is done. These are people who must revise the way they do their jobs for the idea to succeed. They are also those who might be negatively affected by it (more work load, new tasks to learn, and so forth).
- Directly responsible people: those who will have responsibility and accountability for the organizational functions in which the changes must take place. Usually, these are department heads, managers, or executives with nearly unilateral authority over their areas. They are also likely to be the bosses of the intimately involved people.

For our purposes, we'll focus primarily on the directly responsible and intimately involved people. If we can identify who these are in our environment, we'll have a narrower range upon which to focus.

The second question to answer is, "Among the directly responsible and intimately involved people, who might resist this idea?" We need to know, specifically, which people or departments might not like our idea. In essence, we're trying to determine whose ox will be gored as a result of the change. Figure 11.6 provides a list of leading questions that can help us determine the answer.

The next step is to identify the *indications* of resistance. Figure 11.4 shows the various objections people might interpose. All of these excuses appear to be technical in nature, except for the last one (Those whose support we need will never buy in). Having already determined *who* might resist, these indicators should be easier to anticipate.

1. Who stands to LOSE from the change?
2. Who stands to GAIN from the change?
3. Whose STATUS might change?
4. Whose AUTHORITY might be redefined?
5. Whose SECURITY might be threatened?
6. Whose SATISFACTION might be compromised?

FIGURE 11.6   *Who might resist the change?*

The third step is to determine the real reasons for the objections. We must not overlook the possibility that someone's objection is truly based on the conviction that the idea is not technically or economically feasible. It would be stupid to ignore legitimate reservations only because we suspect deeper hidden personal motives. When one of the first five excuses is raised, we must make a concerted effort to reevaluate our thinking and even solicit suggestions that might improve the technical or economic feasibility of the idea. The categories of legitimate reservation (chapter 4) are invaluable in objectively assessing our own—and others'—logic.

At the same time, we must also be open to the idea that the technical objection might be a smokescreen for a more personal reason to resist. If we're reasonably sure that this is the case, we must address the underlying, unspoken reasons for resistance (status, authority, security, or satisfaction). In many instances, this might require personal knowledge of the values, ethics, personality, and leadership style of the person who might resist. Don't be reluctant to seek out this information. There are undoubtedly people in the organization who can provide insight on the motivations of directly responsible and intimately involved people. Be aware, however, that such inquiries themselves can be highly sensitive, so conduct your information search with tact and caution.

Once we're reasonably confident of the real reasons why people might resist the idea, we can set about turning that resistance into cooperation and incorporating the actions we'll need to take into the original plan.

THE POLITICAL FEASIBILITY CONFLICT

Turning resistance into cooperation is quintessential conflict resolution, so the logical next step is to build a conflict resolution diagram around the real resistance issue. Figure 11.7 shows a typical template for such a diagram. Obviously, the specific content of each of the boxes will vary depending on the circumstances. However, the conflicting prerequisites are fairly immutable: change versus don't change. The top requirement is a statement of the desired effects that the change is expected to realize. The bottom requirement is the personal psychological need the stakeholder is trying to protect by resisting the change. The objective is the well-being of all.

The assumptions underlying the arrows between the prerequisites and the requirements are the keys to breaking the conflict. By identifying invalid assumptions that apply to each specific conflict, we can come up with an injection that will enable us to make precisely focused modifications to the original idea. These modifications will preserve the original purpose of the change, but accommodate the psychological needs of the stakeholder as well—a true win-win resolution. What might such an injection look like?

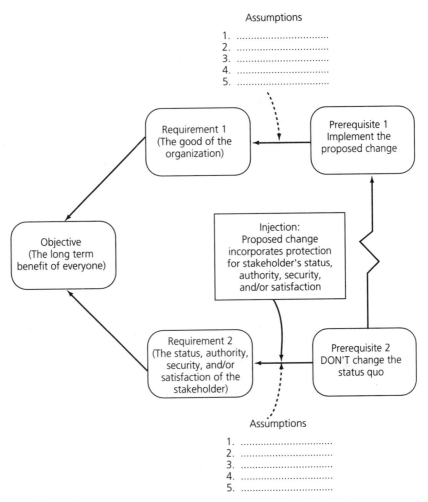

Assumptions

1. ....
2. ....
3. ....
4. ....
5. ....

Requirement 1
(The good of the
organization)

Prerequisite 1
Implement the
proposed change

Objective
(The long term
benefit of everyone)

Injection:
Proposed change
incorporates protection
for stakeholder's status,
authority, security,
and/or satisfaction

Requirement 2
(The status, authority,
security, and/or
satisfaction of the
stakeholder)

Prerequisite 2
DON'T change the
status quo

Assumptions

1. ....
2. ....
3. ....
4. ....
5. ....

FIGURE 11.7 *Conflict resolution diagram: Stakeholders needs are net in the change.*

A HYPOTHETICAL EXAMPLE

Let's say the originally proposed change was to phase out an existing product line (a waning "cash cow," looking more and more like a "dog," according to the widely used classification of the Boston Consulting Group).[6] To replace the old product line, the strategic planning committee has proposed penetrating a completely new market segment with a leading-edge product (a "question mark" that might prove to be a potential "star," according to the same classification). The new idea promises great changes for the company, not the least of which is a complete reorganization of responsibilities in both the production and marketing departments. The directly responsible people in each of these departments, either of whom could slow-roll this idea to death, are not really enthused about it.

The marketing manager sees the potential dissolution of a large branch under her control, to be replaced by a more high-tech but smaller staff (leaner and meaner) for the new product line. The net result will be a decrease in the size of her organization, which she interprets as a diminution of authority. Also, from what people tell us about the marketing manager, it's clear that she is sensitive to threats to her authority.

The production manager realizes that the new technology needed to assemble this leading-edge product is so different from the existing hardware currently used on the production floor that his 30 years of traditional production knowledge will be rendered largely useless. As he has enjoyed a long-standing reputation as an expert in his field, even outside the company, he foresees his status waning. Also, because of the unknown variables involved in ramping up the new line, success is anything but certain. The production manager thinks that if the new production process doesn't meet expectations, he'll be blamed, and the CEO will look for someone with more current experience in the new technology to replace him. So the production manager has a security concern, too.

The strategic planning committee, mindful of the risks in trying to ram this proposal down the throats of the two people most important to the idea's success, prefers to have both on board when they brief the CEO. Between their own personal knowledge of the managers involved and the company grapevine, they have identified the psychological needs (authority, status, and security) that seem to be threatened. They also have a sense of the technical and economic objections the two managers are likely to raise as a smokescreen.

The committee knows that their thinking process analysis has already disposed of the technical and economic objections likely to be raised, but they are also well aware that they haven't addressed the authority, status, and security issues. Several members of the strategic planning committee construct three similar conflict resolution diagrams. The only difference is that in each one, the stakeholder's requirement (R2) is different: in one, it's status, in the second, it's security, and in the third, it's authority. Naturally, the assumptions underlying the bottom arrow are different in each one, too. Under the top arrow, some assumptions remain the same, but others differ between diagrams.

The strategic planning committee arrives at three different injections (modifications they can make to the original proposal) to alleviate the two managers' concerns. The first one adds geographic scope to the marketing effort for existing products, allowing the marketing department to reassign people rather than downsize. The net result is a new product marketing effort with no decrease in staff—a net gain perceived by the marketing manager.

The second injection is a promotion for the production manager to a newly established position of vice-president for operations. In this capacity, he will supervise two other people, one responsible for managing the existing product line (his old job) and the other, newly hired, to bring the new production technology on line. Besides training the new hire in the ways of the company and the other manager to assume his former duties, the production manager (now the vice-president for operations) will be responsible for planning and developing the production advancements of the future for the company. The third injection is the hiring of the new manager to install and supervise the modern production technology.

The final political feasibility strategy: three injections, all technical in nature, but each one designed to overcome a political feasibility obstacle while simultaneously benefitting the company as a whole . . . "a rising tide floats all ships."

The strategic planning committee then goes back to the original future reality tree—the one that validated the idea to develop the new product line in the first place—and incorporates these new injections to trim the negative branches posed by the marketing and production managers' resistance. The injections are folded in seamlessly, so that it appears they were part of the plan all along. Since they do, in fact, lead to new company-level desired effects, the fact that they were inserted to overcome political feasibility problems is virtually invisible to anyone who reads the tree. Only the change agents know for sure.

By now it should be obvious that the thinking process is useful for more than just technical problem solving. We can *construct* common sense with it, but we can also use it to *communicate* that sense to others. The thinking process, as a formal analysis tool kit, has been on the street, so to speak, since 1992, but so far its use has been confined largely to the technical and economic aspects of problem solving. Its use for enhancing political feasibility has barely scratched the surface, yet this is the arena in which the thinking process might realize the most power and influence.

Man is a wanting animal—as soon as one of his needs is satisfied, another appears to take its place. This process is unending. It continues from birth to death. Man continually puts forth effort—works, if you please—to satisfy his needs.

—Douglas MacGregor

NOTES

1. W. Edwards Deming, *The New Economics for Industry, Government, and Education* (Cambridge, Mass.: MIT Center for Advanced Engineering Study, 1993), ch. 4.
2. Robert W. Bailey, *Human Performance Engineering: Using Human Factors/Ergonomics to Achieve Computer System Usability,* 2d ed. (Englewood Cliffs, N.J.: Prentice Hall, 1989).
3. Robert M. Krone, *Systems Analysis and Policy Sciences: Theory and Practice* (New York: John Wiley & Sons, 1980), 42–43.
4. James. L. Gibson, John M. Ivancevich, and James H. Donnelly, *Organizations: Behavior, Structures, Processes,* 7th ed. (Homewood, Ill.: Richard D. Irwin, 1991), ch. 4.
5. H. William Dettmer, *Goldratt's Theory of Constraints: A Systems Approach to Continuous Improvement* (Milwaukee, Wis.: ASQ Quality Press, 1996), ch. 8.
6. Heinz Weirich, and Harold Koontz, *Management: A Global Perspective,* 10th ed. (New York: McGraw-Hill, 1993), 177.

EPILOGUE

In about five years, there will be two types of CEOs: those who think globally and those who are unemployed.

—Peter Drucker

There you have it—the secret to breaking the constraints to world-class performance.

- Five focusing steps that serve as reliable channel markers for navigating into the future: identify, exploit, subordinate, elevate, and repeat
- A set of principles that keeps us everlastingly centered on the only things that really matter in our lives, our families, and our professions: the goal, the necessary conditions for achieving it, and the constraints that keep us from them
- A bag of tools that gives us the confidence that our decisions are the best that we can make them—the categories of legitimate reservation and six logic trees to answer the only three questions important to your success:

> *What* to change
> What to change *to*
> *How* to cause the change

If you expect to be world-class—and remain so—you must be prepared to engage in a race that never ends. This translates to the one trait that the theory of constraints cannot give you: persistence.

The future reality tree in the accompanying figure summarizes everything you've read in this book. You'll undoubtedly notice the striking resemblance to Figure 11.3. This one has been modified to reflect an additional level: the ultimate desired effect. The whole tree is based on the concept of *profound knowledge*. As James Naisbitt once said, "We are drowning in information but starved for knowledge." By applying the concepts in this book, you will be able to identify the important information from the trivial and convert it into knowledge. And knowledge is power.

Genius has limits; stupidity does not.

—Unknown

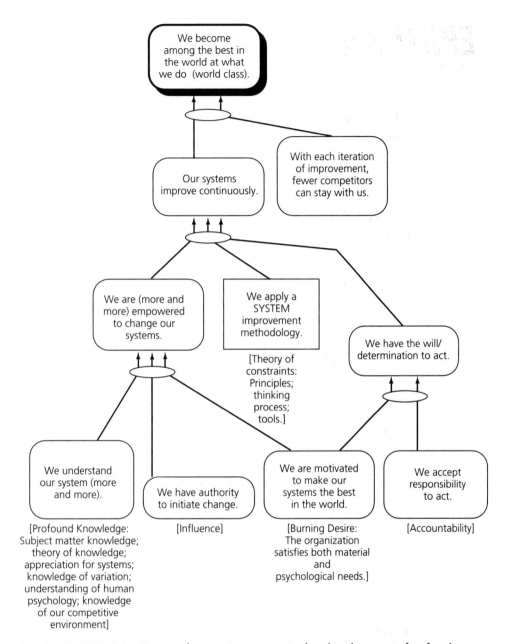

EPILOGUE FIGURE 1 Future reality tree: A summarization based on the concept of profound knowledge.

Appendix A
CAUSE AND EFFECT
An Example

The person with the least expertise has the most opinions.
—Gioia's theory

A humorous message (original source and veracity unknown) circulating on the Internet described the following scenario.[†]

A thermodynamics professor had written a take-home exam for his graduate students. It had one question:

Is hell exothermic or endothermic? Support your answer with a proof.

Most of the students wrote proofs of their beliefs using Boyle's law or some variant. One student, however, wrote the following:

First, we postulate that if souls exist, then they must have some mass. If they do, then a mole of souls can also have a mass. So, at what rate are souls moving into hell, and at what rate are souls leaving? I think that we can safely assume that once a soul gets to hell, it will not leave. Therefore, no souls are leaving.

"As for souls entering hell, let's look at the different religions that exist in the world today. Some of these religions state that if you are not a member of their religion, you will go to hell. Since there are more than one of these religions and people do not belong to more than one religion, we can project that all people and all souls go to hell. With birth and death rates as they are, we can expect the number of souls in hell to increase exponentially.

"Now, we look at the rate of change in volume in hell. Boyle's law states that in order for the temperature and pressure in hell to stay the same, the ratio of the mass of souls and volume needs to stay constant.

"So, if hell is expanding at a slower rate than the rate at which souls enter hell, then the temperature and pressure in hell will increase until all hell breaks loose.

"Of course, if hell is expanding at a rate faster than the increase of souls in hell, then the temperature and pressure will drop until hell freezes over.

"So which is it? If we accept the postulate given to me by Sarah Smith during freshman year, that 'it will be a cold night in hell before I sleep with

---

[†]The author is indebted to Mr. Reg Audibert for transmitting this Internet message. The original source is still unknown.

you and take into account the fact that I still have not succeeded in having slept with her, then number 2 cannot be true, and hell is endothermic."

The student got the only A.

Whether this story is true or not, it provides a unique opportunity to demonstrate how a line of reasoning can be structured in a cause-and-effect tree. No apologies are offered for the validity (or lack thereof) implied in the statements in this tree (Figure A.1). They are taken from the original story, which, if not great theology, isn't half-bad physics.

To read the tree, begin at the bottom of the page. All the blocks are numbered. Begin with the lowest-numbered block. Read the statement

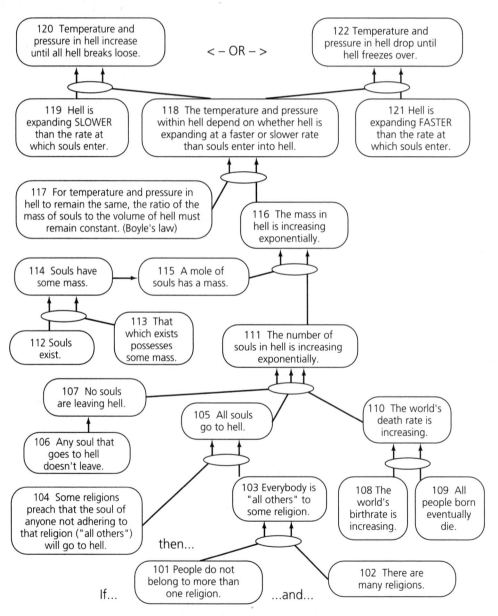

FIGURE A.1   The physics of eternity: Is hell exothermic or endothermic?

within the block, preceded by, If. . . . This is a *cause*. Follow the arrow leading out of that block to the one the arrowhead points to. This is the *effect*. Read the statement in this block, preceding it with, . . . then. . . . Ellipses enclosing more than one arrow signify causes that are dependent on one another. *All* the causes must be read *before* reading the effect, inserting the word *and* between each cause. For example, the first three blocks in the accompanying tree should be read:

> *If (101) people do not belong to more than one religion, and (102) there are many religions, then (103) everybody is all others to some religion.*

Continue reading all cause-and-effect connections this way until the last blocks (ones with arrows going in, but none coming out) are reached.

> *When you're in up to your nose, keep your mouth shut.*
>
> *—Beauregard's law*

Appendix B
THE CHALLENGER ACCIDENT

Who is it that darkeneth counsel by words without knowledge?
—Job 38:2

On January 28, 1986, the space shuttle *Challenger* (Mission 51-L) exploded 73 seconds after liftoff at an altitude of 40,000 feet and a speed of nearly Mach 2.[‡] It was the worst accident in the history of the U.S. space program, probably the worst in the history of any space program. In the aftermath, there was no shortage of second guessing about the cause of the disaster. A distinguished presidential commission was formed to investigate the accident. Most of the public, if they know anything at all about the investigation, is under the impression that some failed O-rings were at fault. But the real causes—the ones that must be addressed if another such disaster is to be avoided—lie much deeper. In fact, the true causes are so deeply rooted that they are not confined to the space shuttle program alone. These same causes are so generic that they could produce a similar disaster in any other space program, or in systems other than the space shuttle.

The entire sequence of events between the original causes and the ultimate effect took nearly 14 years to unfold. Until the last 73 seconds, there were half a dozen or more opportunities to break the deadly chain of cause and effect. The final chance to snatch victory from the jaws of defeat came in a conference call 12 hours before launch. The subject of that conference was the very O-rings that precipitated the ensuing disaster. As Winston Churchill once said, "Man will occasionally stumble over the truth, but usually he just picks himself up and continues on." So it was with the conference call and all the other decision points leading up to it.

The current reality tree in Figure B.1 describes the chain of cause and effect leading up to Mission 51-L. It offers a sobering example of how the thinking process can be used to make sense out of a virtual mountain of information about a very complex situation. Though the tree itself seems

---

[‡]The information used in this Appendix, including that presented in the current reality tree, is derived from *Report of the Presidential Commission on the Space Shuttle Accident* (1986) and "The Final Voyage of the *Challenger*," a case study (9-691-037) by Oscar Hauptman and George Iwaki of the Harvard Business School (Cambridge, MA: June 11, 1991).

very detailed, it still doesn't include all aspects of the situation. Even so, it shows enough to identify the two critical root causes of the disaster:

1. A policy of awarding development contracts to the bidder offering the lowest acquisition cost
2. A leadership that allowed NASA's public image to override safety considerations

The larger the number of people involved in a decision, the greater the pressure for conformity.

—Unknown

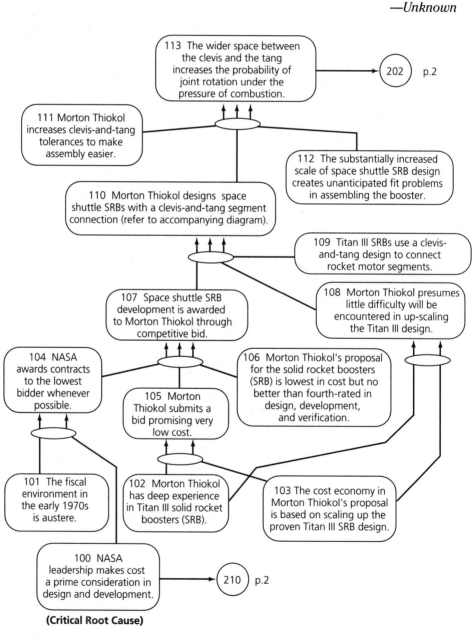

FIGURE B.1.1 Current reality tree: The Challenger Accident.

In the schematic below, the interior of the solid rocket booster is to the right, the exterior to the left. The heavy cross-hatched areas indicate the places where zinc chromate putty are supposed to inhibit the leakage of hot combustion gases into the joint. Should any gases make it past the zinc chromate, the two O-rings (labeled *primary* and *secondary*) are intended to prevent pressure from escaping through the clevis-and-tang.

In up-scaling the design of the casing in 1977 to eliminate problems fitting the upper segment to the lower, the interior space between the clevis-and-tang was increased. This increase in space so degraded the effectiveness of the primary O-ring that in many instances it failed to prevent the escape of hot gases (and internal booster pressure) through the joint. Since the secondary O-ring was never designed to withstand the full force of combustion pressure, it, too, routinely permitted hot gases to escape.

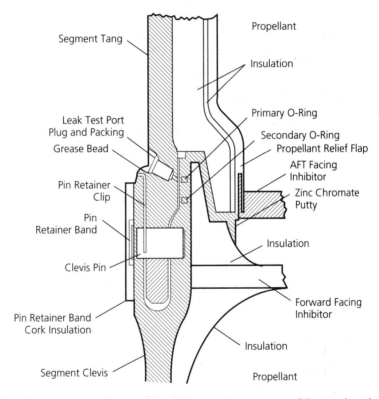

FIGURE B.1.2   Space shuttle clevis-and-tang schematic. *Source: Report of the Presidential Commission on the Space Shuttle Accident (1986)*

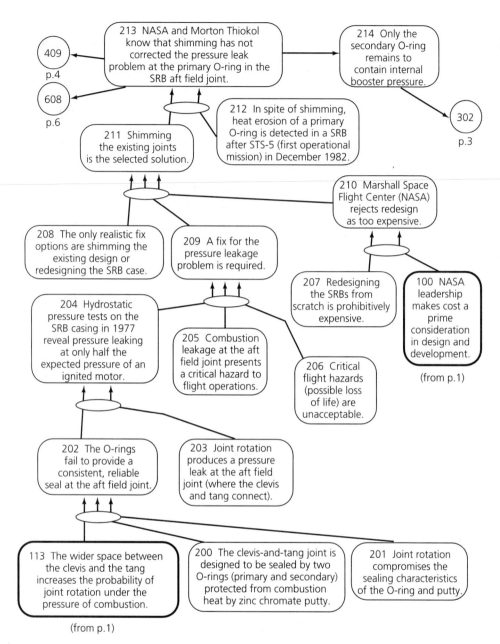

FIGURE B.1.3 Current reality tree: The Challenger accident. (from p. 1)

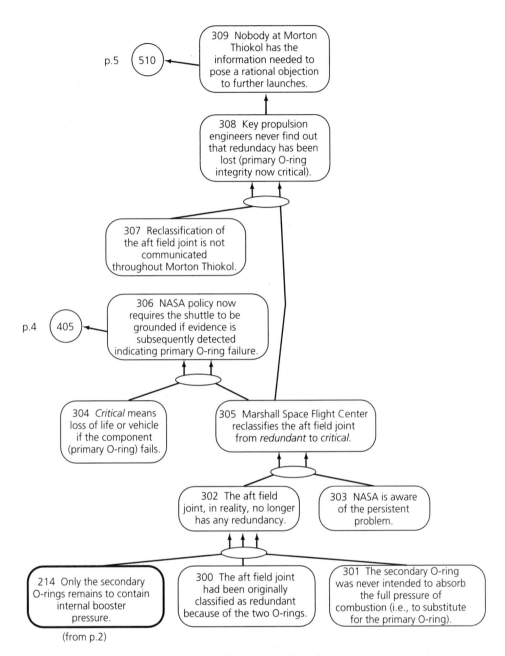

FIGURE B.1.4 Current Reality Tree: The Challenger accident. (from p. 2)

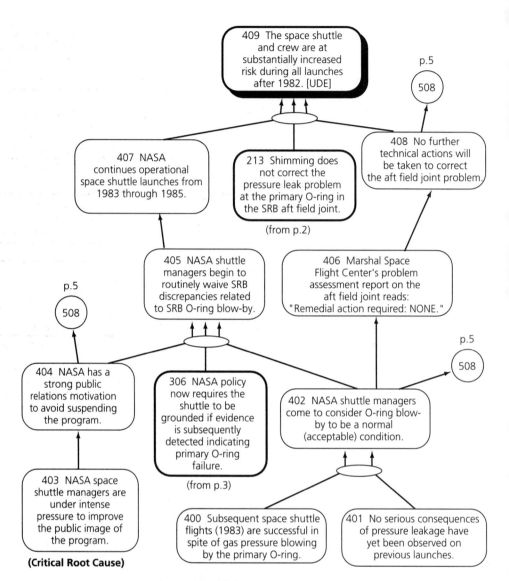

FIGURE B.1.5 Current reality tree: The Challenger accident.

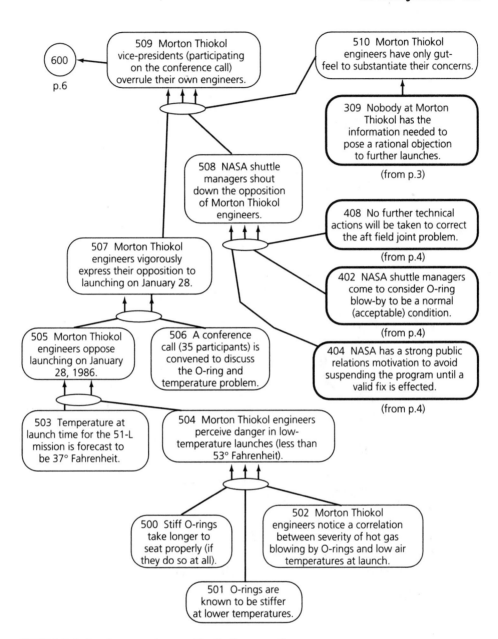

FIGURE B.1.6 Current reality tree: The Challenger accident.

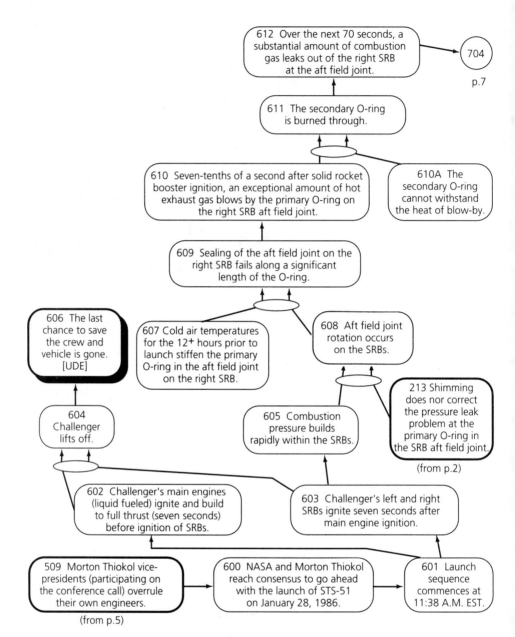

FIGURE B.1.7 Current reality tree: The Challenger accident. (from p. 5)

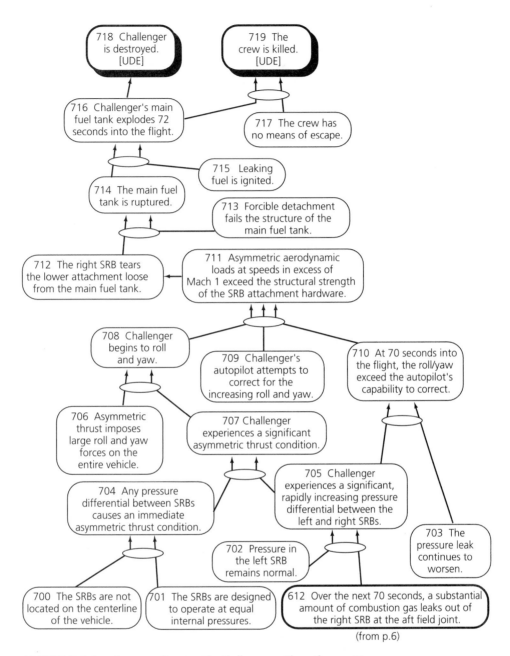

FIGURE B.1.8 Current reality tree: The Challenger accident. (from p. 6)

Appendix C
ILL-ADVISED TAX POLICY
A Knowledge Tree

Politics derives from the Greek word poly, meaning many, and tics, which, as everybody knows, are blood-sucking parasites.
—*Unknown*

Cause-and-effect trees aren't always used only to solve problems. Sometimes they are useful in explaining why events happened as they did. The tree in Figure C.1 is such an example. Because it happened in ancient history, the problem is far beyond a fix at this point. But the lessons of this tree can be instructive nonetheless, if our desire is to avoid falling into the same trap again. Some of these lessons might include the following:

- Sometimes well-intended decisions produce disastrous consequences.
- Always look for the possible long-term negative outcomes of any policy you contemplate instituting.
- Economic problems don't confine themselves to the economic arena alone.

Cause-and-effect analysis of historical events, such as this one, can be a particularly useful teaching tool if our objective is to learn from the mistakes of others without having to repeat them ourselves.

Public money ought to be touched with the most scrupulous conscientiousness of honor. It is not the product of riches only, but of the hard earnings of labor and poverty. It is drawn even from the bitterness of want and misery. Not a beggar passes, or perishes in the streets, whose mite in not in that mass.
—*Thomas Paine*

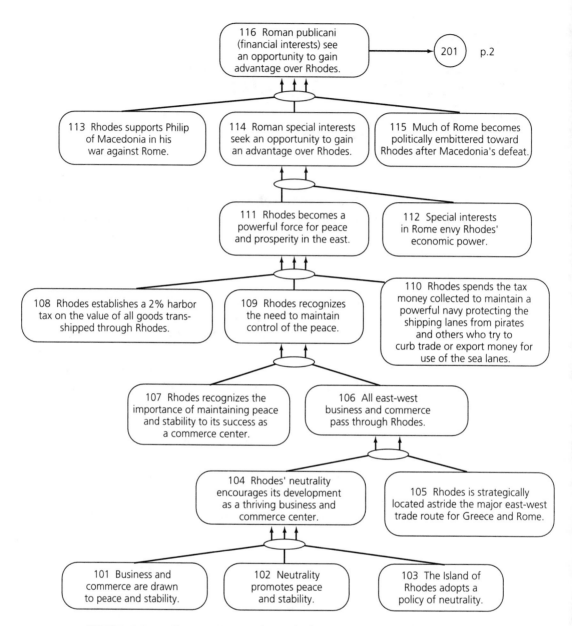

FIGURE C.1.1   The system impact of tax policy: Free trade isn't always free. . . .

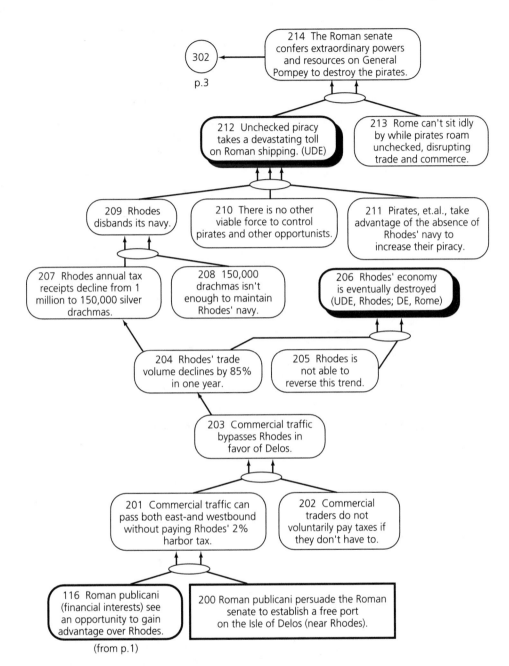

302
p.3

214 The Roman senate confers extraordinary powers and resources on General Pompey to destroy the pirates.

212 Unchecked piracy takes a devastating toll on Roman shipping. (UDE)

213 Rome can't sit idly by while pirates roam unchecked, disrupting trade and commerce.

209 Rhodes disbands its navy.

210 There is no other viable force to control pirates and other opportunists.

211 Pirates, et.al., take advantage of the absence of Rhodes' navy to increase their piracy.

207 Rhodes annual tax receipts decline from 1 million to 150,000 silver drachmas.

208 150,000 drachmas isn't enough to maintain Rhodes' navy.

206 Rhodes' economy is eventually destroyed (UDE, Rhodes; DE, Rome)

204 Rhodes' trade volume declines by 85% in one year.

205 Rhodes is not able to reverse this trend.

203 Commercial traffic bypasses Rhodes in favor of Delos.

201 Commercial traffic can pass both east-and westbound without paying Rhodes' 2% harbor tax.

202 Commercial traders do not voluntarily pay taxes if they don't have to.

116 Roman publicani (financial interests) see an opportunity to gain advantage over Rhodes.

200 Roman publicani persuade the Roman senate to establish a free port on the Isle of Delos (near Rhodes).

(from p.1)

FIGURE C.1.2 The system impact of tax policy: Free trade isn't always free. . . . (from p. 1)

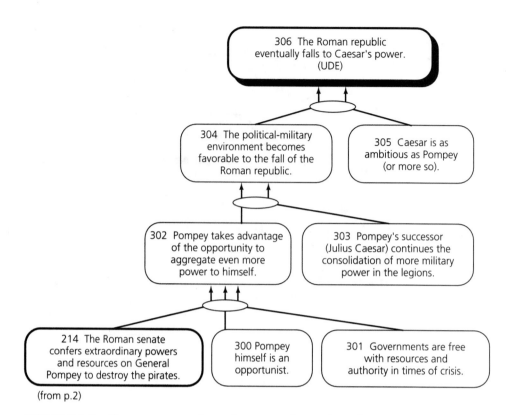

(from p.2)

FIGURE C.1.3   The system impact of tax policy: Free trade isn't always free. . . .

Appendix D
VECTOR ONE CORPORATION: "WHY IS OUR TQM EFFORT FAILING?"
A Case Study

We know where most of the creativity, the innovation, the stuff that drives productivity lies. It's in the minds of those closest to the work. It's been there in front of our noses all along while we've been running around, chasing robots and reading books on how to become Japanese—or at least manage like them.
> —*John F. Welch, Chairman*
> *General Electric*

THE SCENARIO

The Vector One Corporation manufactures servo controls for robotic machines and other computer-controlled unattended equipment. The 35-year-old company shifted from making electromechanical devices to the high-technology devices during the 1980s as Japanese companies, such as Hitachi, began introducing numerically controlled, flexible manufacturing machines.

Vector's organizational structure had always been a traditional vertical hierarchy with a chief executive officer (CEO) and chief operating officer (COO) overseeing three traditionally structured divisions: engineering, production, and marketing and sales. These divisions functioned adequately in a vertical hierarchy until heavy competition from the Japanese began eating into Vector's market share. Between 1986 and 1989, Vector's share of the servo-control market dropped 50 percent, with attendant financial losses. During that time, Vector's executive management watched in frustration as Japanese, and even other American competitors, began introducing newer and more effective servo-control products, sometimes two or three generations of improvements, while Vector struggled to launch one.

Even that one had problems. Besides an inordinate number of in-house test failures for both electrical and mechanical reasons, warranty returns and customer complaints soared for shipments of the new Vector model that happened to pass final testing. Vector's market share was free-falling, but even more ominously, so was its historical reputation for excellence.

Vector's COO, vice-president for engineering, and senior production manager attended a Deming four-day seminar in 1989 and came away convinced that they needed to rethink the way they approached quality. Using Deming's fourteen points[1] as a foundation, they eagerly embarked on a company-wide effort to upgrade quality in all areas. The work force responded to the changes the management instituted with cautious optimism and willing cooperation.

By 1991, quality had shown some modest improvements. Warranty returns and customer complaints were down by 25 percent. However, during the same time, Vector's market share had dropped another 10 percent. Layoffs ensued. Vector's leadership, remembering admonitions from the Deming four-day seminar that quality improvement was a long-term effort requiring patience and persistence, redoubled their efforts to improve. They limped along for another two years, adding design of experiment (DOE), quality function deployment (QFD), and concurrent engineering (CE) to the statistical process control (SPC) that they had previously introduced. Vector was creating a regular alphabet soup.

Profits and market share fluctuated, with improvements posted in one quarter followed by some backsliding in the next. By early 1994, Vector's market share was still hovering between 7 and 8 percent—far from management's expectations of the recaptured glory of the early 1980s. They were at their wits' end. What were they doing wrong? Their quality efforts, in which they had invested hundreds of hours and thousands of dollars in training, were producing modest quality gains, at best. But the breakthrough they had all hoped for—a steadily increasing quality improvement curve—eluded them. Worse, their efforts seemed to have little or no impact on the bottom line. One consultant after another advised Vector to change *this* in production, or *that* in engineering, or something else entirely in marketing and sales. *Tiger teams* were established to blitz individual processes in hopes of finding the solution. Nothing seemed to work.

At an executive meeting in mid-1994, the CEO posed the question that was on everybody's mind: "Why is our TQM effort failing?" Nobody had an answer. It wasn't until a mid-level mechanical engineer sent a memorandum up the chain-of-command three weeks later that eyebrows began to rise. The engineer posed three questions in her memo:

- What is the goal of this company?
- What are the necessary conditions we must satisfy to achieve that goal?
- What is the one constraint that keeps us from achieving the goal?

The engineer went on to point out that in her informal discussions with colleagues and production personnel, nobody else seemed to know for sure what the goal was, either. They all knew what the mission and vision statement were, but nobody could articulate one basic, overriding goal—one measurable thing that everybody could focus their attention on. There were quarterly objectives and quotas, and everybody paid close attention to be sure they always met them. But, she said, nobody she had spoken to really understood how—or even whether—the things that they did each day contributed to the benefit of the company.

The engineer attached an unusual one-page diagram to her memo, the likes of which her department head had never seen before: something called a current reality tree (Figure D.1). It so intrigued the department supervisor that he passed it, along with the memo, to the vice-president for engineering, who in turn forwarded it to the chief operating officer.

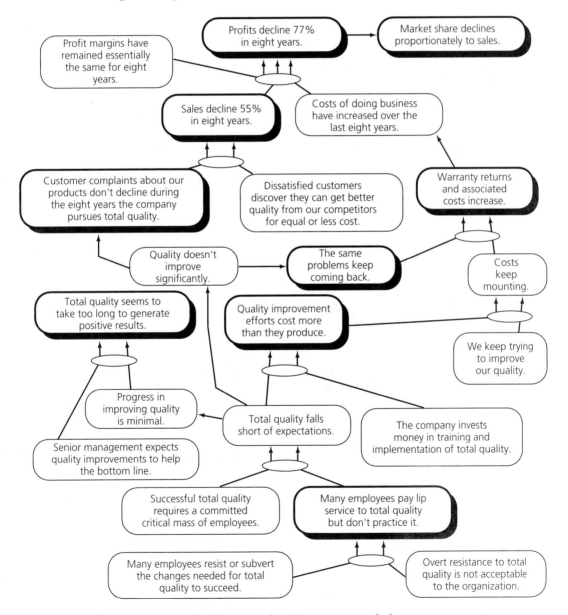

FIGURE D.1 "Why Vector One's Quality Efforts Are Failing" (First version, attached to engineer's memo).

At an informal meeting in the executive conference room, the chief operating officer began by acknowledging that the engineer's memo had caused him to ponder the question of the company's goal. He admitted that the goal was *not* clearly stated in any of the total quality policies or guidance the quality advisor had published, and he recognized that a goal was different from either a mission or vision statement, both of which the company had spared no effort to disseminate. "So, what *is* our goal?" he asked, opening discussion among the three vice-presidents. They concluded that their goal should be profitability, because that's what the company's owners—the stockholders—would probably say it was if they were asked.

"In that case," the chief operating officer continued, "what happens to customer satisfaction? And market share? And competitive advantage? These are important, too. They're in our mission statement because they're important." After some discussion, the engineer suggested that perhaps these were *necessary conditions* that had to be satisfied in order to realize profitability. The chief operating officer and the vice-presidents were inclined to agree.

"Now comes the tough question. Do we have a constraint that keeps us from achieving profitability? And if so, what is it?"

The chief operating officer looked around the table, but nobody spoke for about 15 seconds. Then the engineer offered an opinion. "I believe that every system has a constraint somewhere—something that keeps it from doing better than it does. Maybe that constraint is inside the system, but it could also be outside. I think ours might be inside. Either way, if we don't do something to break that constraint, we'll never do any better."

THE CURRENT REALITY TREE

The executives digested this for a moment. Then the vice-president of production spoke up. "I was intrigued by this flowchart you prepared. How did you come up with this?" The engineer explained that it was part of a technique she had learned in graduate school and that it was a logic tree rather than a flowchart.

"I began with a list of undesirable effects—indications that our company wasn't living up to either our business or our quality expectations. Some of these I've observed myself. Others I've been told about by fellow employees. Some of them I got from our last five annual reports. And I worked those back down to some causes."

The chief operating officer winced when she mentioned the annual reports. "Is there any doubt in anybody's mind," he inquired, "that our marketing and sales people are the equal of anybody else's? Does anybody really believe that the market itself has gone soft?" The three vice-presidents shook their heads. "Then I have to believe that the reason for our problems is within our own walls. And the evidence seems to point rather convincingly to our quality." They reviewed the list of undesirable effects attached to the logic tree.

- Market share declines proportionately to sales.
- Profits decline 77 percent in eight years.
- Sales decline 55 percent in eight years.
- Warranty returns and associated costs increase.
- Customer complaints about our products don't decline during the eight years the company pursues total quality.
- Total quality seems to take too long to generate positive results.
- Quality improvement efforts cost more than they produce.
- Many employees pay lip service to total quality but don't practice it.
- The same problems keep coming back.

The chief operating officer said, "This tree is very interesting. But why did you stop it where you did? I think you're on the right track, but it seems clear to me that the real causes of our quality problems are deeper than this. Why are our employees resisting?"

The engineer explained that she was at the limits of her personal knowledge of how the company worked, having been on board for only six months. The other demands of her job prevented her from spending more time to learn about the intricacies of production and marketing and sales. Her instinct told her, however, that the problem was a system problem, not just an engineering or production issue, and to solve a problem that crossed departmental lines, more expertise from the other areas involved would be needed. But with that added knowledge, the constraint could probably be identified.

The chief operating officer decided to form a cross-functional team to analyze the problem and suggest a strategy. He asked the vice-president of engineering to offload the engineer's routine duties to someone else so that she could devote full time to expanding the one-page current reality tree into a complete picture of the situation. The team was formed the next day.

Ten days later, they delivered a detailed tree (Figure D.2) to the CEO, the COO, the chief financial officer (CFO), and the vice-presidents for engineering, production, and marketing and sales. The engineer presented the current reality tree using an overhead projector and explained it to the executives.

"The first thing you'll notice is that this tree is much more detailed than the first one you saw (Figure D.1). As we worked on the problem in a group, we discovered that some things had been overlooked. And, of course, we dug more deeply into the problem.

"Second, we found that what we thought was a single path between the root causes and the undesirable effects was actually three paths that converge at both the top and the bottom. The left-hand path is on the first

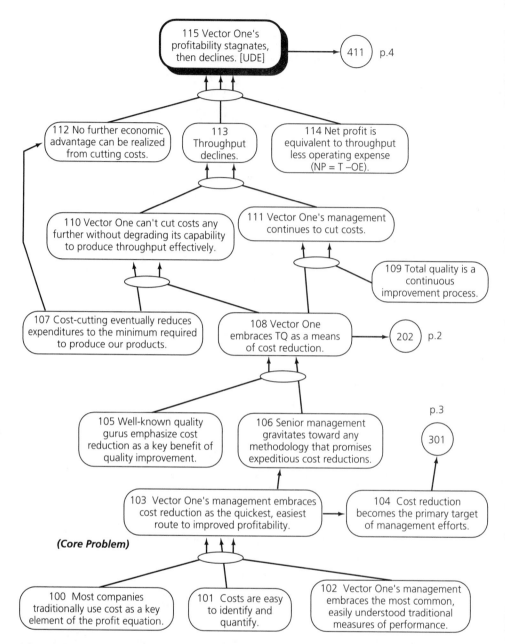

FIGURE D.2.1   Vector One's current reality tree.

page (Figure D.2.1). The center path is on the second page (Figure D.2.2). The right-hand path is on the third (Figure D.2.3), and the three paths converge at the undesirable effects on the fourth page (Figure D.2.4).

"We were surprised to find that all three paths and all the undesirable effects originated from one core problem, which is highlighted on the first page. Our conclusion is that Vector One has been using total quality for the *wrong* reasons. We've been focusing on *cost reduction*. This misplaced emphasis has caused the growth of these three branches, culminating in the undesirable effects. The left-hand branch traces the problems associ-

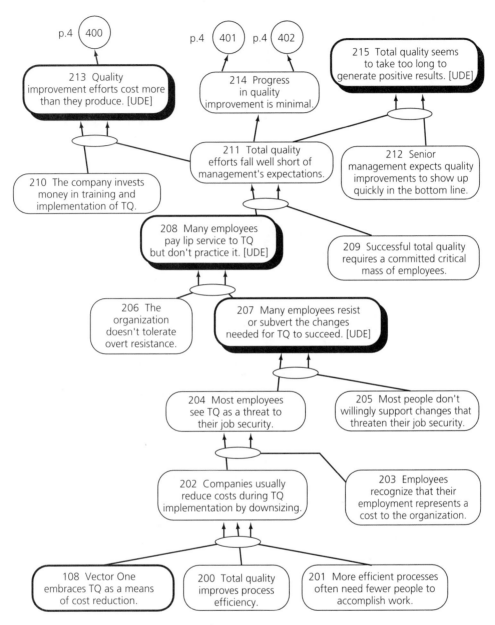

FIGURE D.2.2 Vector One's current reality tree.

ated with cost cutting. The center branch shows how our emphasis on cost cutting actually causes counterproductive behavior by our employees, and the right branch reveals how a cost-reduction focus has given rise to a faulty measurement and reward system. Our use of the wrong performance measures causes us to reward the wrong employee behavior.

"The crux of our problem, block 103, is that we're not applying our corporate efforts to the task that will do us the most good: *increasing throughput.*"

After some spirited discussion, the executives agreed that the team had accurately identified the core problem. The question was, what should be done about it? And who should do it?

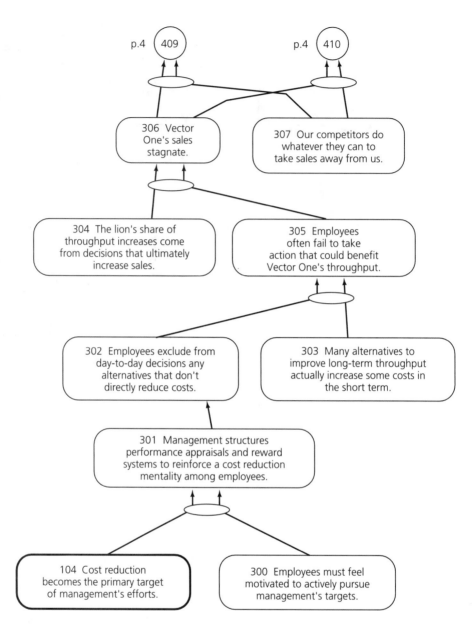

FIGURE D.2.3   Vector One's current reality tree. (from p. 1)

THE CONFLICT RESOLUTION DIAGRAM

The CEO, lips pursed and squinting at the current reality tree the engineer has just presented, brought the conversation back on course. "Intuitively, something has been telling me that we might have been going down a blind alley, focusing on cost cutting the way we have. But it wasn't really clear to me until I saw this tree. The question is: If what we're doing is wrong, then what *should* we be doing?"

The engineer hesitated a moment, watching for one of the executives to say something. When none did, she took a deep breath. *What the heck . . . it's only my job!* "Maybe the way to answer that question is to

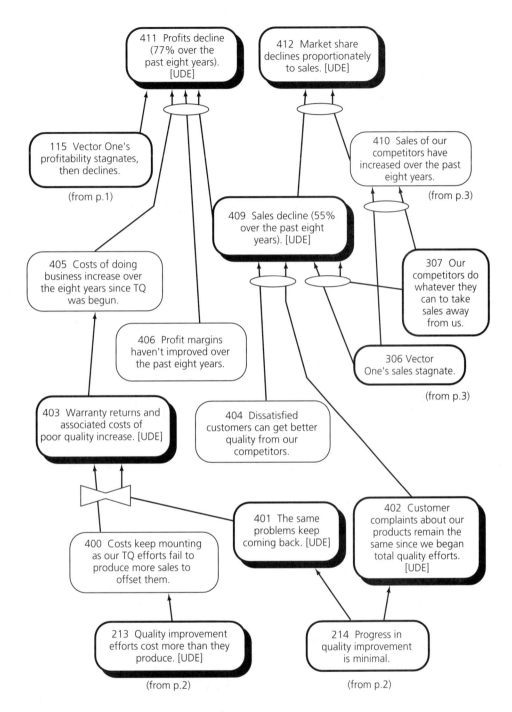

FIGURE D.2.4 Vector One's Current reality tree.

consider why this focus on cost reduction exists in the first place. Would you like to see what our team came up with?" Around the conference table, executives leaned forward perceptibly.

"Once we were reasonably sure we'd found the core problem, we asked ourselves, If this is *causing* our undesirable effects, what situation would make them go away? We brainstormed this a while and decided

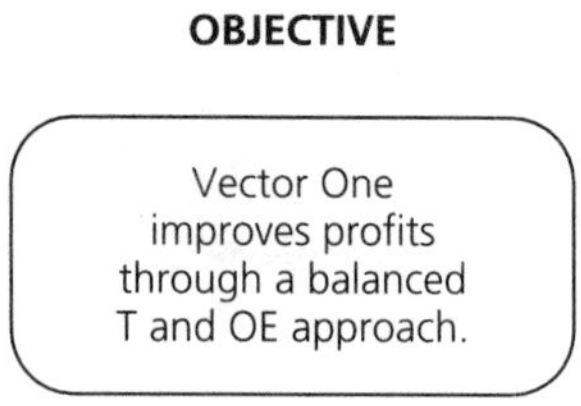

OBJECTIVE

Vector One
improves profits
through a balanced
T and OE approach.

FIGURE D.3 Vector One's objective.

that the *opposite condition* of this core problem could do it. That, we decided, was what *should* be happening, but wasn't. In other words, if we'd had this opposite condition instead of the core problem, the undesirable effects wouldn't have happened in the first place.

"We decided this opposite condition would be our objective. We tried several different formulations of an objective statement, and we finally settled on this."

The next slide she put on the overhead projector stated: Vector One improves profits through a balanced throughput and operating expense approach (Figure D.3). "From our standpoint, it seemed that the problem wasn't that we've been trying to cut costs. It was that cutting costs *alone* was all we've been emphasizing, thinking that this would take care of our competitiveness problem all by itself. So we decided the objective should be a balanced effort, emphasizing increased throughput, but not ignoring operating expense, either." She let that sink in for a moment.

"Then we asked ourselves, Why haven't we been able to operate under such a balanced approach? We found two possible reasons. One was that we've just been ignorant of the core problem, and now that we know about it, the company could immediately change things. The second was that some hidden, underlying conflict was perpetuating the core problem. We discounted the first reason. There has been too much discussion about declining sales over the past year for us to believe that everybody's just been blind to it. That left us with conflict as a possible answer."

She changed to a new slide. This one showed the objective, with arrows from two other statements leading to it (Figure D.4). "Then we asked ourselves, What necessary conditions must we satisfy for Vector One to be profitable? The answers, we decided were *effectively control operating expense* and *expand throughput significantly*. We derived these from the formula net profit equals throughput of the entire company minus operating expense ($NP = T - OE$). Throughput is further defined as total sales revenue less the total variable costs of sales ($T = SR_T - VC_T$).

"Notice here that we now have *two* cost-related elements in these equations: variable and fixed. The fixed costs are obvious—that's the operating expense in the upper necessary condition. The variable costs aren't so obvious because they're implicit in the throughput necessary condition. The variable costs could be considered product-related costs, while the fixed costs might be considered process-related costs, or overhead. We considered both of these conditions—controlling operating expense and increasing throughput—to be necessary in order to maximize long-term profit." The engineer glanced over at the chief financial officer, looking for nonverbal feedback, and finding none.

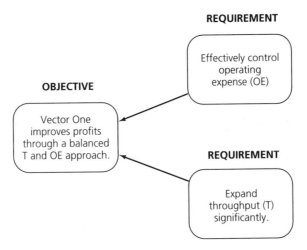

FIGURE D.4   Vector One's requirements.

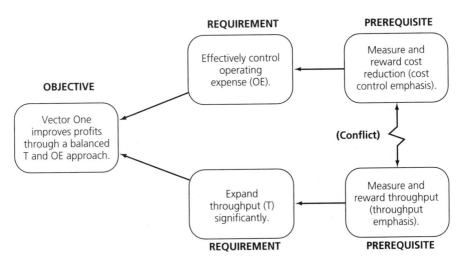

FIGURE D.5   Vector One's prerequisites.

The CEO spoke up. "You mentioned something about conflict. I don't see a conflict here."

"You're right," the engineer replied. "These requirements are both *necessary* for attainment of the Objective, which means, by definition, they can't be in conflict. But the actions we consider ourselves obligated to take to satisfy these necessary conditions *are* in conflict." The engineer replaced the slide with a new one (Figure D.5) "In other words, the conflict lies not in what we're trying to satisfy, but in what we think we must *do* to satisfy them. And it's this tug-of-war that essentially neutralizes any possibility of achieving the objective.

"In order to effectively control operating expense, we feel compelled to measure and reward cost reduction. But in order to expand throughput significantly, we need to measure and reward increases in throughput. This company hasn't been operating as if it can do both at the same time."

The chief financial officer spoke up. "Well, I don't see why not. That's what we pay sales commissions for. We reward the sales force for getting us more orders. And we reward the operations people for keeping our production costs down. We've also rewarded our staff for reducing overhead. I don't see a conflict here."

The engineer shifted uncomfortably from one foot to the other. "Yes, we have definitely been rewarding cost reductions, both on the line and in the staff. But more orders don't directly equate to increased throughput. *Payments* for those orders by customers do. And we've been unable to make that translation. We've lost orders because we've consistently missed delivery due dates. We've repromised so many times, our credibility is largely shot. And when we have delivered, a high percentage of our products end up returned to us for repair or replacement—our quality problem again. The money that we spend to fix these problems directly offsets the profits we would have realized from the sale in the first place, which is the same as increasing the cost of the sale. So rewarding the sales force alone for generating more orders isn't the same as increasing throughput. Improvements to throughput are the result of a chain of dependent events that start with the order and end with our depositing the customer's check into our bank account. But it's between order and delivery that the process breaks down.

"We lose a lot of customer good will and loyalty for the problems these warranty returns cause our customers. So we lose repeat business, and there's no way I can think of to quantify that—I just know it's hurting us. But I don't need to be telling you this. It was all in the current reality tree."

The CEO smiled at the engineer's deftness in deflecting the CFO's shot. "Okay, so what do we do about this? We have to reward cost reduction, don't we? And we have to reward throughput improvements, not just increased orders. But improvements cost money, which is the antithesis of cost reduction. I see the conflict now, but how do we resolve it?"

The engineer pressed on. "For us to come up with an idea to break this conflict, we had to determine what assumptions we were making about *why* we thought we needed to measure and reward cost reductions to keep operating expense under control. And we had to do the same for the throughput side. The reason we need to expose these assumptions is really twofold.

"First, we all operate under some kinds of assumptions every day. Most of the time, we aren't even consciously aware of them, but we make these assumptions just the same. Second, our assumptions are sometimes flawed, maybe even completely invalid. But since we don't continually— or consciously—evaluate those assumptions, we often make mistakes because of them. So in trying to break this conflict, we had to make an assumption about conflict itself. We assumed that if all the underlying assumptions on both sides were valid, we'd have an unbreakable conflict. But we're pretty sure that's not the case, because there are other companies out there that have faced the same problem we're facing, and they're not having the trouble that we are. If the assumptions were all valid and immutable, the other companies would be in the same boat we are.

"So our thinking about this conflict was that if we could expose all the unspoken assumptions behind each side of the conflict, we'd be able to find some that were invalid—or could be *made* invalid somehow. And that would give us some clues about what we could do to break the conflict. And here's what we came up with (Figure D.6).

R1-to-O: *For Vector One to improve profits through a balanced T and OE approach (O), it must effectively control operating expense (R1) because*
1. Changes in operating expense flow directly and immediately to the bottom line.
2. Less operating expense is always desirable.
3. Tight cost control is necessary for profitability.

P1-to-R1: *In order to effectively control operating expense (R1), Vector One must measure and reward cost reduction (P1), because*
4. Cost control always means cost reduction.
5. Cost reduction actions are always an effective means of cost control.
6. Cost reduction is the best way to improve profitability.
7. Costs can be reduced indefinitely without adverse effect on system performance.
8. Unfocused rewards don't reinforce desired behavior.
9. To be effective, rewards must be based on measurements linked directly to individual or small group performances.
10. Local efficiencies must be managed to reduce costs.
11. What is measured and rewarded gets done.

R2-to-O: *For Vector One to improve profits a through a balanced T and OE approach (O), it must expand throughput significantly (R2) because*
12. More throughput is always desirable.
13. More throughput always improves profit.

P2-to-R2: *In order to expand throughput significantly (R2), Vector One must measure and reward throughput increase (P2) because*
14. Effects of actions taken to increase throughput are measurable.
15. Increasing throughput is the best way to improve profitability.
16. Throughput can be increased indefinitely without adverse effects on system performance.
17. Unfocused rewards don't reinforce desired behavior.
18. To be effective, rewards must be based on measurements linked directly to individual or small group performance.
19. What is measured and rewarded gets done.

P1-to-P2: *On one hand, Vector One must measure and reward cost reduction (P1); on the other hand, it must measure and reward increase of throughput. It can't do BOTH because*
20. Increasing throughput often increases costs.
21. Decreasing costs often degrades throughput.
22. Emphasizing throughput precludes rigorous cost control.
23. Emphasizing cost control limits capability to increase throughput.
24. People are confused when opposite behaviors are rewarded simultaneously.

FIGURE D.6 Vector One conflict assumptions. The author is indebted to Dr. John Caspari for the use of this conflict resolution diagram

"We decided that assumptions 1 through 3 were the reasons why control of operational expense was needed for profitability, R1 to O on the diagram. And all of those assumptions seemed valid to us. The same was pretty much true for assumptions 12 and 13 concerning the importance of increasing throughput, R2 to O on the diagram. It's when we get to the next link, P1 to R1, that we start finding questionable assumptions.

"We found eight assumptions behind the idea that Vector One must measure and reward cost reduction in order to control operational expense. Of those eight, numbers 4, 5, 6, 7, and 10 seemed invalid at face value."

The vice-president for operations broke a lengthy silence as everyone read through the assumptions. "Well, I'll certainly agree that number 7 is invalid. We can't keep reducing our costs. We've already hurt our production capacity with the cost reductions we've absorbed up till now."

The chief financial officer added, "I'd agree that number 4 is invalid. And while I might be tempted to challenge you on number 6, it's tough to do the way you've got it worded there. It would be very hard to defend the idea that cost reduction is the best way to improve profitability. But I'm not so sure about number 5. Cost reductions *are* an effective means of cost control. That one's not invalid."

The operations vice-president countered before the engineer could say anything. "Okay, if that's valid, then I shouldn't be able to point to a situation where our cost reductions actually increased costs, should I? But that's what happened last year. Remember when we started cutting out redundant inspections? That was a cost reduction *bennie* promised by TQM. And what happened three months later? We had to recall 4000 servo controls. That cost us four times what we saved by cutting out the inspections!"

The CFO and operations man exchanged several comments before the CEO brought the discussion back on course. "Okay, let's table that for now. What about number 11—Local efficiencies must be managed to reduce costs? That's valid, isn't it?"

The engineer nodded. "Yes, we can certainly cut costs in the short term by managing local efficiencies. And our bottom line will look better in the next quarterly report. But in the long run, how do we know when enough is enough? Can we be sure that we've stopped short of degrading our ability to generate more sales? This really points to another assumption, one we've failed to list here, but one we routinely make about our business: *the efficiency of the entire company is always the sum of the local efficiencies of each part of the company.* That one really invites a challenge. If the sales department generates 10,000 orders a week, that would be pretty efficient. And it would completely bog down our production line with backlogs. Our customers would scream when we didn't deliver on time, and we'd lose business. That's not very efficient from the company perspective, but it sure would be from the sales department's alone."

The engineer noticed the CEO glance at his watch and continued. "In the interest of time, let me quickly summarize. We found one assumption on the other side, between P2 and R2, number 16, that might possibly be challenged, and two more, numbers 22 and 23 between P1 and P2 that we considered invalid. But clearly, the weakest part of the conflict was the link between P1 and R1—it had the most assumptions we thought were either invalid at face value, or that could be made invalid. So we focused our attention on generating ideas that could break the conflict on that side.

"We began with the idea that the two requirements are nonnegotiable: we *have* to control operational expense and we *have* to increase throughput. We thought we'd probably have to measure and reward our employees for the things they did to increase throughput. We didn't see a way around that, although we certainly looked for one. So we asked ourselves, How can we control our operating expense without having to measure and reward people for cost cutting?"

The CFO nodded. "We've *got* to keep a handle on the operating expense. I'm open to suggestions on how we might make that happen without rewarding cost cutting. After all, if we don't have to pay a reward for that, we've just saved some more costs!"

The engineer showed a new slide (Figure D.7). "This is the last slide I have for now. We settled on two ideas that we thought would simultaneously do the trick. The first is to prepare a sensible operating budget for fixed expenses—one that everybody can live with for the year—and consider it fixed at that level. No increases, but no decreases, either. Since expenditures won't increase, they're essentially under control. At the same time, we want to make it clear to everybody that we're no longer

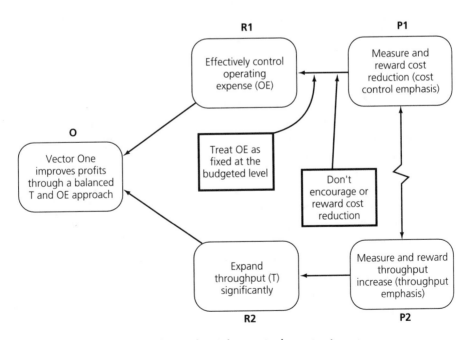

FIGURE D.7 Vector One conflict resolution diagram (with injections). The author is indebted to Dr. John Caspari for the use of this conflict resolution diagram

encouraging or rewarding people for cutting operational expenses. We've got as lean a machine as we can make it with a sensible operating budget, so there would be no rewards for trimming it any further. Instead of further cost cutting, we can devote our attention to increasing throughput by improving our quality, minimizing our variable production costs, and reducing our order-to-ship cycle time. Those are the things we'll reward."

The CEO raised one eyebrow. "Well, it *looks* promising. But will it work? And how do you know that these ideas will be effective? That's what I want to know before we decide to proceed. We can't afford any more false starts on this. I've got another meeting to attend. Let's reconvene on Friday to continue this discussion."

THE FUTURE REALITY TREE

On Friday, at 8:30 A.M., the CEO joined the rest of the executive staff and three members of the cross-functional team in the company executive conference room. "Okay. Where did we leave off on Monday?" The engineer reviewed the conflict resolution diagram, concluding with the two injections the team had created to break the conflict:

Injection 1:   Treat operating expense (OE) as fixed at the budgeted level.
Injection 2:   Don't encourage or reward further OE reduction.

The chief financial officer's brow furrowed as the second injection was read. "I understand the first injection—I can live with that. But why shouldn't we reward our employees if they find ways to reduce cost even more? That seems counterintuitive. It's traditional in companies everywhere: Pay for cost-cutting suggestions."

The team member from production operations spoke up. "Perhaps I can explain that one, since it was my idea. First of all, you're right about it being traditional to give financial incentives for cost reductions. But we had to ask ourselves whether that practice might be hurting our long-term performance in the interest of a quick—but usually small—boost to the bottom line. In the case of variable costs, the ones directly involving the product, we can still realize worthwhile savings by reducing some costs. Scrap reduction comes to mind. The higher our reject rate during inspection, the greater our expense in lost material if the rejected part can't be reworked. We still have a long way to go in that area. And we'll still reward our employees for reducing some of these so-called throughput costs.

"But operating expense—fixed costs of doing business—that's another story. We've been shaving fixed costs for eight years now. All the fat is gone, and it's been gone for some time. We just haven't realized it, so we've continued to cut operating expense. And in so doing, we've cut muscle—our ability to generate throughput.

"For example, as sales have fallen off, we've laid off highly qualified production workers. Even if our sales increased, we can't replace them, at least not easily. They've already found jobs elsewhere. And what's available on the job market now isn't very much use to us. Most of our new hires have reading and basic math deficiencies. We're not equipped or inclined to deal with that problem.

"Since we don't really know for certain where that fine line is between fat and muscle, we're suggesting that we not reward ideas that might hurt our ability to recover. We don't want to encourage more cost cutting, but we don't want to encourage more spending either. Instead, we'll apply the traditional incentives and rewards to those decisions that are likely to help us generate more revenue."

"How can production workers do that?" challenged the vice-president for sales and marketing. "They don't sell anything!"

"No," allowed the production man, "but the decisions they make directly affect the success of your sales force. What would happen if, instead of rewarding cost cutting, we rewarded people for doing things that would reduce the manufacturing cycle time? In other words, we delivered the orders your sales force generated *earlier* than the customer expected? Would we get paid sooner? Yes. Would that customer like that kind of service enough to maybe buy from your salesperson again? Probably. So the reward we pay to reduce cycle time, rather than decrease cost, actually generates more revenue over the longer term.

"Here's another example. What if we reward our production people for improving the first-time quality of our products? That action might actually *increase* variable cost because it may require upgrading to a better quality raw material. But if it reduces our warranty returns by 20 percent, it saves money in the long run. Not only is scrap reduced internally, but we don't anger customers. And satisfied customers usually come back with repeat business for us. This isn't new. We've been through all this when we started on our quality efforts years ago. We preached quality—we just didn't put our money where our mouth was."

"Okay," said the CEO, "let's assume for a minute that there are good reasons to adopt these two injections. How do we know for sure that they'll work?"

The engineer spoke up. "We've tried to validate these two ideas logically. Basically, we built an unbroken chain of cause and effect, much like the current reality tree. We started with these two injections and followed them, step-by-step, to their logical conclusions: the effects we desire to have, which, not coincidentally, all negate the undesirable effects from the current reality tree. That's not an accident.

"We began with the injections at the bottom of this future reality tree and the effects we wanted at the top. The rest of the effort was devoted to filling in the middle, from bottom to top. Along the way, we found that several other actions or decisions would be necessary, or the cause and effect would lose momentum and never reach the desired effects. Here's the result of that effort."

The engineer then presented several slides detailing each cause and effect leading to the desired effects (Figures D.8.1 through D.8.4).

"Notice that our two injections don't appear at the very bottom of this tree. They're several levels above it. Originally, we started the tree with the injections from our conflict resolution diagram. But as we tested the tree for logical sufficiency, we discovered that there were a few other things we'd have to do to ensure that we sustained our capability to generate throughput (number 107). These additional actions are numbers

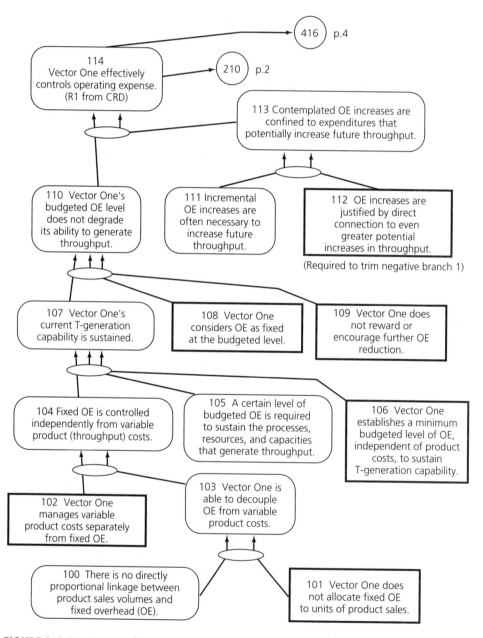

FIGURE D.8.1 Future reality tree: Vector One. The author is indebted to Dr. John Caspari for his insightful contributions to the content of this future reality tree

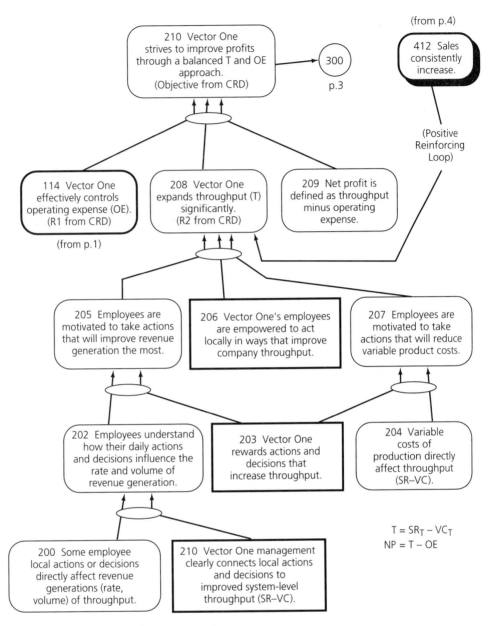

FIGURE D.8.2 Future reality tree: Vector One.

101, 102, and 106. This is homework that must be done before we can expect 108 and 109 to produce number 110. Another way of summarizing this is to say that we have to do things to sustain our existing capability to generate T, and then we have to make sure we don't do anything new to degrade it."

The vice-president for production operations said, "This all looks very clean, all the way to the top of the tree. Maybe too clean. What about replacing worn-out equipment? And what about new technology? I don't see that addressed here."

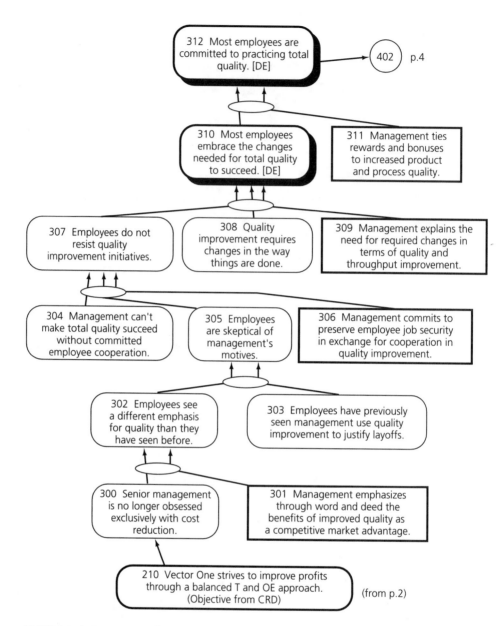

FIGURE D.8.3 Future reality tree: Vector One.

The production team member stood up again. "That's a good point, boss. Clearly, this tree doesn't speak to those issues directly, though we did talk about them. In fact, we look at capital acquisition separately, whether its straight replacement or new technology, as investment. That's a separate category from operating expense. The way we manage that won't change. We'll do cost-benefit analyses to determine whether we can amortize the investment over a reasonable time, just as we always have. The difference here is that we'll apply the same reasoning to any contemplated increases in operating expense."

"He's referring to block 112 on the future reality tree," the engineer added. "As we scrutinized the logic of the tree, someone pointed out

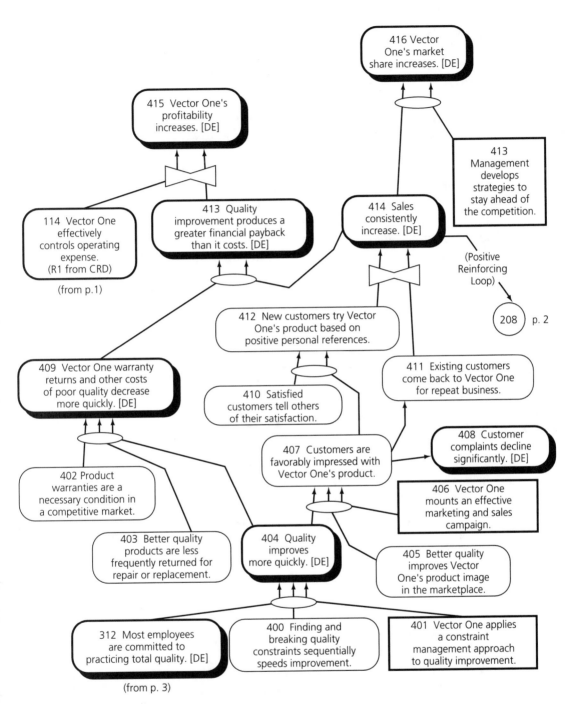

FIGURE D.8.4 Future reality tree: Vector One.

that if we maintained operating expense fixed at the budgeted level (108), it could create an adverse consequence that we don't have now. There might come a time when we *need* to increase operating expense, perhaps to break some internal constraint. For example, we might need to go to overtime or a second shift. That's not investment—it's pure operating expense. If we're confined to a fixed budget, it could create problems for us. We traced that line of reasoning out through what we call a negative branch. Here's what it looked like (Figure D.9). We saw that if we established a mechanism for evaluating possible operating expense increases, we could allow enough flexibility in the policy to increase the budget during the fiscal year as long as there was a verifiable logical connection between the OE increase and a much greater improvement in throughput. So, in essence, we created another injection to trim the negative branch that had grown on our tree, even before it got started."

The chief operating officer interrupted. "I think I see some potential problems with your injection number 206, on page two, the one about empowering employees to act locally to improve Throughput. We've got employees that don't have a clue about how to do that. I can foresee all kinds of chaos *that* might create!"

The three cross-functional team members stared silently at block 206 for a few moments. "You're right," replied the engineer. "We never thought about that. Thank you for bringing that to our attention. Yes, that could

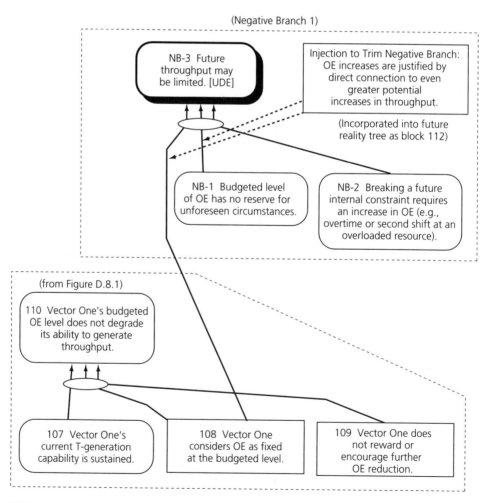

FIGURE D.9 Negative branch 1: Vector One future reality tree.

cause the rest of the tree above that point to break down. If we could come up with a way to neutralize that problem, could you buy into the rest of the tree?"

The COO looked at the tree again. "Yes, I think I could. But it would have to be a pretty well thought out intervention."

"Let us go back and work on it," the engineer said. "We'll build another negative branch and try to trim it. Then we'll come to your office to get your approval on the results." The COO nodded.

"One other thing I should point out," the engineer continued, "is the positive reinforcing loop that developed in the future reality tree. Notice that the desired effect on page four, block number 412, says, Sales consistently increase. An increase in sales constitutes an increase in throughput, as long as variable costs remain under control. And that's essentially the same content as block 208 on page two. If this were all one big diagram on a single page, the positive feedback characteristic of the loop would be more obvious. The input to block 208 comes from an effect that is really 11 levels above it. That's why we call it a reinforcing loop. Every pass through the tree makes the causation in 208 stronger—and that's good!"

There was a period of silence as the executives contemplated the future reality tree, the negative branch, and the positive loop. At last, the CEO said, "Well, it works for me." The others signaled their agreement. "Now the question is, how do we make all this happen?"

"We've already started working on that," the production team member volunteered. "We'll be ready to show you the results in about a week."

THE PREREQUISITE TREE

Ten days later, in the absence of the CEO, the chief operating officer convened a meeting of the senior executives and the cross-functional team. "The boss didn't want to delay this meeting for his return, so we're going ahead with it. When we adjourned last time, the question was how this plan to put the company on a throughput footing was going to be carried out. I understand you have something to show us."

The engineer went to the overhead projector. "Yes, we do. There's good news and . . . well, not exactly bad news. Let's just say that we're not as far along as we'd hoped to be." The COO looked at the engineer and raised an eyebrow.

"Last time we met, we left thinking that converting the future reality tree to a step-by-step action plan was going to be relatively straightforward. It turned out to be a little more difficult than we'd expected. We had 16 injections—changes the company would have to make—in the future reality tree. About half of these can be done with the stroke of a pen—in other words, immediate policy changes. The other half require significant homework and the completion of some preliminary activities before they can be considered in effect. It was these for which we underestimated the time required. It'll take us the better part of the next three weeks to finish those."

"Only three weeks?" the chief operating officer snorted. "We were eight years getting ourselves into this mess. If you think you can finish the job in that time, I think we can be patient for another three weeks."

The engineer nodded and continued. "I think we can come up with a proposed plan in that time.

"Our first job after the last meeting was to examine the sixteen injections, one at a time, and assess how difficult it would be to achieve them. We set aside the eight that looked fairly easy and concentrated on the more complicated ones. Seven of those still remain to be addressed. We've got one ready to show you today."

"Seven to go?" said the vice president for operations. "It took ten days to figure out the first one, and you expect to do the other seven in three weeks?"

"We've got two things going for us," the production member of the cross-functional team said. "First, we picked the toughest injection to start with. At least, I think it's going to be the toughest, because there's a bit of a culture change involved." A couple of other members of the team nodded their agreement. "Second, there's a learning-curve factor at work here. We struggled with these next two trees, but now that we have a better idea of what we're doing, the rest will go much faster."

The engineer showed a new slide. "This is a prerequisite tree (Figure D.10). We decided that the first step should probably be to figure out what obstacles to implementation stood in our way. This tree does that. It's a little different from the other logic trees you've seen so far. It's intended to show only those factors that would prevent us from proceeding right now, and the things we'll have to do to overcome them. But perhaps most important, it tells the *sequence* in which we'll have to attack the obstacles.

"At the top of the first page is our objective, the injection from the future reality tree that we want to make happen. In this case it's:

Vector One's employees are empowered to act locally in ways that improve company throughput, inventory, and operating expense.

What we're aiming for is a work force that knows what the company needs to have done and can naturally do the right thing without needing continual guidance from management.

"There's obviously much more to making that happen than just the stroke of a pen. In fact, though it's a simple statement, the actions needed to make it happen are somewhat more complicated.

"We identified three major obstacles to having our employees be reasonably autonomous in their work, yet ensuring that they do what's good for the company. Each of these was the culmination of a separate branch of lesser obstacles that have to be overcome in sequence.

"The first obstacle (number 100) was that our employees can't act effectively—do the right thing—without thoroughly understanding what

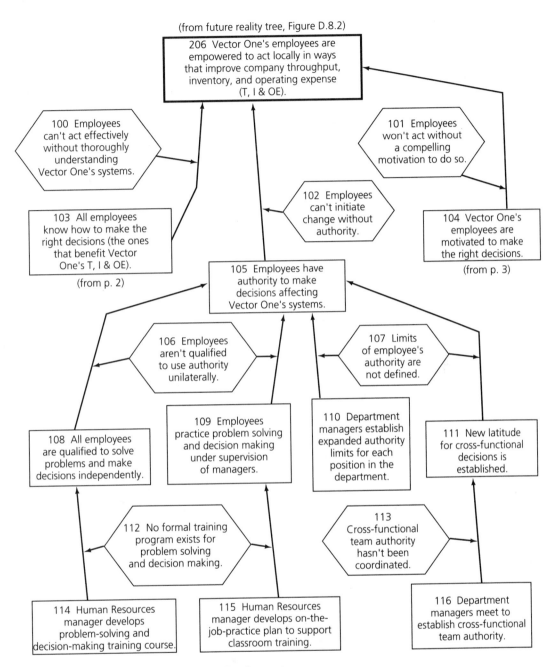

(from future reality tree, Figure D.8.2)

206 Vector One's employees are empowered to act locally in ways that improve company throughput, inventory, and operating expense (T, I & OE).

100 Employees can't act effectively without thoroughly understanding Vector One's systems.

101 Employees won't act without a compelling motivation to do so.

102 Employees can't initiate change without authority.

103 All employees know how to make the right decisions (the ones that benefit Vector One's T, I & OE).

(from p. 2)

104 Vector One's employees are motivated to make the right decisions.

(from p. 3)

105 Employees have authority to make decisions affecting Vector One's systems.

106 Employees aren't qualified to use authority unilaterally.

107 Limits of employee's authority are not defined.

108 All employees are qualified to solve problems and make decisions independently.

109 Employees practice problem solving and decision making under supervision of managers.

110 Department managers establish expanded authority limits for each position in the department.

111 New latitude for cross-functional decisions is established.

112 No formal training program exists for problem solving and decision making.

113 Cross-functional team authority hasn't been coordinated.

114 Human Resources manager develops problem-solving and decision-making training course.

115 Human Resources manager develops on-the-job-practice plan to support classroom training.

116 Department managers meet to establish cross-functional team authority.

FIGURE D.10.1   Prerequisite Tree: Vector One Corporation.

it is we want them to do. This means they not only have to know how to do the tasks associated with their jobs, they also have to know how their decisions will benefit the company as a whole.

"Second, they don't have the authority (102) to act independently— to do the right thing without having to get permission for every little change. In spite of our total quality efforts, we haven't really pushed

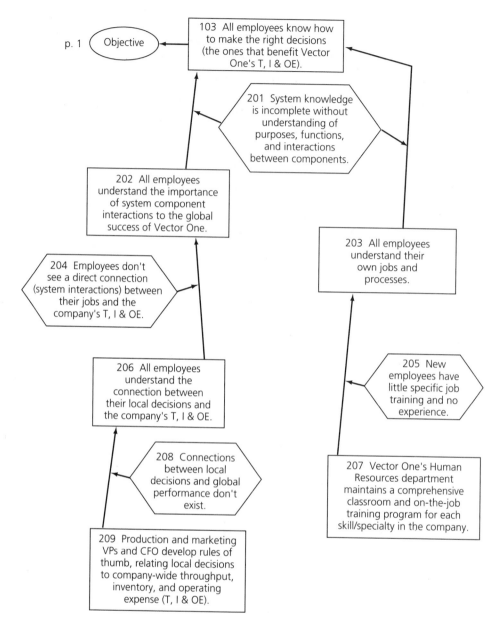

FIGURE D.10.2 Prerequisite tree: Vector One Corporation.

much authority down to lower levels. Almost everything seems to require management approval.

"Finally, we're not sure they *want* to do the right thing (101). Given our recent history layoffs and poor sales, lack of a motivated work force could be a real obstacle. If they think they might not be here very long, they're not likely to care much one way or the other. If we can overcome these three major obstacles, we'll have an empowered work force that will perform as we would, if we were in their shoes."

"That's probably the most concise expression of the challenge any company has in work force performance," the COO said. "Know how to

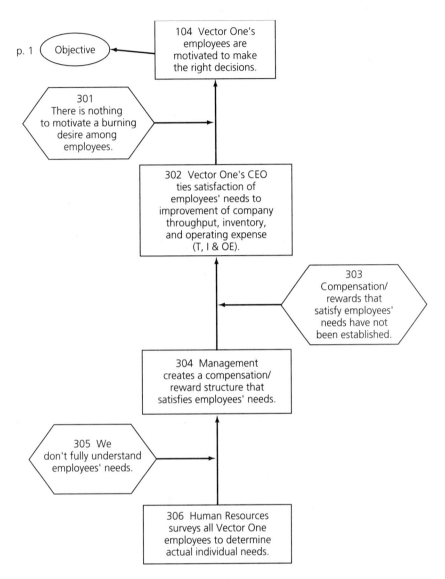

FIGURE D.10.3 Prerequisite tree: Vector One Corporation.

do the right thing, have the authority to do it, and want to use that authority the right way. So how does that happen?"

"Each of these obstacles is overcome by an intermediate objective of some kind. These are indicated in blocks 103, 104, and 105. But even those are somewhat idealistic, and each of them has its own separate branch of obstacles that must be overcome (Figures D.10.1 through D.10.3). But you'll notice that the obstacles and the intermediate objectives become progressively more discrete and specific the farther down each branch we go." The engineer then traced each branch all the way to the bottom.

"Remember," she summarized, "these are only the roadblocks—those things that stand in our way. They don't include everything that needs to be done. For that we need a transition tree."

THE TRANSITION TREE

"We happen to have the transition tree for this injection," the engineer said. "It's on the handout in front of you (Figure D.11). This is a lot like the future reality tree, except that as you can see, it's much more detailed. The branches of this tree—all six pages of it—conform generally to the

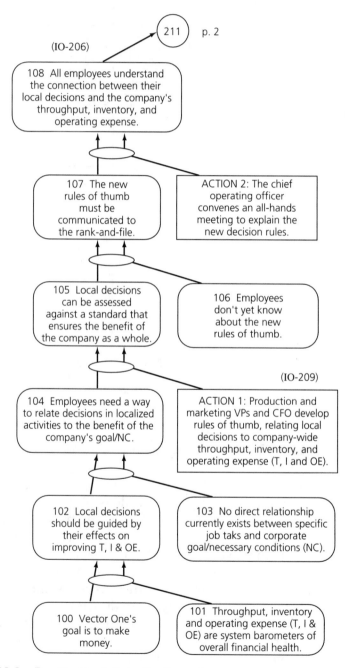

FIGURE D.11.1 Transition tree 1: Vector One Corporation.

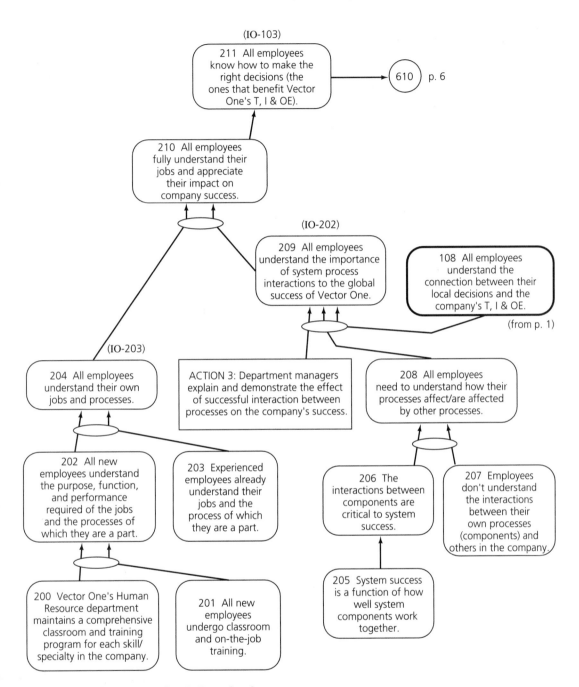

FIGURE D.11.2   Transition Tree 1: Vector One Corporation.

three-branch structure of the prerequisite tree. In fact, I've labeled those blocks that correspond to numbered intermediate objectives on the prerequisite tree. Block number 108 on the first page of the transition tree is also intermediate objective 206 on the prerequisite tree.

"It's pretty clear that this tree contains a lot more step-by-step guidance. There are 15 discrete actions that must be taken, indicated by the

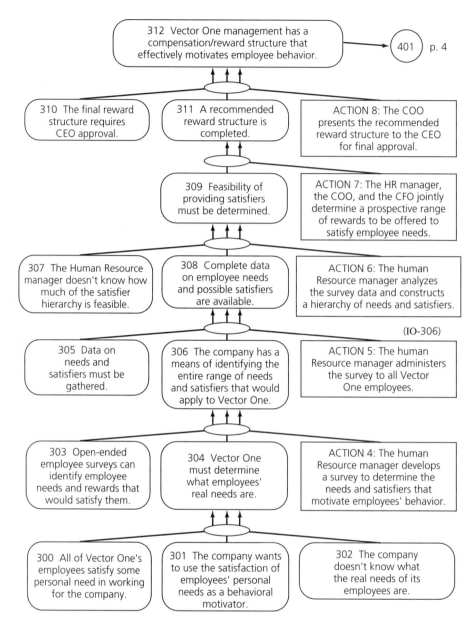

FIGURE D.11.3 Transition Tree 1: Vector One Corporation.

square-cornered boxes on each page. If each of these actions is completed, the injection from the future reality tree will be achieved.

"Notice, too, that each action box also assigns accountability—it tells *who* is responsible for completing each action."

"I see that," said the chief financial officer, "but I don't see any kind of deadline associated with these actions. Shouldn't there be one?"

"Good point," the engineer replied. "Time is not an element in these trees, only logical sequence. One thing has to happen before another,

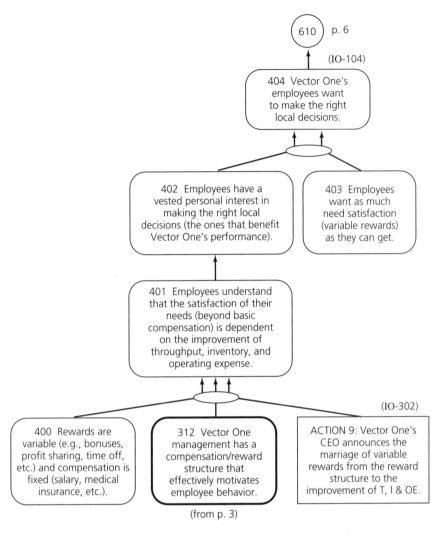

FIGURE D.11.4 Transition tree 1: Vector One Corporation.

and where branches converge, the actions in both branches must all be completed in sequence before the convergence occurs. But that's as close to time as these trees ever get. However, it's fairly easy to reduce these actions and effects to activities and nodes on a project diagram. The last page of your handout shows this (Figure D.12).

"Notice that it looks like a typical PERT chart, but without the time computations and a critical path identified. Those elements would be easy to add, and the actual implementation of our future reality tree could be managed as a project. In fact, I would recommend doing so. This is a very simple activity network, but it contains all 15 actions that must occur to execute injection number 206 from the future reality tree."

The vice-president for marketing spoke up. "Will there be charts similar to this for all the injections?"

p. 6

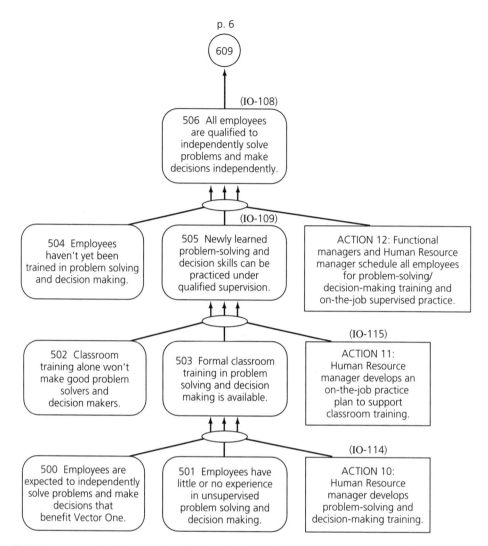

FIGURE D.11.5 Transition Tree 1: Vector One Corporation.

"Not for all of them," said the production team member. "Remember that eight of them didn't need prerequisite or transition trees. But seven more do. That's what we expect to accomplish in the next three weeks."

"It looks like a lot of work," said the chief financial officer. "Is it worth it?"

"You tell me," said the COO. "We've seen the current reality tree. It took us eight years to get into this hole we're in now. You've seen the future reality tree. It looks like the way out—we all agreed on that. Do we dare try to execute those changes without a well-thought out implementation plan? I seem to remember my father telling me that a smart carpenter measures twice and cuts just once. If we can work out the details in three weeks, why not take the time to be sure the job's done right?"

To the engineer, the COO said, "Better get to work on those other prerequisite and transition trees. The CEO will want to see them at the next meeting. Better schedule that one for a full afternoon. . . ."

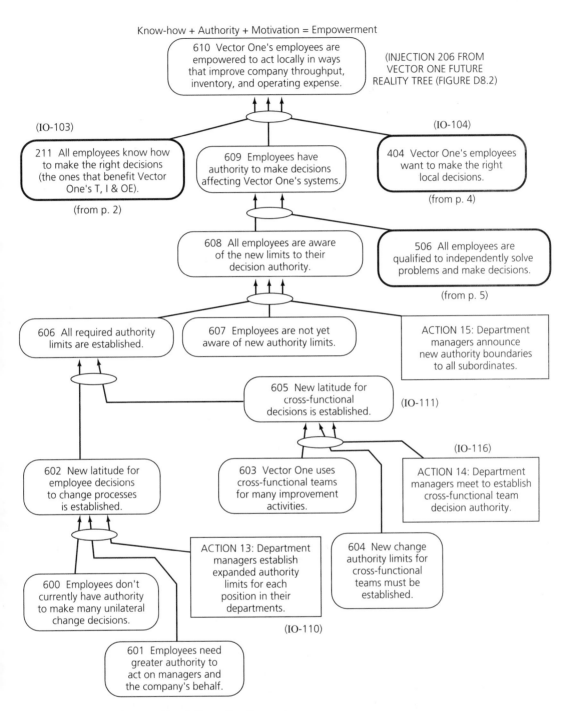

Know-how + Authority + Motivation = Empowerment

610 Vector One's employees are empowered to act locally in ways that improve company throughput, inventory, and operating expense.

(INJECTION 206 FROM VECTOR ONE FUTURE REALITY TREE (FIGURE D8.2)

(IO-103)

211 All employees know how to make the right decisions (the ones that benefit Vector One's T, I & OE).

(from p. 2)

609 Employees have authority to make decisions affecting Vector One's systems.

(IO-104)

404 Vector One's employees want to make the right local decisions.

(from p. 4)

608 All employees are aware of the new limits to their decision authority.

506 All employees are qualified to independently solve problems and make decisions.

(from p. 5)

606 All required authority limits are established.

607 Employees are not yet aware of new authority limits.

ACTION 15: Department managers announce new authority boundaries to all subordinates.

605 New latitude for cross-functional decisions is established.

(IO-111)

(IO-116)

602 New latitude for employee decisions to change processes is established.

603 Vector One uses cross-functional teams for many improvement activities.

ACTION 14: Department managers meet to establish cross-functional team decision authority.

ACTION 13: Department managers establish expanded authority limits for each position in their departments.

604 New change authority limits for cross-functional teams must be established.

600 Employees don't currently have authority to make many unilateral change decisions.

(IO-110)

601 Employees need greater authority to act on managers and the company's behalf.

FIGURE D.11.6 Transition Tree 1: Vector One Corporation.

When you find people who know their job and are willing to take responsibility, keep out of their way and don't bother them with unnecessary supervision. What you may think is cooperation is sometimes nothing but interference.

—Unknown

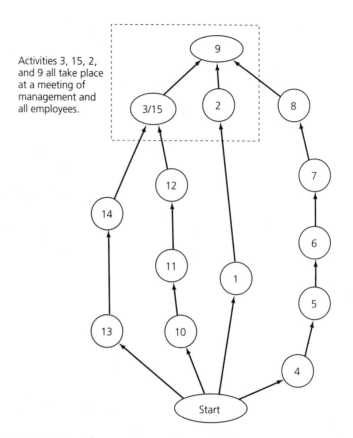

Activities 3, 15, 2, and 9 all take place at a meeting of management and all employees.

FIGURE D.12 Vector One's first transition tree Converted to a project activity network.

NOTES

1. Deming, W. Edwards. *Out of the Crisis.* Cambridge, MA: Massachusetts Institute of Technology Center for Advanced Engineering Study, 1986.

INDEX

Page numbers of figures are in italics.